91819

Building Web Applications with ADO.NET and XML Web Services

D1411144

Building Web Applications with
ADO.NET and XML Web Services

Building Web Applications with ADO.NET and XML Web Services

Richard Hundhausen

Steven Borg

Cole Francis

Kenneth Wilcox

Gearhead Press™

Wiley Publishing, Inc.

Publisher: Robert Ipsen
Editor: Theresa Hudson
Consulting Editor: Donis Marshall
Developmental Editor: Kathryn A. Malm
Managing Editor: Angela Smith
New Media Editor: Brian Snapp
Text Design & Composition: Wiley Composition Services

Published by Wiley Publishing, Inc., Indianapolis, Indiana
Published simultaneously in Canada

For general information on our other products and services please contact our Customer Care Department within the United States at (800) 762-2974, outside the United States at (317) 572-3993 or fax (317) 572-4002.

Wiley also publishes its books in a variety of electronic formats. Some content that appears in print may not be available in electronic books.

The Gearhead Press trademark is the exclusive property of Gearhead Group Corporation.

Library of Congress Cataloging-in-Publication Data:

ISBN: 0-471-20186-3

Printed in the United States of America

10 9 8 7 6 5 4 3 2 1

A Note from Gearhead Press

Gearhead Press is dedicated to publishing technical books for experienced Information Technology professionals — network engineers, developers, system administrators, and others — who need to update their skills, learn how to use technology more effectively, or simply want a quality reference to the latest technology. Gearhead Press emerged from my experience with professional trainers of engineers and developers: people who truly understand first-hand the needs of working professionals. Gearhead Press authors are the crème de la crème of industry trainers, working at the companies that define the technology revolution. For this reason, Gearhead Press authors are regularly in the trenches with the developers and engineers that have changed the world through innovative products. Drawing from this experience in IT training, our books deliver superior technical content with a unique perspective that is based on real-world experience.

Now, as an imprint of Wiley Publishing, Inc., Gearhead Press will continue to bring you, the reader, the level of quality that Wiley has delivered consistently for nearly 200 years.

Thank you.

Donis Marshall
Founder, Gearhead Press
Consulting Editor, Wiley Publishing, Inc.

Gearhead Press Books in Print

(For complete information about current and upcoming titles, go to www.wiley.com/compbooks)

Books in the Gearhead Press *Point to Point* Series

- *Migrating to Microsoft Exchange 2000* by Stan Reimer, ISBN: 0-471-06116-6

- *Installing and Configuring Web Servers Using Apache* by Melanie Hoag, ISBN: 0-471-07155-2

- *VoiceXML: 10 Projects to Voice Enable Your Website* by Mark Miller, ISBN: 0-471-20737-3

Books in the Gearhead Press *In the Trenches* Series

- *Windows 2000 Automated Deployment* by Ted Malone and Rolly Perraux, ISBN: 0-471-06114-X

- *Robust Linux: Assuring High Availability* by Iain Campbell, ISBN: 0-471-07040-8

- *Programming Directory Services for Windows* 2000 by Donis Marshall, ISBN: 0-471-15216-1

- *Programming ADO.NET* by Richard Hundhausen and Steven Borg, ISBN: 0-471-20187-1

- *Designing .NET Web Services Using ADO.NET and XML* by Richard Hundhausen and Steven Borg, ISBN: 0-471-20186-3

- *Making Win32 Applications Mobile: Porting to Windows CE* by Nancy Nicolaisen, ISBN: 0-471-21618-6

- *Programming Windows CE Wireless Applications* by Barry Shilmover and Derek Ball, ISBN: 0-471-21469-8

- *Mastering SQL Server 2002 Security* by Mike Young and Curtis Young, ISBN: 0-471-21970-3

- *Microsoft.NET Security Programming* by Donis Marshall, ISBN: 0-471-22285-2

Contents

Introduction

In 1998, Microsoft submitted a draft specification of what would later be named the SOAP protocol. XML 1.0 had only just become a full recommendation. Given that the contributors worked on the COM and MTS teams, it was no wonder that Microsoft initially wanted this new protocol to support its Windows DNA 2000 solution. It would be only a matter of time, however, before this protocol, mated with a mature XML schema language, would form the headwaters of XML Web services.

Industry embraced HTTP and XML. Today, these two protocols are as ubiquitous as Kevin Bacon. They are used everywhere, on all operating systems. Pick a platform, and you'll not only have access to an HTTP Web server and XML parser, but you'll have choices. Every platform from the IBM big-iron systems down to handhelds can serve up Web and XML documents.

Sure, there were "Web services" before 1998. Companies have long been able to serve up a URL or IP socket to their business partners that, when called, would execute a CGI or ISAPI application, call a service, or run a waiting script. These services could then return something meaningful to the calling party, in text, binary, or one of several MIME types. The net effect (sorry, bad pun!) was delivery of presentation-quality data. The idea of remote code over the Internet is not new.

Remote scripting took this one step further by enabling clients to call server-side script functions directly from client-side DHTML script running in a Web browser. Once everything was configured, your HTML page could embed functionality such as this:

```
function btnQuoteOfTheDay_onclick() {
 var obj = RSGetASPObject("http://hundhausen.com/functions.asp");
 var result = obj.QuoteOfTheDay();
}
```

Even the idea of SOAP was not new. SOAP borrowed from the idea of COM Internet Services (CIS), which supported the tunneling of DCOM calls through existing TCP port-80 traffic. While CIS was a great technology and rescued many projects doomed by the installation of firewalls, it still assumed a Windows environment, or at least a DCOM-friendly piece of software, on the other end of the wire.

If you are asking yourself why we needed another protocol, we might ask you how successful you have ever been at deploying DCOM applications across your enterprise. Assuming that you had the support of all of your various domain administrators (good luck), mastered dcomcnfg.exe (it can be done), and had read that one MSDN white paper on passing DCOM through a firewall (long live Michael Nelson, whoever you are), then you stood a chance.

What makes these new Web services interesting is SOAP. SOAP is just a protocol specification that defines how to invoke methods on servers, typically over HTTP. It provides an extensible way for applications to communicate using simple XML messages over the Web. Regardless of operating system, brand of parser, or language, the messages themselves are the standard. The SOAP specification goes on to mandate a specific XML vocabulary that defines parameters, return values, and exceptions. This means that two software developers with completely different backgrounds, platform preference, and love for software companies can coexist peacefully in the world — and work together efficiently. Clients written in Visual Basic .NET can easily invoke services running CORBA on Unix boxes, while Windows Scripting Host (WSH) clients can call mainframe code and access DB2. Even your Macintosh boxes can access Perl Web services running on Red Hat Linux. The list goes on and on.

This brings us to a landscape where every major Web server software manufacturer and tools vendor not only speaks XML and SOAP, but is providing SDKs and IDEs to build and deploy Web services efficiently, thus making business prospects limitless. The possibilities of what you can do with these cross-platform Web services are more interesting to us than how you build them.

How This Book Is Organized

We debated how best to approach writing a Web services book. Some authors were busy writing high-level, how-to books. Other authors had committed to writing the low-level technical "plumbing" books. As developers, we really appreciate this second group of authors as they pledged to hunt down the fast-moving SOAP and related specifications, then stake them to paper.

We opted to present a case study. In our opinion, this is a better way to demonstrate not only what Web services are, but also how a typical wired business can leverage them in business-to-business (B2B) commerce. If that approach fits your needs, look no further. You've picked up exactly the right book.

We will study Hutchings Photography, an online warehouse of stock photography images. Like other photography agencies, Hutchings Photography started out shooting photographs for hire. Through the years, these photos, along with others shot purely on speculation, were kept in reserve to support the growing needs of their clients. Publishers, Web designers, and even other photographers need to license photographs. The idea of licensing stock photography as a business is not new. Even the idea of searching for stock photography on the Web, licensing it, and immediately downloading the images is not new. What is new is the application of Web services to this business concept.

Hutchings Photography would like to become more of a wholesaler of the images than a retailer. In other words, it would like to move from a business-to-consumer (B2C) business model to a B2B model, dealing directly with other online stock houses that can broker and distribute licensed images on its behalf. Blend the fact that Web services can support the myriad of various operating systems and languages in use by these stock houses with the fact that Web services are about revolutionizing the B2B world, and you have a business-oriented case study begging to be written.

The first section of this book, Chapter 1, introduces you to Web services and their related technologies. This chapter walks you through a bit of history and the challenges that have faced developers in the past when building distributed applications across the Web. You will also be introduced to SOAP, the key protocol that enables Web services, and to a few security concerns.

The second section covers the Web service provider case study, covering the analysis, design, construction, registration, and deployment of Hutchings Photography's Web service. Because Hutchings Photography is the owner of the Web service, we refer to it as the Web service provider. In this section, each chapter builds on the previous chapter, taking you from cradle to grave.

Chapter 2 introduces the Hutchings Photography case study from a business perspective, pointing out problems with the original manual process — even the company's first attempt at automation with a Web site.

Chapter 3 covers the conceptual design of the system and introduces you to Object Role Modeling (ORM). Only Web services with a strong database back end will be successful, so we start with the data tier. We walk you through each discrete step of the Conceptual Schema Design Procedure (CSDP) so that you can build a bullet-proof, normalized, and efficient physical database model using Visio for Enterprise Architects.

Chapter 4 extends our database design, covering the implementation of the physical design in Microsoft SQL Server 2000. Hutchings Photography takes advantage of many of the new features of SQL Server 2000; we showcase them in this chapter. In addition, we show you how to create a database maintenance plan to protect your database's integrity and keep it running efficiently.

Chapter 5 introduces ADO.NET, the cornerstone of any .NET Web service. We cover the XML capabilities of ADO.NET, then we begin to walk you through the design and construction of the Hutchings Photography data layer using ADO.NET's Connection, DataAdapter, and DataSet objects. We build our WebData component in Visual Basic .NET and showcase the advanced features of Visual Studio .NET so that you can see how quickly you can build a data service.

Chapter 6 covers the construction of our Web service. To demonstrate the flexibility of the .NET framework, we use C# in this chapter, calling our WebData component. We show you all of the syntax and attributes used to code a Web service, including proper testing techniques. Caching is also discussed as a way to improve performance.

Chapter 7 rounds out the section on the Web service provider. Here, we discuss the benefits of using the Universal Description Discovery and Integration (UDDI) framework as a means of advertising and discovering Web services. Businesses that want to promote their Web services can make use of public or private UDDI services. We also cover the Web Service Inspection Language (WSIL) as a way for a company's Web server to describe the Web services that it contains.

The third section of the book looks at the Hutchings Photography Web service through the eyes of the Web service consumer. The first consumer of the Web service is Hutchings Photography itself. In this section, we cover two distinct Web applications that utilize the Hutchings Photography Web service.

Chapter 8 looks again at the case study from the perspective of Hutchings Photography's business partners. We revisit some of the issues from Chapter 2 and look to the concerns that its partners have had with using its Web site and licensing its stock images. We discuss security and trust issues as well as how we addressed them. Carrying on with our discussion from Chapter 7, we discuss the concept of anonymous partners, which are visitors to our Web service that found us either through a UDDI or WSIL registration, or by word of mouth. Finally, we introduce the two consumer Web sites that we will build in Chapters 9 and 10.

Chapter 9 walks you through the construction of Hutchings Photography's Web site. Yes, the company is its own consumer, much like an outlet store for a major manufacturer. Although its business model changed to focus on becoming a stock photography provider, it still wants to be able to license its own photographs. One part tutorial and one part revelation of best practices, this chapter is full of code samples and techniques for referencing, calling, and processing the image and metadata returned by the Web service. You will learn about binary encoding, XML schema validation, and testing and deploying a Web application.

Chapter 10 is unique in that it provides a divergent view from the one Microsoft proselytizes. Although we use Microsoft .NET and Visual Studio .NET throughout the book to build our Web service, we wanted to practice what we preach regarding cross-platform operation with Web services. This chapter looks at Penguin Photos, a partner of Hutchings Photography that runs Red Hat Linux and uses Borland's Kylix software to build its Web site. We walk through the construction of the Linux Web site. Along the way, we discuss a few issues involved with consuming a data-intensive Microsoft .NET Web service from a non-Microsoft platform.

The fourth section of the book looks at two important topics: security and performance. Although they are not specific to our case study, we want to cover these important issues, which are applicable to any Web service.

Chapter 11 covers security, both the traditional mechanisms provided by IIS and new ones provided by ASP.NET. Because Web services in .NET are just ASP.NET applications, they abide by the same configuration rules as other Web applications. We look at the security tweaks you can make in the web.config file and discuss how to build your own credential store, allowing or denying certain users. We finish the chapter by showing you how to build a client application to test your security mechanism.

Chapter 12 discusses Web service performance testing and tuning. We begin by illustrating the many areas where you can tune the performance of a Web service. Our tips include design changes, such as supporting asynchronous service calls and callbacks, and being smart about the scope of the data you return. We point out areas in Windows, Component Services, and IIS 5.1 where you can monitor and tweak performance. Finally, we leave you armed with tools to audit and monitor the performance of all aspects of your Web service, including Microsoft's Application Center Test (ACT) and the Advanced .NET Testing System (ANTS).

Who Should Read This Book

As mentioned, this book is a case study. This means that it will appeal to developers, IT specialists, and even business professionals. The common thread is an interest in the benefits derived from exposing your business by using Web services. We sprinkle a fair amount of technology, terms, and code throughout the book.

To fully benefit from the construction chapters, you should have an understanding of Visual Basic .NET, Visual C# .NET, XML, HTML, and even a little SQL. Even a seasoned .NET developer, however, will find new and useful information in our pages.

If you are interested in building Web services using Visual Studio .NET, you should read Chapters 1 through 7. If you are interested in consuming Web services using .NET or other non-Microsoft platforms, you should read the third section, Chapters 8 through 10. If you are interested in securing, testing, and tuning ASP.NET Web services, you should read Chapters 11 and 12. If you are primarily interested in the business aspects of our case study, you should read Chapters 1, 2, and 8. But our hope is that you'll read the entire book, cover to cover, as well as download and analyze our models and source code!

Tools You Will Need

If you want to follow along in each chapter, building database models, writing stored procedures, compiling code, and deploying our Web services and applications, you will need access to the following products:

- Microsoft .NET Framework
- Microsoft Visual Studio .NET (Enterprise Architect Edition recommended)

- Microsoft Visio for Enterprise Architects (for Object Role Modeling)
- Microsoft SQL Server 2000
- Advanced .NET Testing System (Red Gate Software)
- Borland Kylix 2.0 (to implement a Linux Web application in Chapter 10)

What's on Our Web Site

All of our models, code, database, and even working examples of the Hutchings Photography Web service are available at our Web sites. Our construction chapters go light on the code to give your eyes and our publisher a break. Instead, we refer you to our companion Web site to download the code in its entirety.

It's best to start with Wiley's Web site, as it is the official source for the book's errata:

```
http://www.wiley.com/compbooks
```

Our Web service project, fully documented and available for download, is hosted on a separate server:

```
http://code.hutchingsphotography.com
```

Summary

We hope this book provides you with a unique perspective on the power and benefit of Web services. We didn't want to write a reference book or step-by-step instructions to build a Web service. Instead, we trust that you'll agree that we found a nice balance between the two and wrapped it up in a real-world, meaningful case study.

The Internet, of course, is here to stay. Businesses that are currently on the Internet, and even those that are not, will want to investigate Web services as a way to broaden their customer base. Whether you are a consultant, staff IT professional, or the CEO of your firm, we wish you success with your Web service project and hope it opens new doors for your business.

CHAPTER 1

What Are Web Services?

Years ago, in the Dark Ages before XML Web services, getting disparate systems to talk to one another was difficult—sometimes very difficult. At first, that didn't matter. Nearly all applications were meant to stand alone on a single machine, and if they needed to interact with another program, doing so involved passing a floppy disk from one person to another. Even after computers were originally networked, the majority of computing was done inside the confines of one box. Sure, data was passed from one computer to another, but computers didn't use each other's processing power.

With the advent and popularization of powerful database software, things changed. When you accessed a database, you asked the machine hosting the database to do some processing and return the results of that effort. This proved to be a winning tactic. More applications sought to take advantage of server power. Those of you who've been in the industry for a while will remember the shift to a client/server architecture. Of course, to communicate with the server, the client needed to be able to speak the same language as the server. For instance, to communicate with SQL Server, the client needed to understand Tabular Data Stream. This became a problem, so harkening back to the wise words of David Wheeler, a layer of indirection was added. In this case, it was Open Database Connectivity

(ODBC). This allowed any client that could speak ODBC to access any database server that could speak ODBC.

NOTE David Wheeler, a chief architect for the EDSAC project in the early 1950s, said, "Any problem in computer science can be solved with another layer of indirection." Wise words! And written back at the origins of computer science.

This worked for a while, and newer layers of indirection were developed, such as OLEDB and JDBC. But while this approach proved very successful, it served a limited audience. Providing these useful indirection layers took considerable industry support. This meant that as software developers working within a single organization, we had difficulty creating servers that could easily interoperate with numerous, diverse clients. If we wanted to create some code with functionality that could be invoked by another machine, we were in for a difficult time. A few technologies evolved to assist developers, including DCOM from Microsoft, CORBA from the Object Management Group, and, later, RMI from Sun Microsystems.

These new technologies were fairly good . . . as long as you were communicating with other systems using the same platform—and even that could be rough. How many of you tried to make DCOM talk to CORBA? How about making CORBA talk to DCOM? Or DCOM talk to RMI? And how many of you tried to make CORBA talk to CORBA? Yep, even that could be hard. No matter how you sliced it, getting a Microsoft Windows machine to talk to a Unix machine in any meaningful way was a headache.

Thus, the introduction of XML Web services. Like the technologies before it, XML Web services are a layer of indirection. This time, however, the method of invoking functionality on another machine is done through plain text using standard W3C protocols. In one significant way, this is a step backward—binary protocols can be much faster than an XML Web service. This disadvantage, though, is more than made up for by the ease with which different platforms can communicate with one another.

This benefit is simple to demonstrate using Visual Studio .NET. You can create a project that references code running on a Linux machine in some guy's garage in Peoria in just a few steps. Literally in minutes, you can create a meaningful application that is actively running code and receiving data on a machine running an entirely different operating system.

Now that you've seen what XML Web services can do, how do you use them? In reality, Web services are nothing more than code running on someone's platform that has an entry point allowing you to activate that code using a special XML document. In the most common case, you're sending an XML document in a format called the Simple Object Access Protocol (SOAP) over HTTP. The server has a listener waiting for a SOAP packet. When it receives one, it opens it up, and if everything is in order, it executes the native code. It then takes the results from that code, packages it into another SOAP packet, and returns it to the client. That's it. So, what's the fuss? Nothing, really; it's very simple. What makes it exciting is that this is an industry standard that is being adopted by every major technology firm.

To be concise, Web services are nothing more than code that has been encapsulated by an envelope of reserved words written to a Web Service Definition Language (WSDL) and a Web Service Meta Language (WSML) file. The WSDL and WSML files describe the code, methods, parameters, and data types available for use.

This chapter focuses on Web services and SOAP. It discusses the background of Web services, how SOAP fits into the picture, and how distributed programming was accomplished prior to Web services. The chapter discusses the background of Web services and how they are more robust when compared to their RPC predecessors. Furthermore, the chapter discusses the pros and cons of using SOAP through Web services and provides you with information as to what types of businesses can benefit using SOAP.

Last, the chapter discusses applying security to Web services. This topic is also discussed at length in Chapter 11, "Securing the Web Service."

SOAP (The Web Service Protocol) and the General Protocol Pecking Order

The Simple Object Access Protocol, better known as SOAP, was introduced to the public in 1998 when Microsoft released its Microsoft SOAP Toolkit 1.0. The objective was to find a simple interoperable technique to receive and transfer a wide range of data across the Internet using well-defined data types.

SOAP was created as a collaborative work orchestrated in part by the following companies: Microsoft, IBM, Lotus Development, Userland Software, and DevelopMentor. Also, a well-known standards body, the W3C (World Wide Web Consortium), recognizes and endorses the effort as a protocol that has already received recommended status. Please read www.w3.og/TR/SOAP/ for more details.

Before we delve too far into SOAP, let's discuss the order of nature in the protocol world. Only a fraction of all protocols that exist are listed in the next paragraph, but many of those that are listed here are well known and require no explanation after their introduction.

The Transmission Control Protocol/Internet Protocol, better known as TCP/IP, is ultimately responsible for the creation of other TCP-backbone protocols: HTTP, DHCP, SOAP, Telnet, Rlogin, DNS, FTP, RSH, IMAP, NFS, SMTP, POP3, NNTP, SNMP, SSH, most chat protocols, and most X Window network communications.

FTP, HTTP, and SMTP are three of many widely known standard protocols that are generally supported within an organization and that rely on TCP as a standard transport mechanism. FTP, HTTP, and SMTP are interactive protocols that can trigger events by either programmatic contribution or encountering a manual user transmission of meaningful information. We will focus on these protocols in this section because they are the protocols with which most people are familiar.

In the set of circumstances surrounding the HTTP protocol, programmatic contributions offer a robust way to exchange information between a client and a server, and Component Services are committed to processing information in a very efficient manner. For example, the IIS Server does an excellent job handling HTTP user requests and responses as well as interpreting and executing ASP requests. Because of the special relationship of IIS with MTS and COM+, known as Component Services, server-side resources can be pooled, including connections to the database and COM+ transactions.

In effect, the SOAP protocol overcomes the barriers discussed previously in this chapter regarding earlier attempts at creating custom TCP-based solutions. Because the SOAP protocol uses XML and the TCP protocol to bypass firewalls, it masks itself as an HTTP response or request and is easily passed through virtually all firewalls.

Hence, without TCP/IP, the HTTP protocol could not exist. You might think of the SOAP protocol as a third-tier protocol and FTP and HTTP as second-tier protocols, depending on the TCP protocol that provides for physical transmission. (See Figure 1.1.)

The TCP/IP protocol negotiates handshaking and RPC (Remote Procedure Call) across an intranet and the public Internet. Handshaking is simply the method by which two programs, through their interfaces, determine the type of relationship that exists between them. (See Figure 1.2.) RPC is a way for the programs of one computer to actually execute code on another computer.

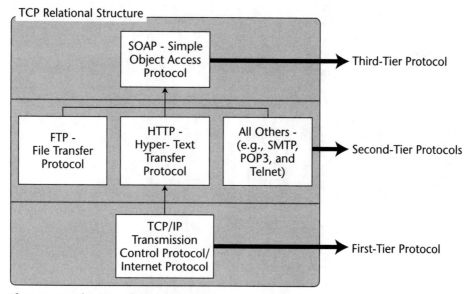

Figure 1.1 The TCP relational structure.

If the server offers both incoming and outgoing communication, as with TCP/IP, then the relationship between the entities is bilateral, or mutual. If the server is nothing more than a receiver and processor of information without returning a confirmation of processes' success or failure back to the client post-process, as with UDP (User Datagram Protocol), then the relationship is parasitic, or unilateral. In the case of XML Web services, we're virtually always dealing with bilateral relationships.

SOAP is not a first-tier or second-tier protocol (see Figure 1.1) because it depends on a second-tier protocol for translation capabilities across the Internet—HTTP. In turn, the HTTP protocol depends on the TCP transport. Instead, SOAP sits atop the other protocols. It uses its own standard specifications supported by its own specific reserved words, designated numbers, and so forth. What makes SOAP really powerful and noteworthy is that it supports language and platform interoperability through XML. Another factor that makes the SOAP protocol remarkable is that the developers of the protocol brought structure and reusability to an age-old practice where standards were not always possible.

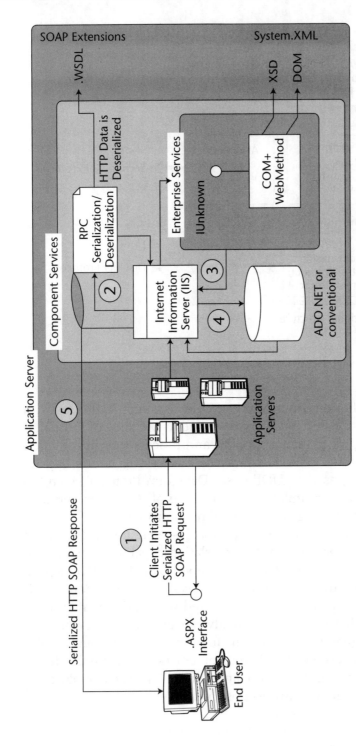

Figure 1.2 The SOAP process flow diagram.

Before COM, Web Services, and XML

From the authors' personal experiences, one of our earliest tasks was to provide some remedial-level interoperability that involved the Microsoft Winsock control. At that time, Winsock was all the rage in Internet communication. The ActiveX control allowed you to connect and bind to a server via TCP/IP. The server was often another application created using the Winsock control, but that provided logic and processing by supplying the IP address and port of the host.

The host was most likely another application that you created to communicate specifically with the client, as most client/server code at the time used a parser that was built exclusively to handle the data that the client would send across the Internet.

After initiating the conversation with the server, the client control had to contain logic to handle callbacks from the server. Also, the server was responsible for handling the requests of the connected clients, forcing the server to queue the requests when more than one thread accessed the same function to prohibit unanticipated collisions, ultimately resulting in an unnecessary application failure.

Once the server parsed the request of the client, usually sent as a comma-delimited or fixed-length string, it could do just about anything it wanted with it, including validations, database inputs and selects, and even returning information to the user in a string format.

Provided you didn't do anything thickheaded on the server, like run the contents of the input parameters through the command line, everything was good. Additionally, the server environment could be controlled. If a client request did not contain the correct header information and structure, then the request could be terminated and the client's connection could even be closed if needed. This was how our earlier attempts to accomplish transaction-based programming using a form of remote procedure calls were accomplished.

One of the earlier hurdles when writing code to communicate with remote servers was the firewall. This is ironic because it is still a major problem for some Internet applications and software today. The firewalls on the client might prohibit the call from ever making it to the outside world if the port required by the server was blocked by the client's firewall, never even making it as far as the server.

This same scenario could be true for a server application. A client/server handshake might never take place if the Winsock server sat behind a firewall. To challenge this issue usually meant using port 80. After all, most companies left this port open on the firewall to meet their standard business needs. Doing so also forced the developer to write the packet data in an HTML format to trick the firewall into believing the information was a valid response to a client request via HTTP and required a server application to intercept and interpret the packet of information. It was difficult to use port 80 because you needed to create a proprietary port-80 listener on the server, which was often banned (wisely, in our opinion) by network administrators.

Another trick was to use the FTP protocol as a transport mechanism for communication between client and server applications. The FTP protocol was standard, and most companies left ports 20 and 21 open for FTP communication, making it fairly easy to create a file and send it to a host FTP server.

An application on the server would be responsible for grabbing the file, opening it, parsing the contents, and processing the information. Once again, this process involved the use of the Winsock, or equivalent, control for TCP/IP capability. And that suffered the same problem as using HTTP—you needed to provide your own listener that had to run on the server.

The Lineage of Web Services

TCP/IP began as a low-budget development effort pioneered by an association of allied researchers for the promotion of United States Department of Defense Advanced Research Project's Agency Network (ARPAnet) and was instituted in 1975. It has since progressed to a worldwide standard, recognized for bringing to life the first-tier electronic peer-to-peer communication process known as TCP/IP. For this reason, the TCP/IP protocol is ultimately responsible for spearheading the influence for the development of many of the previously mentioned second-tier protocols, as well as the creation of SOAP.

Unlike its sidekick, the UDP protocol, TCP offers a reliable manner in which to exchange true client/server information. UDP, developed as a one-way protocol, is responsible for simply broadcasting messages to a host system without binding, also known as handshaking, with it. A UDP packet is simply broadcasted to an IP address and, optionally, a port, so it never physically binds to a host TCP/IP server and therefore never returns a response code to the user who initiated the broadcasted message.

Thus, the initiator cannot be 100 percent certain that the request made it to the server unless an additional request is sent to query for the answer. Also, because the UDP protocol never binds to the server, IP addresses are easily masqueraded, making it potentially untrustworthy. Regardless, despite the drawbacks of the UDP protocol, it is still widely in use today. For instance, the Simple Mail Transfer Protocol (SMTP), on port 25, supports UDP, making it possible to transmit emails while impersonating the identity of an alternate IP address.

Despite the downfalls of the UDP protocol, there are some advantages to using it. For instance, because it lacks a binding process, the protocol saves processing time, so a UDP packet can be quickly delivered to a client or server process. The protocol is also available to software developers who might use it when building custom applications, including gaming software and data-driven, peer-to-peer, UDP-based, noncritical applications that are built for speed but can tolerate some degree of inaccuracy. Last, without a binding process, server-side state cannot be maintained in a UDP transmission as it can be with the TCP/IP transmission.

SOAP-based Web service HTTP transports are built on a unique foundation. In some ways, their transmission characteristics emulate the efficiencies associated with the UDP protocol by allowing you to call a remote Web service only once to send the data (because the data is generally so small in terms of bytes). In many other ways, they emulate transmissions associated with the TCP/IP protocol, allowing you to keep state if necessary and to track return information to the user to confirm HTTP requests. Effectively, it is like having the best of both worlds.

Why Web Services Are Superior to Winsock and DCOM

The following subsections discuss the history of Winsock and DCOM.

Winsock

Writing a basic client/server application that leveraged TCP through the Microsoft Winsock control was not a problem, but your efforts were duplicated for each application server you wrote. Here are some additional reasons why this was a painstaking way of accomplishing distributed application programming:

- There was no standard parser.
- Server code applied specifically to the client that it was built for.
- Maintenance was a hassle.
- Firewalls would stop you cold unless you formatted your transmission in an HTML-like format.

- Writing applications to communicate via FTP took time and were I/O expensive.

- Distributions of the client application were a nightmare. Any time changes needed to be done on the client, the effort would have to be replicated on the server and setup diskettes would need to be made all over again.

Consequently, this method experienced severe shortcomings, as the server application was limited to parsing the application for which it was written. Another downfall of the FTP method was that you had to read and write to a file.

I/O operations are expensive, so to perform this task on a laboriously busy server could spell performance problems, potentially generating its own brute-force denial-of-service attack against itself if it became too busy handling I/O-intensive client requests.

The final problem with the FTP method was that the response time from the server was often not real time. The fact that the application had to perform I/O processing, and that it often scheduled a task or service running intermittently to look for available files within a specific folder, made the real-time performance slower than the TCP method.

The writing was on the wall: The world was in dire need of a new protocol, one that is TCP compliant, is standard across all platforms, and overcomes the problems associated with historical ways of communicating with remote applications.

Furthermore, a language was needed to transport data from application to application. It no longer made sense to write string parsers that were tied to specific applications that would need to be rewritten to accommodate each new application's data structure.

As a result, the technical world has changed. The efforts to continually improve efficiency and decrease complexity have introduced a latecomer to the protocol kingdom, an appellation celebrated by the acronym SOAP. Its fortitude relies completely on the well-known XML standard.

DCOM

Remote Procedure Calls (RPC) are intended to allow individuals to run processes on distributed systems. The primary downfalls of RPC are security and configuration. The following attacks might be possible when allowing distributed RPC communication:

- Port mapping
- Spoofing

- Traffic sniffing and stealing
- Denial-of-service attacks

Additional problems and issues can occur, such as these:

- Firewall configuration and maintenance can be a hassle, and improper configuration can ultimately prohibit valid packets from reaching their host destination. SOAP is nearly unstoppable, utilizing HTTP and port 80 to communicate.
- DCOM uses RPC to communicate and requires marshalling, thereby reducing efficiency.
- COM DLLs must be exported as .exe or .msi and distributed to the remote DCOM callers, so maintenance and updates can be a hassle.

With SOAP, developers can focus more on architecting and developing scalable solutions and concentrate less on network configuration issues. SOAP acts as a service-level provider, allowing you to expose only the methods that you want to expose over a secure, standard protocol. Special ports do not need to be opened for access as they do with RPC. The developer is in complete control.

The Microsoft SOAP Toolkit versus Built-in Support

When Microsoft SOAP Toolkit was released in 1998, its main objectives were to provide experimental capabilities for interoperability between language-independent clients and to create Web services that leveraged a lightweight protocol requiring only a minimal amount of information to be carried across the wire and a minimal amount of effort to accomplish the mentioned tasks.

Prior to the existence of SOAP calls, Action settings, Response.Redirect, and Server.Transfer calls on an ASP page forced the entire page to be submitted to the Internet Information Server (IIS) for processing. If your intentions were to navigate to an entirely new page, then this behavior was acceptable. If your intentions were simply to update a field in a table on an otherwise static page, then this behavior was costly. Running entire pages through IIS for processing takes time. If your Web application utilizes DCOM objects, then you can expect some latency.

ASP pages are fundamentally scripted, so the code was never compiled until the page was processed through IIS. Also, if out-of-process components were used, then they were referenced by the server in a just-in-time manner. Instancing those components took additional time.

For Visual Studio 6.0 developers, the SOAP Toolkit is available for download at http://msdn.microsoft.com/downloads/default.asp?URL=/ code/sample.asp?url=/msdn-files/027/001/580/MsdnCompositeDoc.xml.

The SOAP Toolkit 2.0 provides a more robust Web service creation experience. It includes a client-side component that can be used to raise calls across the Internet, contains a wizard that automatically generates required .wsml and .wsdl files, and handles communication marshalling across the Internet. If you are developing with Visual Basic 6.0 and want to turn your DLLs into Web services, the SOAP Toolkit 2.0 is literally the only way to go.

In .NET, SOAP is inherently part of the .NET Framework, so creating and calling SOAP-based Web services is even easier than using the SOAP Toolkit and client-side components associated with Visual Studio 6.0. Once you install the framework, you have effectively established the foundation for SOAP Web services.

The .NET Framework is free to download. If you want to experiment with Web services but don't know where to start, go to http://msdn .microsoft.com/downloads/default.asp?url=/downloads/sample.asp? url=/msdnfiles/027/000/976/msdncompositedoc.xml&frame=true and download the .NET Redistributable Framework. It contains all the ingredients that are needed to run .NET Framework applications and includes the CLR, the .NET Framework Class Library, and ASP.NET.

The download is only 21 MB, but pay attention to the hardware, software, and installation requirements. Later in this book we delve into building .NET Web service consumers and providers, demonstrating how you build them, and documenting how they work.

Several non-Microsoft development environments provide built-in SOAP support. Because SOAP is now an industry standard, you can also expect ever more platforms and products to support it.

The Pros and Cons of SOAP

Prior to .NET, leveraging SOAP on the client required the client to have the SOAP client component installed on the client's PC to initialize the SOAP object and make SOAP-based Web service calls. Although the SOAP Toolkit doesn't require much space on a user's machine, Internet options sometimes need to be tweaked to support client-side calls. For the general user, this could spell problems.

In addition to this, the SOAP-based Internet calls support a limited number of data types. If a developer is expecting unconventional in, out, or return values, then programmatic modifications might be needed to meet the SOAP specification.

Not all PC equipment is created equal. For users of very low-end systems, client-side processing could spark trouble. If extensive client-side processing is performed on these PCs, it might cause them to crash or, at best, slow to a crawl.

Pros

Here are some of the advantages of SOAP:

- SOAP is a lightweight protocol, allowing the client to submit only necessary pieces of information as transient data to the server instead of requiring an entire Web page to be submitted, although it is flexible enough to support server-side processing from a page request, if necessary.

- SOAP, unlike many other distributed communication solutions, can be easily integrated on the client and server PCs. With .NET, the effort to communicate in a client/server scenario is minimal.

- SOAP can be leveraged as an internal or external type of HTTP communicator without changing the code to adapt to both topologies. Internal communication is known as remoting, whereas external communication is known as Web services.

- SOAP is a protocol that sits atop the host HTTP protocol. Because HTTP is a well-known and widely used protocol, remote Web-based communication is no longer a challenge.

- SOAP is documented as a recommendation by the W3C.

- SOAP is recognized and used by many well-known software vendors.

- SOAP solves the problem of transporting data through firewalls for server-side processing of user requests.

- SOAP used in .NET is almost transparent. It's like writing functions: It is literally as easy as referencing a DLL in your application.

- SOAP in .NET is built into the framework, so there is nothing else to install. The developer establishes the Web reference, and Microsoft IntelliSense can help you do the rest. The code is similar to referencing and calling a local COM+ DLL. (See Figure 1.3.)

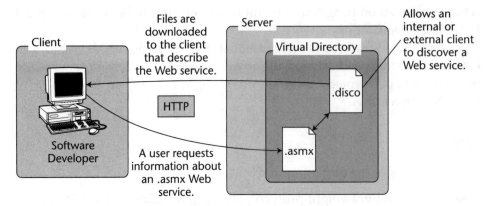

**The above example depicts non-proxy, the scenario for non-proxy Web service classes only.

Figure 1.3   How Web services are discovered.

Cons

Here are some of the negatives associated with SOAP:

- SOAP standards provided by the W3C are merely recommendations (as are all the standards provided by the W3C), so some companies might drive their own SOAP initiatives and internal standards, making it difficult or impossible to communicate with processes of different application languages and platforms. By doing this, they will be defeating the purpose of interoperability, something that many individuals and groups are hoping the SOAP protocol continues to permit.

- SOAP is still hounded by data type limitations. It still is not possible to pass an unlimited number of data types via HTTP. Most intranet and Internet communications can be accomplished using three or four different data types, but if a special circumstance arose that required a special user-defined data type (UDT), SOAP could not be the solution.

- SOAP can expose a lot of functionality, depending on the code you write. If you write code allowing a Web service to format your C: drive and expose it as a Web service, don't be surprised if it someday gets called!

NOTE If you are building Active Directory applications using Web services, be ultra-careful about what functionality you provide to those who are accessing your XML Web service.

What Types of Businesses Should Use Web Services?

The following types of businesses should consider Web services:

- New businesses seeking to provide functionality to other developers using the Internet.

- Any business that already has an Internet presence. These businesses can leverage the advantages of SOAP-based Web methods in their applications.

- Any business that is currently using Winsock or RCP as a method of remote communication.

- Companies that have diversified software project initiatives by IDE, operating system, or both. By default, Web services are as secure as internal remoting objects because they can be exposed only to members of the domain you choose. Authentication methods include Basic, Windows, Digest, Forms, and Passport. You control who has access to your Web methods programmatically.

XML Web Services Security in .NET

When considering .NET for Web services and SOAP, the first thing most people think about is security. Many people believe there isn't any security wrapped around Web services. True, security isn't readily visible to the user and is usually configured internally to the server, but that doesn't mean Web services aren't secure!

Another concern is that Web services are publicly exposed. This leads people to believe that anyone can simply reference a Web service and begin using its public methods. This, too, is an unfounded concern. In fact, we can even use Windows authentication to restrict the users of our Web service to only those people who have valid user accounts on the same domain as the server.

At first, it is easy to conceive of .NET Web services as functions on the Web that anyone can use at any time. The truth is that anyone with information pertaining to the location of the .asmx Web service file can reference a published or unpublished Web service. Referencing a Web service and using a Web service, though, are two entirely different things.

If the authentication and authorization nodes stored in the Web.Config file are modified to protect a public Web method, then the user of the Web service might be in for a shock when the Windows Authentication dialog box appears, a Passport Authentication screen pops up, a form login emerges, and so forth. In general, we don't want to use any type of authorization that forces human interaction, because XML Web services are meant more for computer consumption than for human consumption, but it is something we may consider using.

The Web.Config file is an autonomous security file, containing more built-in methods of authentication than the Internet Information System's (IIS) Internet Security Manager (ISM). The only way to configure Passport Authentication in IIS is through the Web.Config file. Every available method of authentication and authorization available in IIS is also available for modification in the Web.Config file, and the Web.Config file actually supports even more methods of authentication than are available in the IIS ISM. We will discuss these methods further in later chapters.

Other Types of Security Measures

Suppose we are a full-service brokerage firm that offers real-time stock quotes to our clients on the Web. The Web service operates using a unique identifier as an input parameter and then returns an XML structure containing the stock quotes.

The fact that we are offering only stock quotes might not warrant the need for using encryption software to disguise the information because this information is common knowledge and readily available to the general public at many Web sites. The fact that we are offering this as a service available only to our clientele, though, might warrant some form of secrecy. After all, the stock quotes that are returned to our users will most likely reflect either the stocks held in their portfolios or ones they are interested in purchasing.

As a result, it might be advantageous to hide the input parameters of the Web service, making it difficult for unauthorized individuals to use the service. By keeping the parameters hidden and simply exposing a string without a definitive structure, you keep individuals from being able to use the service.

After all, if external viewers do not know what the required XML structure is to use the service and do not have access to code behind the Web service, then chances are they will send invalid XML structures and unacceptable values.

As a result, an XSD document can be established to automatically deny them access before any true processing ensues. Also, the unauthorized individual has no idea what type of string the method is expecting. The viewer of the exposed Web service is left wondering if the expected input is a number, a serial code, alphabetic characters, XML, or something else.

In addition to this, using a single string parameter in your Web service's input parameter can also keep the expected information disguised. By exposing a list of parameters, you could be giving away your business to your competitors. After all, if your competitors are aware of what data you are capturing they might be able figure out the services you are providing, making it easy for them to replicate the Web service and reduce the income that you are generating from your customers.

Summary

In this chapter we defined SOAP, provided examples demonstrating the protocol hierarchy, and discussed how things were done prior to the existence of Web services. We discussed the lineage of SOAP, Web services versus DCOM and Winsock, the SOAP Toolkit, the pros and cons of SOAP-based Web services, what entities should use Web services, high-level .NET Web services security, plus additional security measures that you can use to make your applications more secure.

More importantly, we also discussed the reasons behind XML Web services and why they are an excellent choice for implementing remote invocation requirements. We also discovered what types of problems are suited to Web services and presented a brief introduction to Web services in .NET.

The Hutchings Photography Business Model

XML Web services are ideal for many business-to-business (B2B) applications. Before XML, dissimilar systems had to agree on a proprietary data format to transact their commerce. For those firms that didn't start up a full-blown EDI system, CSV and XLS files ran their order processing. XML provides a common, self-describing data format, which is sorely needed for B2B commerce. Add to that the routing and discovery capabilities that SOAP, WSDL, and UDDI provide, and you've got an infrastructure ripe for any number of new or improved B2B ventures.

XML Web services allow for specific functions to be published and used between two businesses. Application Service Providers (ASPs), which have become popular in the last few years on the Internet, may now publish their services with an even finer level of granularity in a framework that is both intuitive and universally accepted. These ASPs were typically browser/server applications where the calls to the service were fairly complicated and embedded in the client-side processing. Not only did this approach reveal a bit too many details to the users about the transactions taking place, it was proprietary in nature and suffered browser compatibility problems, as does any code running client-side in a public Internet browser. The solution to the continued success of these ASPs was to embed the calls on the server side so that the two businesses were communicating server to server, with the client or consumer seeing only the end product.

Another issue with ASPs is a matter of trust. Successful service providers don't encroach into gray areas of commerce where consumers start to feel threatened. The public demands its privacy and thus will not gravitate toward applications that require sensitive information to be stored on a foreign system. This goes beyond the concern that people have about storing their credit card numbers on another party's server. With B2B applications, other worries include a firm storing important files on another system that is out of its control. These can be customer lists, files, business information, transaction histories, databases, or other forms of hosted data—critical systems that keep a business in business—sitting on someone else's hardware. The client may have no insight to the durability of the data center, the maintenance and backup procedures (or lack thereof), or the expertise of the staff.

These are the sorts of issues that keep firms from buying into some of the more elaborate ASPs. Because there hasn't really been a standard way of transporting data, some of the more interesting ASPs required the client to park its data on their servers. The fear is that the client's data will be located in only one location—a location not controlled by the client, which could become a single-point-of-failure issue.

XML Web services address this point because they are entirely stateless, meaning that the client does not need to host any confidential data on the service's system and that the server doesn't need to host any proprietary connection information on the client. Once the connection endpoint (typically a URL) is known, all required information can be passed to the XML Web service with every call. This behavior is reminiscent of the Windows API, in which you knew of the function in the API and you called it without any fanfare. Add to this the cross-platform capability of the XML format of the SOAP message and return value, and you've got a stage on which to build or upgrade thousands of proprietary systems on the Internet.

Hutchings Photography

Hutchings Photography is an assignment and stock photography business in New Rochelle, New York. The business of stock photography is becoming increasingly popular, especially in today's modern, wired world of constant advertising and marketing. Stock photography describes a business model whereby the proprietor manages a large number of photographic images. These photographs are then categorized into any number of different themes, indexed, and then offered for sale to buyers for their specific needs. Essentially, stock photography turns photographs into a commodity.

In the beginning, Hutchings Photography was purely an assignment photography business, fulfilling contracts for various clients. Over the past 30 years, several hundreds of thousands of negatives, slides, and prints have amassed in their archives. A prosperous stock photography company, however, is not the one with the most images, but the one with the best marketing.

As with any automation project, a solid analysis of the existing process can discover loopholes, areas of inefficiency, and areas of redundancy. While analyzing Hutchings Photography's manual process, many questions were asked that the proprietors had never thought of or had not felt a need to address. Writing software, as was explained to them, is a very explicit process, and all of the business rules and processes need to be identified and implemented.

The Manual Process

Hutchings Photography added the stock photography service virtually from day 2. As soon as the staff had a few photos in storage, they would ponder those as alternatives for current assignments. Not until they arrived at a store of several thousand photos did it become worthwhile to put a process in place to sell these photos. Pioneers in this field, Hutchings Photography approached it as any other customer relationship business.

The original, manual process (see Figure 2.1) shows the physical steps taken from first contact with the client through the delivery of the images.

We will take a look at each step in the process in detail and provide a useful example so that you can see how a stock photography licensing transaction flows from beginning to end.

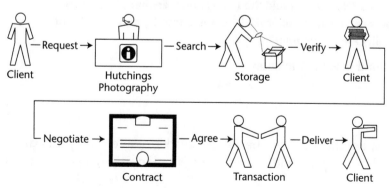

Figure 2.1   The stock photography retail process.

Requesting

The first step in buying stock photography is for a client to have a need. The client then needs to make a request. This request can come in the form of a phone call, fax, or email to the stock photography house directly or through one of its brokers. It is important for the request to be as specific as possible. There are thousands of photographs, each of which will have to be evaluated. If you were to compare the client's request to a SQL query, it's important to get that WHERE clause as specific as possible to restrict the number of results. Knowledgeable staff or an efficient filing system can aid in this task.

Traditional marketing and word of mouth are mechanisms used to get the name Hutchings Photography into the marketplace. In addition, as soon as clients begin licensing and using Hutchings' images, the copyright notice on the correspondence, frames, and images themselves becomes a mode of marketing as well. Earlier copyrights simply read *Copyright (c) Hutchings Photography*, but now read *Copyright (c) HutchingsPhotography.com*, which corresponds to its Web site's URL. This type of marketing is known as *viral marketing*, a technique whereby the product itself passes along the marketing message as it is being observed by individuals. Assuming the product is professional and appealing, this type of marketing has the potential for exponential growth, much like a virus.

EXAMPLE   **Kristen, a marketing consultant for an environmental group based in New York City, visits Hutchings Photography. She saw one of its photographs in a popular magazine and contacted the editor, who forwarded her the contact information. Kristen speaks with Amy and indicates that she is looking for a photo of a family engaged in recycling. Amy, who has knowledge of those types of photographs in the files, asks additional questions to help narrow the range of possible images and find a match with an image in inventory, such as "How old should the family members be?", "How many family members can be in the photo?", "Can the photo be outdoors?", and "What nationality are the people?"**

Elapsed time for this step: 12 minutes.

Searching

Before the advent of the Internet, dial-up networks, or even computer databases, stock photography shops executed long-running, carbon-based queries against three-dimensional devices (read: humans manually looked for images in storage boxes). With any luck, the photographer or office manager would have an eidetic memory or maybe an efficient filing system that would make Melvil Dewey proud. Quite often requests for these photos are denied because of ignorance of their existence or the inability to retrieve such images from the bowels of the filing system.

A categorization system was created and continues to be honed. In the early days, those images that were retained from photo shoots could be filed and categorized on sticky notes. Through the years, a more methodical system has been installed, one that translated into software without pain. Here are a few of the image categories used at Hutchings Photography: Amusements, Animals, Arts and Crafts, and Weather. These categories are broken down again and again, further refining the category.

Beyond this system of categories, however, it's up to the operators of the business to know what images are in each of the categories. Misfiled slides, slides that are currently checked out, or slides that are correctly filed under other categories deemed more appropriate are all reasons why the desired image is not found and commerce is lost.

Hutchings Photography implemented a manual card file system, much like the one you'd find in a public library (see Figure 2.2). With this system, every image was identified by a unique, numeric ID. This ID was a simple expression of MMDDYY##, where MM equaled the month of the photo shoot, DD equaled the day of the photo shoot, YY equaled the year of the photo shoot, and ## equaled the photo number taken that day. Each card would also list the topic, subtopic (if any), title, description, and any other descriptive information.

EXAMPLE Amy takes Kristen's written request and heads to the file cabinets. She has in mind the photo of a mother and her daughter carrying a large recycling bin full of plastic containers to the street. Amy had used this photo only a few weeks prior and is fairly sure that the slide was returned. She decides to look first in the ecology files and, after several minutes, gives up. Thinking about the content of the photo she has in mind, she looks again in the family cabinet, specifically for activities. Again, no luck. Finally, she remembers that the last client to use the image had wanted it for the teamwork angle of the photo, not the recycling or family aspects. She looks in the business cabinet and successfully locates the image among others in the teamwork and cooperation folders.

Elapsed time for this step: 19 minutes.

Topic – Ecology   Image # – **05189615**

Sub-Topic – Recycling

Title – **Mother, daughter and dog recycling plastic**

Description – Shot of mother, daughter and northern breed dog,
        possibly a malamute; all standing near the curb and handing
        a blue recycling bin of plastic containers to a man near the
        back of a recycling truck; Fall time, clear day

Models – Jane Smith (mother), Suzie Smith (daughter), Bob Jones
        (driver)

Source – Richard Hutchings, Photographer

Format – Reversal, 120mm, Kodak 100 SW, 150mm Lens

Media Type – Chrome/Slide

Shot for Stock – No

Shot for Assignment – Yes (1996, ACME Publishing)

Restrictions – Do not release until May 2000; Models cannot be used in
a derogatory or defamatory manner; A written, signed model release is
on file (document # 1.5.219)

Usage History –

Client	Media Usage	Date	Fee
_____	_____	_____	_____
_____	_____	_____	_____
_____	_____	_____	_____
_____	_____	_____	_____

Figure 2.2   Sample of current filing system.

Verification

Once the prospective images have been located, the client must see them
before approving and licensing can begin. This step is referred to as verification and can take several forms. Ideally, the client will look directly at the
image and decide if it's suitable. Potential clients, however, can be located
anywhere in the world. Restricting the verification to local clients greatly
reduces Hutchings' marketplace.

Other options were to use the telephone or fax to describe an image. This approach could deliver only so much detail to the client, and it often frustrated the chances of sale. This type of verification was a deal-breaker when it came to enforcing a contract where the purchasing party hadn't seen the image directly before licensing. The ideal solution was to deliver a high-quality reproduction that conveyed the original image's detail, yet protected the rights of Hutchings Photography.

Getting a copy of the image to a remote client became the big challenge. Sending the original would be taking quite a risk. To balance the protection of rights with the trust of marketing, the ideal solution was to generate a watermarked positive and overnight it to the customer. This took time and money, which often weren't recouped by the sale of a license.

Remote clients who have worked with Hutchings in the past have developed a level of trust in the proprietors' judgment. A description over the phone or fax is often sufficient for the client to be satisfied. If the client has a solid relationship with Hutchings, then the company may just send several of the slides over to the client and let the client choose among them. These types of relationships are uncommon and will present a challenge when building the automated process.

To summarize, the options for verification are:

In person.   Client reviews the original slide, negative, or print at Hutchings Photography.

Mail.   Valuable clients receive original images and others receive a second-generation copy.

Fax.   Photocopies of the images or printouts are faxed to the client.

Phone.   The images are described over the phone.

Email.   With the introduction of email, images can be scanned, watermarked, and delivered.

EXAMPLE   Amy returns with the slide to Kristen, who studies it and agrees that she likes the content. Kristen asks if she could take the original back to her office for the meeting in two days. Amy asks some preliminary questions about the environmental firm and their potential use of the image. Amy then makes a subjective decision that doing business with Kristen's firm is worth the risk of sending the original out the door for verification. Amy has Kristen sign a liability statement indicating the penalty for not returning the image or returning it damaged and the method of payment. Kristen signs the agreement and leaves with the original slide.

Elapsed time for this step: 15 minutes.

Negotiation

Once a client has verified the image and is interested in licensing it, the negotiations begin. For 95 percent of these transactions, a standard license agreement and fee are used. This agreement is typically spelled out on the bill of sale itself—no formal contract is even used. Hutchings realizes that stronger legal language should be used because the images are the capital of the business. Occasionally, however, the client wants to license the image for multiple or unique purposes, or the image is of such tremendous value that a special license must be negotiated.

Often, clients will want to license the image in such a way that Hutchings promises not to license the image (or similar images) to the client's competition. This can be a very specialized negotiation, listing each of the known competitors or just the industry itself. The negotiation might also list the states or regions where the exclusion applies.

In addition to identifying how and why the image will be used, this negotiation step includes recording all of the client's information, such as the type of business, address, phone numbers, managers, and years in business. For larger contracts, financial statements are sometimes requested. Because each license is a kind of partnership, Hutchings Photography must keep its reputation in mind.

Hutchings Photography has several categories of license to choose from. Some are more liberal in how the client can use the image and cost more. Others are more restrictive in how the client can use the image and cost less. The bottom line is that the image will be licensed such that the more substantial the intended use and the more exposure Hutchings has for its popular images, the higher the fee to use the image.

Hutchings Photography licenses its images in four ways:

Rights protected (explicit use).   Hutchings Photography spells out exactly how the image will be used, and the rights are assigned for only that use. These rights are specific, and no other use is allowed. Both the purchaser and the intended purpose are explicitly identified, typically on the invoice. This form of license can also be enhanced, often for an additional price, to include an exclusivity clause to have the purchaser's rights protected as well, such that Hutchings guarantees not to license the image to a competitor (limited buyout). This would be considered the baseline license.

Flat rate (nonexclusive, multiuse).   The purchaser pays a single price and, in turn, is granted the permission to use the image for any number of purposes for a range of dates. With this kind of license, only the purchaser is explicitly identified. This kind of license would cost about five times the cost of the rights-protected license.

Royalty free.   The purchaser pays a single price, sometimes for a batch of several photographs and, in turn, may do pretty much anything with them short of going into business against Hutchings. Royalty free doesn't mean free, although exceptions are sometimes made. No image, regardless of the negotiated price, however, may be resold. This kind of license would cost about 10 times the cost of the rights-protected license.

Buyout (outright sale).   This is extremely rare, but it can happen when the client wants to own the image outright. Although it is more common in the business of assignment photography, occasionally, stock photographs are sold outright as well. Clients may also opt to buy out all *similar* images as well. Because Hutchings would be ending its ability to derive income from an image, prices to purchase outright can be up to 20 times the cost of the rights-protected license.

Based on the type of license and other factors of the negotiations, license, damage, and other fees are articulated to the client. Here are some examples:

Usage.   This is the core price for licensing the image. For most sales, this usage fee is a flat rate per customer, but often Hutchings varies the fee based on special circumstances of the client, such as budget, number of images being licensed, and the chance to do future business with the client.

Replacement.   The value of each original image must be identified during negotiations. The default value is $1,500 per image. For a unique or exceptional image, this value would be higher.

Holding.   If the client receives the original image, he or she is required to return it by a specific date. Failure to do so will result in a daily or weekly fee.

Damages for failure to include credit.   The client is required to display the image's copyright notice on or near the image when it is used. Failure to place the notice, or placing the wrong notice, will result in a damage fee, which is typically two to three times the cost of the usage fee. The client can request the copyright not to be displayed, which can result in a higher usage fee.

Damages for manipulation of the images.   Unless otherwise stipulated, Hutchings' images may not be digitally or mechanically manipulated. Doing so may result in a damage fee.

Research.   Research fees apply if Hutchings Photography has to research any existing usages of images by one or more firms, typically competitors. Research fees are based on an hourly rate and may be recovered by the client.

Shipping and handling.   Hutchings passes the shipping and nominal handling fees through to the client, especially for rush or courier services.

Ideally, Hutchings and the client should come away from the negotiations with a feeling that they both have won. This is very possible with an in-person negotiation, but more difficult when responding to email, fax, or other forms of automated dialogue.

EXAMPLE   Kristen returns to Hutchings Photography a few days later and meets with Peter to negotiate the license of the image. Peter determines that Kristen's needs are special and beyond the scope of a standard license, so he begins to go through the options with her. Kristen explains that her firm wants to use the photograph in three distinct ways: on the cover of its annual report, on all fliers used in North America for the next year, and as the main graphic on the company's Web page. Kristen also explains that her firm doesn't want Hutchings Photography to license this photo or any similar photograph from the same shoot.

Peter asks Kristen many questions, such as the languages and areas of the world where the report and the fliers will be distributed, as well as the amount of traffic, current and expected, on its Web site. Because Kristen has asked for special protection, Peter must list all of Kristen's firm's competitors that are to be excluded. Fortunately, Kristen has brought a list of 12 names.

Peter types up a contract detailing the client, the image, the intended usages, the protection clause, and the copyright information. Kristen has brought her own contract as well, which lists the expectations that her firm has of Hutchings Photography.

Elapsed time for this step: 45 minutes.

Agreement

Agreeing to the terms of the contract is a small but essential component of the transaction. Although contracts can be updated and superceded, the agreement step is where both parties certify the terms of the contract with a signature. It is also in this step that Hutchings Photography must verify that the individual agreeing to the contract and signing it is a valid representative of the client.

Authenticating the individual comes down to a matter of trust. Hutchings Photography must make a subjective decision as to whether the person signing the agreement is capable of sealing the deal. In other words, will the client's firm pay the forthcoming invoice after it has been negotiated by this person? Hutchings Photography can make its decision based on several factors, such as possession of a purchase order, use of a company credit card, or a person's title in the company.

As trivial as this step may seem, it is important to separate it from the negotiations and delivery steps when we start looking at the automated systems.

EXAMPLE   Kristen and Peter review both contracts one last time. Peter inquires about payment, and Kristen produces a signed purchase order from her firm. Seeing this, Peter feels more confident about Kristen being an authorized agent of the company. He goes on to explain that payment is required within 30 days of the invoice date. They both sign copies of the contracts.

Elapsed time for this step: 5 minutes.

Delivery

Once the contract has been signed, Hutchings Photography delivers the image. If the client still has the original from the verification step, there is no delivery to speak of. Had the client verified the image by some other means, Hutchings must locate, package, and deliver the image to the client.

Depending on the format requested by the client, this step might also include some media manipulation. For example, Hutchings Photography may have only a *chrome* (slide) of the image, but the client requested a four-part color separation. Hutchings Photography would then be required to convert the image to the requested media.

With the increasing popularity of professional digital photography, the delivery vehicle mechanism is simplified as the image only needs to be emailed, FTPed, or burned to a CD-ROM. The digital format, however, introduces many areas of possible manipulation that a client might request: resizing, color depths, formats, cropping, digital effects, and so forth.

EXAMPLE Because Kristen's firm has a staff of media professionals, she doesn't require any manipulation services from Hutchings Photography. Because she already has possession of the original slide, there isn't any delivery to speak of, just the signing of the forms.

Elapsed time for this step: 0 minutes.

The Automated Process (World Wide Web Version)

After reading the previous section, I'm sure you've identified several areas that could be aided by software automation. If you are a seasoned analyst, you've probably also noticed a few areas where the process is loose. These would be areas where the business rules might be painful to implement. Our example business deal took 96 minutes of processing to complete—and this was a smooth, simple transaction. Hutchings Photography knew that it desperately needed automation in its business!

In the late 1990s, Hutchings Photography bit the bullet and turned to the Web to offer a portion of its images to qualified buyers (see Figure 2.3). This version was a traditional Windows DNA architecture, using Active Server Pages, Microsoft Transaction Server, and Microsoft SQL Server. The software served up basic HTML pages, using style sheets and themes. The end result was a slick interface with a middle tier and back end firmly rooted in Microsoft technologies.

Because Hutchings' standards are high and its licensing requirements are strict, the purpose of the public Web site was more for exposure and less for commerce. The goal for this version was to get as many thumbnails and watermarked images digitized and online as possible for the public to find the images they were looking for and then to contact Hutchings Photography about the licensing. Later improvements included the ability to set up a custom portal for a customer and have his or her lightbox (see accompanying note) set up for perusal.

NOTE A *lightbox* is a portal or a personal folder on a Web site where the operators of the site, or even the users themselves, can place images for which there is interest. The idea of a lightbox is similar to that of a shopping cart, with the exception that the users may not necessarily be able to purchase from the lightbox, but rather just verify the images. With Hutchings Photography, the lightbox was an extension of the verification step.

A true e-commerce Web site was never planned, but one eventually came into being, albeit never quite the way Hutchings intended it. The e-commerce portion was added to serve the partners.

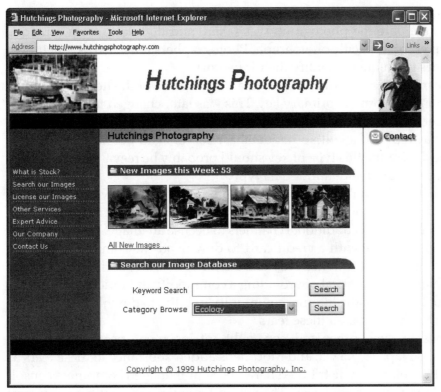

Figure 2.3   The main page of HutchingsPhotography.com.

One of the first big challenges with the Web site was to digitize all the photos and provide sufficient metadata about each one. This metadata consisted of all the important properties of the image, such as the photographer's name, copyright, year, title, and any keywords. Most of this metadata could be taken from the filing cards (see Figure 2.2). All photographs are identified, cataloged, and searched according to this metadata. The automated search is a replacement for a human doing the searching. The Image ID is returned with, more important, a thumbnail or watermark of the image itself. In a way, the metadata may take more time to procure and thus be more valuable than the photograph itself. After all, you're not going to sell many steaks if they're not on the menu.

Without the right combination of descriptive keywords, prospective customers won't locate the images. These keywords were not part of the original, manual system so they had to be assembled by a human looking at the photograph and making decisions. As far as identifying a particular photograph goes, until there is a system such as ISBN for photographs to hand out unique IDs, photographers must rely on some combination of their name, the date the photograph was taken, and its title to form a unique identifier for a specific photograph. Photographers may also use their own schemes to uniquely identify their inventory.

The original image database used a combination of the items previously mentioned to form its primary key. This was later changed to an ascending number, or Identity value in Microsoft SQL Server. With the chance of someday replicating with other database servers and possibly performing offline data entry, this type of key should probably be reevaluated, possibly making it a Uniqueidentifier data type.

Hutchings' initial thinking was that anyone with a browser can visit its Web site, search and view thumbnails of its photographs, and then contact Hutchings through traditional channels to license an image. The staff didn't want just anyone with a credit card to download the company's images. Knowing that the Internet provides a near real-time distribution vehicle, Hutchings was skeptical of providing a commodity as liquid as a graphical image. The fear of the Internet community's ability to download and reproduce the images fueled these fears.

News of such organized copyright infringement peer-to-peer (P2P) efforts as Napster, Kazaa, and Morpheus added substance to these fears as well. P2P refers to a distributed network of unmanaged computers consolidated for a specific purpose. The network may or may not have a central server. The purpose of the P2P conglomeration may be quite dignified, such as SETI@home (http://setiathome.ssl.berkeley.edu), which links computers in the Search of Extra Terrestrial Intelligence (SETI). The purpose of the P2P may also be rather insidious, such as with Napster and its various clones—all networks built for the purpose of sharing files, such as music, video, software, and digital images.

This kind of thinking will keep Hutchings' intellectual property safe, but it will not yield the sales that the Internet promises. Even without the Internet, a percentage of paying clients will make illegal copies, and some of those copies will end up in nonpaying clients' hands. Knowing the trade-off of risk versus reward, Hutchings Photography started adding real-time commerce to the Web site in 1999. Visitors could browse the images they wanted, select them, choose the terms that best suit them, provide a credit card number, and agree to the contract online. The image, devoid of the watermark, would be made available for download in one of several digital formats.

Early Commerce Model

In the early stages of the Hutchings Photography Web site, we looked at alternate ways of allowing partners, brokers, and other stock photography consortiums to host the photography metadata and watermarked thumbnails, but not the unspoiled images themselves. The plan was for consumers to visit a partner's Web site, search through the combined database of all photographic metadata, and review interesting thumbnail images. When a consumer located a photograph that he or she wished to license, the commerce was transacted at the partner's Web site; the untouched image was fetched from a secure FTP site and made available for download. Later, the partner mailed a business check for the transaction. Figure 2.4 shows a flowchart describing the process of this early commerce model.

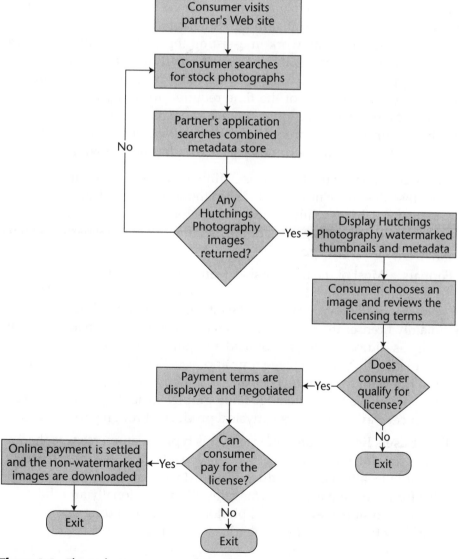

Figure 2.4 The early commerce model.

Hutchings Photography would continue to license its images from its studio using the phone, fax, email, and in-person visits. The firm was pleased to receive additional exposure through its partner Web sites, even though additional setup was required to implement this. The extension of the Web site to the partners seemed like a good solution, but there were a number of problems.

Problems with the Original System

Commerce flowed, and Hutchings Photography licensed some images through the partners' Web sites. The percentages licensed through partnerships, however, were equivalent to those licensed through the Hutchings Photography Web site itself. Either Hutchings was working with the wrong partners, or all the work in assisting the partners with their sites, migrating and transporting the metadata and thumbnails, and assisting with the application code was not paying off as it should have. If anyone had actually done a study of the time required to set up a partner compared to the amount of revenue generated, these partnerships would never have been launched. The process of getting a partner integrated with the Hutchings Web site must become easier. Consider the following issues:

Lopsided effort.   Hutchings was definitely making its partners happy because they were now able to boast thousands of additional photos in their databases while someone else supported the headache. It seemed that Hutchings was doing all the work and the partners were gaining all of the exposure.

Formats.   Most of the partner sites were interested only in offering immediate-download, soft-copy images in JPEG, TIFF, or GIF format. Hutchings Photography, like other stock photography houses, mainly licenses its works in original positive or negative format, typically as slides. These types of media require more time to procure, more handling, and postage time and fees. For that reason, partners did not want to be involved with anything more tangible than a downloadable file. Hutchings Photography struggled to find an economical way to offer these physical products through partner sites.

The abusers list.   A consequence of this type of commerce was the need for Hutchings Photography to keep a list of consumers that would illegally use its products. This list was small and inconsequential for the most part, but it was referred to occasionally and did manage to stop a few licensed photographs from ending up in the hands of firms that abused their licenses. Hutchings Photography never got to the point of distributing this list to its partners. It wasn't even sure it wanted to.

Adding or removing images.   Different partners had different photographs on their Web sites. Hutchings Photography would have to remember that partner 1 had 1,200 specific images, partner 2 had 700 specific images, and so on. If a new image was added to the main database, it would have to be manually made available to each of the partners, such as by asking them to visit the New Photos page. On the other hand, if Hutchings outright sells an image under a buyout agreement, it would have to contact each of the partners to verify that it no longer markets that photo.

Updating metadata.   When new photographs were made available, the metadata had to be distributed to all of the partner sites. This process was automated but still required customization, as some partner Web sites wanted comma-separated value (CSV) files and others wanted Excel spreadsheets (XLS) and later XML formats. Hutchings Photography was not large enough to dictate its own file format—yet.

Updating thumbnails.   Every partner agreed that JPEG images were the way to go. The fact that there was a small loss of quality for the sake of the JPEG compression was fine as these were just thumbnails. The problem was that each partner wanted its thumbnails a certain size to better fit within its pages. We did, however, automate this conversion procedure, but it was still a push process and not a pull process. When a partner wanted to revamp its Web site, it would have to submit a manual request and we'd convert the new thumbnail formats as a batch and then email, FTP, or mail a CD-ROM to them.

Updating business rules.   If Hutchings Photography ever changed its business rules, such as discounting or changing the verbiage of their licenses as a whole or for certain photographs, it was difficult to propagate those rules to the partner's Web site. This difficulty was compounded when a partner blended its business rules with those of Hutchings Photography, especially when the partner was not running on a Microsoft-supported platform.

Lost commerce.   Although it never happened, there is the chance that a partner simply forgot to send in its payment to Hutchings Photography. Because the partner's Web site was an autonomous agent, it was able to conduct the transaction and deliver the image to the client without Hutchings' knowing.

It's All about the *Right* Partnerships

The stock photography business can be very location transparent. A consumer, searching for the perfect image, could certainly find and license directly from the photography house, or the consumer might contact one of the photographer's preferred agents or brokers. In the latter case, our consumer could find the same photo for a different licensing fee and set of stipulations. Although each layer or broker means more exposure for the stock house to advertise and sell its photographs, it also typically equates to less profit, as every person along the commerce pathway tacks on a finder's fee and an individual set of rules and regulations.

As long as the important legal facts about the photograph remain intact, where a consumer finds the photograph for sale becomes less important. Progressive photographers, wanting to see their images licensed to a wider audience, are quick to grasp this concept. In their opinion, the reward for having exposure to more potential consumers outweighs the risk of hosting their unprotected, unwatermarked images on a virtually unknown Web site.

WARNING To have partnerships in which other Web sites are able to completely handle the commerce cycle on Hutchings' behalf, those Web sites need access to the raw, unprotected images themselves.

In order for a partner's Web site to allow the consumer to license and eventually download an image, all of the photographer's images must be made available in a virgin, unwatermarked form. Sophisticated Web sites can watermark an image on the fly (see Figure 2.5), as visitors browse the thumbnails, but it would be impossible to un-watermark an image on the fly. By hosting so many of the photographer's cherished images, a great deal of trust is extended to the partner, as there could be many thousands of images, each worth hundreds of dollars in licensing fees. That's an expensive loss if a compromise occurs.

For this reason, full-blown partnerships like this are few. More often than not, Hutchings Photography was merely listed as a link from a pseudo-partner's Web site and labeled "click here for more great photographs." This sometimes did more harm than good, as a really great photography house such as Hutchings was reduced to a blasé hyperlink on a page—a page that already had good photographs right there to browse. Human psychology suggests that visitors will search what is directly in front of them, possibly settling for another product, rather than shopping around on a nonspecific link.

Figure 2.5   An image with the Hutchings Photography watermark.

The Automated Process (Web Service Version)

We used our initial implementation plus fixes here and there as a model for our next version. The plan was for the next version to directly benefit by implementing XML Web services. With an experience of failures, and some successes, a more successful system will be designed—one that is more open to partners and yet keeps our data more secure on our own servers.

Fortunately, our staff has a firm understanding of Visual Basic and VB Script. The legacy version of the Hutchings Photography Web site was a traditional Windows DNA application, using Active Server Pages to handle the server-side processing and ActiveX DLLs to do the heavy lifting. SQL Server 2000 will be used as the database management system.

The new commerce model was designed with XML Web services in mind. We will continue to integrate with our partner Web sites. Our new approach will be 100 percent application-to-application calls rather than the hybrid it has been in the past. Previously, some of our partners' code accessed our resources, and some of our code accessed our partners' resources. It always depended on the situation, including who had the more talented professionals available. Using XML, we will now be able to easily communicate with applications on non-Microsoft platforms, such as a Linux server running Apache.

It's important to remember that Web services are called by other programs and not directly by humans. The Web methods that we will implement on the Hutchings Photography site will ease the partner's ability to spin up their commerce site. The partner Web sites, however, will continue to process the payment.

A New List of Goals

The goal of the company hasn't changed. It's still to market and license its stock photography to as many customers as possible. The goal of the automated system, however, has changed a bit.

The previous version catered too much to the partners when it should be more balanced. Because Hutchings Photography was a bit late to the Internet, it was eager for as much exposure as possible in a short time. This led to many integration projects that were over and above what would be expected of a partner. For example, it's a fairly rare thing when a partner performs gratis programming for another partner. This was not uncommon with our partners.

By implementing the various steps of the process as Web services, partners can easily make a call to the Hutchings Photography Web service endpoint and have the data they are looking for returned. All the data, business rules, and contract terms will be hosted within the Web service.

Web Services

The following is a list of functions to be supported by the Hutchings Photography Web services. The eventual implementations will be different; but at a high level, this is a list of functionality that we will need.

ReturnThumbs()   Supports the searching and verification steps; returns image as thumbnail that can be custom sized for a partner's Web site.

ReturnImage()   Supports the searching and verification steps; returns image as larger, watermarked image.

RequestContract()   Supports the negotiation step; returns license agreement for perusal.

NegotiateContract()   Supports the negotiate step; end user can counter with an offer or special conditions.

CheckNegotiateStatus()   Supports the negotiate step; end user or partner can check on a specially negotiated contract.

AcceptContract()   Supports the agreement step; the contract is submitted by an authorized representative of the client and the pristine image is returned.

ReturnReferenceTables()   Supports the partner by providing all reference data for population of the partner's Web site.

All the partner Web site must do is make the appropriate method call to the Web service. Because the Hutchings Photography site will support HTTP-GET, HTTP-POST, and SOAP-formatted Web service calls, the partner is free to implement its Web site in whatever language it is comfortable with. The returned information will be in XML format so, again, the partner may use whatever parsing engine it is comfortable with.

Centralized Data

Having the pristine images hosted on a partner's Web site, no matter the level of trust in place, still makes everyone nervous. There are liability issues as well as the risk of exposing the images to pirates. As a result of upgrading the Web site to a Web service, Hutchings is able to centrally locate everything on its server. All access to the images, whether using thumbnails, watermarks, or the virgin images themselves, will be possible only through the exposed Web services.

This security mechanism is similar to locking down the tables in SQL Server so that nobody but the System Administrator has access to the tables. All access to the tables is then made available through stored procedures. The Transact SQL code can handle any exceptions or business rule violations explicitly.

New photos are instantly available to a partner's Web sites searches. Removed photos are instantly removed from searches. No longer does Hutchings Photography need to contact the partners individually to inform them of inventory changes.

Centralized Business Rules

By forcing all partners to call the NegotiateContract() and SignContract() Web methods, Hutchings is able to manage the code behind those calls centrally. The next partner that makes the call will see the new material. If Hutchings decides to pull a photograph from its stock database, it can do so by setting a flag, and the next query will not find that image. This kind of real-time software business rule maintenance can be a silver bullet when problems arise with a particular photograph or its various verbiages. For example, if Hutchings finds that the market as a whole has been abusing copyrighted material, it may decide to strengthen the wording of its contract.

Consolidated Image Formats

In order to attract more partners, Hutchings Photography realizes that it must offer its digital images in a number of popular formats. Fortunately, the GDI+ capabilities of the .NET Framework provide many such capabilities. Hutchings will support JPEG, GIF, and TIFF formats electronically in addition to their physical media, such as chromes and negatives.

Centralized Abusers List

To be able to centrally manage a list of companies, clients, individuals, credit card numbers, and so forth that have been known to abuse licensed material is a bonus. When a partner makes a call to NegotiateContract(), enough information about the client must be passed with it to make a query against the list of abusers. If any hit is returned, the deal is off. The XML returned by the NegotiateContract() method would contain the reason why the contract was denied.

Put the Effort on the Partner

Backed by the powerful standards of XML, SOAP, and HTTP, not to mention the XML Web services marketing dollars of Microsoft, partners will quickly buy into a solution that is made available to them. They will be prone to invest in a programming effort to consume XML Web services, thinking that they will be doing it again and again in the future.

Once Hutchings Photography hosts these Web services, essentially our job is done. Sure, there will still be some marketing to prospective partners and possibly some shared expenses in migrating current partners over to the Web service way of doing things. Also, resourceful partners may want to craft their own Web services to screen existing stock photography databases. This would result in even more potential hits for a given search.

Commerce Tracking

Partners will continue to perform their own e-commerce. Credit cards, purchase orders, checks, or money orders will be accepted and handled by each partner according to its own rules. Hutchings Photography simply wants to be the back end. By using Web services, however, the commerce is able to be tracked because each contract request and acceptance will be passed through the Web service, and auditing will be enabled. At the end of the period, Hutchings will be able to review the number of SignContract() Web method calls that were executed and reconcile that number against the accounts receivable from the partners.

Distributed Processing

Not every partner can invest in quality hardware or network connectivity. Hutchings Photography, as the sole source of the Web service code, must do this to become and remain profitable. Partners also do not necessarily need to invest in expensive firewalls, security, and other infrastructure technologies.

Depending on how a partner's Web site is designed, it could be calling the Hutchings Web methods asynchronously along with other stock photography databases, especially those also running Web services. We speculate that there will be partners that basically run their queries like many of the comparative shopping bots. Each Web site searched would be a separate thread of execution, all returning to the central application to assemble a master list of returned images.

A Partner Regardless of Platform

An XML parser now exists on every platform that might be participating in Web browsing or hosting. There are several varieties of XML parsers available, as well as Web service SDKs. This pervasiveness guarantees that any platform out there can consume a Web service call. With some creative programming or the running of a wizard (as it is with .NET), partners can connect to our Web service, read our WSDL to understand the interface of our Web methods, and then make the call using the lowest common denominator, which is support for HTTP-GET protocol.

Integration with .NET Passport

We're planning to integrate our Web services with Microsoft's .NET My Services in a later version. We're interested primarily in the Passport service. By using Passport, authentication can be expedited with a single call to Microsoft's Web service. This is automation that the client, the partner, and Hutchings Photography will welcome.

Chapter 3 focuses on the conceptual and logical design of these services. Chapters 5 and 6 focus on the physical implementation of the database access components and the Web services themselves.

A New Database Design

Early on, Microsoft SQL Server version 7.0 was selected as the back end of choice for the Hutchings Photography Web site. This database has served

Hutchings' intranet applications as well as its Web site well. SQL Server 2000 will replace version 7.0 for the new system. SQL Server 2000's integration with XML, scalability, and powerful tools make it an ideal choice as the back end of a .NET Web service application. ADO.NET includes a customized .NET Managed Provider for SQL Server, which will greatly improve our connected layer performance.

Many lessons have been learned from the original database design. The original database was what we refer to as a "Big MAC with cheese, supersized" (a large Microsoft Access database with many bad denormalization traits and "the cheese" upsized directly to SQL Server). The Excel spreadsheet guru fires up Microsoft Access and starts building tables that act like spreadsheets. Yes, those columns named Keyword1, Keyword2, Keyword3 ... Keyword20 are a dead giveaway.

Remember that the new Web machine is going to centrally locate all of the images and metadata on one server or farm of servers. For this reason, the database design will need to have a high-performance query mechanism. Reliable indexes, database maintenance, and optimization techniques will play a large role in keeping this server running efficiently and scaling properly. Remember that no processor upgrade or addition of RAM can compare to the performance gained by sound database design and having the right index.

One discussion that came up early was whether to store the images as BLOBs (Binary Large OBjects) in a table or as files on a server. The arguments for and against these approaches will be detailed and we will demonstrate how to retrieve image data using XML.

Here are some other areas to address in the new database design:

Query processing.   Identify the ways to implement the many searches to be executed.

Stored procedures.   Determine the extent to manage our data changes through stored procedures.

Tokens.   Generate, track, and expire tokens (GUIDs) for requested and signed contracts.

Authentication.   Authenticate the user by manipulating these tokens.

Returning data.   Consider ways to embed image data in the XML being returned by the Web services.

Returning license terms.   Identify how to store and compose the contracts and licensing terms.

Chapter 3 focuses on the conceptual and logical design of the database. Chapter 4 focuses on the physical design of the database.

Summary

Hutchings Photography is excited and ripe for an upgrade to XML Web services. The existing system works fine, generates revenue, and promotes the firm's name and reputation as a professional stock photography house. The staff feels, however, that the current system never bloomed like it should have. Maybe it was due to the fact that it is so hard to maintain, especially when it comes to serving all of its various partners' requirements.

Making the move to a 100 percent XML Web service site will allow Hutchings to make some long-needed changes to its database and infrastructure as well. It's not so much that its existing database and code need to be overhauled, but with .NET there are just so many better and classier ways of doing things. Hutchings Photography wishes to exploit them as much as possible.

Conceptual and Logical Design

The database design used by the Hutchings Photography XML Web services is straightforward, but we want to share our conceptual and logical design steps with you, detailing why we built the structure the way we did. Along the journey, we will introduce some new techniques and tools care of Microsoft and Visual Studio .NET Enterprise Architect.

We're probably all familiar with the idea of a logical model. It's supposed to be your starting point—some nontechnical or semi-technical document that graphically or grammatically illustrates your design. There are many types of logical models. Some are meant to help discuss the database aspects of your application. Others help with coding. There are also many formal, and rather expensive, logical design languages, constructs, and tools out there. Some support only basic flowchart and reporting; others include full-blown code generation and project management.

Regardless of the tool you use, the goal of logical design is to inspire you to think before you code. Whatever software or nonsoftware tool you choose, you're smart to go through a thorough analysis and logical design phase of your project (both database and code) as opposed to the "sit and prototype" method of software construction.

Logical Modeling

Logical models are useful because they represent your soon-to-be-physical database design and, depending on the tool you use, may allow you to generate a somewhat tangible, printable diagram, showing all the key players in your system. This can be an effective documentation tool or, better yet, sales tool. It's rather difficult to show a customer or your manager a database that is under construction because it's just a collection of bits and bytes. It's nice to have a large document hanging on the wall of your cubicle to reflect your hard work or entice the client to continue with the next phase.

Programmers and project managers alike can use logical diagrams as deliverables for a project milestone. These diagrams, although technically useless to the database application itself, represent the fact that you've spent many hours designing the database, planning the relationships, and anticipating the many data business rules. You print the diagram and deliver it to the client. On larger database design efforts, especially those managed by nontechnical types, the delivery of these diagrams may just keep the wolves from the door, so to speak.

Figure 3.1 shows a portion of the Northwind SQL Server database modeled as a logical diagram. Logical models do more than make pretty posters. This type of modeling is a good technique for designing transaction processing systems, where a high degree of database normalization is required to enforce consistency. *Normalization* is the process by which you minimize the amount of duplicate data and white space in a database. If you are modeling a Decision Support System (DSS) where users will be performing more queries than data entry, you might consider breaking a few of the traditional rules and denormalizing the database.

Entity Relationship (ER) modeling is a type of logical modeling that helps guide its designer into constructing a database with minimal data redundancy. One-to-many and many-to-many relationships are identified and then separated by data element into tables and joined by key values. If the ER modeling software is powerful enough, it may also have features to validate the model for logical and physical errors and inconsistencies, which may be reported as errors or just warnings.

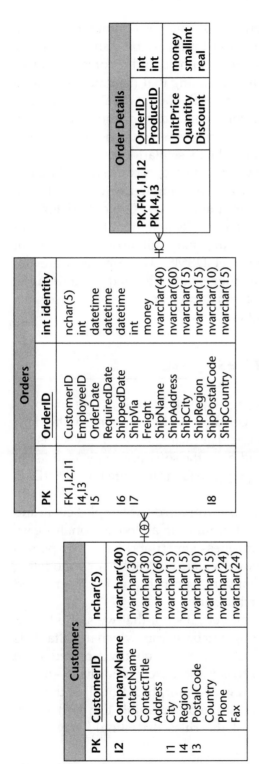

Figure 3.1   Logical model of a portion of the Northwind database.

Large databases can make it nearly impossible for a human to scan the design visually and identify all of these problems by hand. Generally accepted database design standards can be upheld and enforced. The tool may also validate the model physically, meaning that the database design must adhere to the rules and regulations of the target database platform. Oracle databases, for example, limit you to one *Long* (memo text) column per table. Physically validating a reverse-engineered database is especially important if you are migrating to a new database platform.

When modeling, be sure to know your audience, because formal logical models, such as ER diagrams, can be a source of ambiguity to nontechnical people. Although the intention is for them to be "logical" diagrams, exempt from the physical details of final implementation, they are sometimes far from logical looking. The drawings may still incorporate some of the gritty technical aspects of the target DBMS. These aspects are not expressed in any kind of a natural language, but rather require training in database design to understand. Conceptual modeling, as you will see in a moment, is free from these complications.

From Napkins to Hard Drives

Logical designs can be created using sophisticated software, such as Microsoft Visio. Your designs can also come to be by using a standard whiteboard or even a napkin. The benefits of using a tool like Visio is the ability to click a couple of buttons and have the software analyze and spin up the physical design for you, even going so far as to write the DDL (Data Definition Language) code for you.

Whiteboards, however, are nice because you can draw simple "circle and line" diagrams and incorporate instant input from all lookers-on. It's easy to hand the dry-erase pen to your business expert and have that person add notes and examples. Napkins, however, are our choice for a modeling platform, mostly because it means that you're probably sitting in a relaxed environment and can focus on the architecture.

With the Hutchings Photography models, it's not that we started completely from scratch. We had an existing database from which to delta. This database, however, was a version 1.0 design, originally upsized from Microsoft Access, and it was created to support exactly one client—us. As our business rules changed and we grew and morphed, not all of the coding of these business rules was placed in the best possible tier. With deadlines and other priorities, so many of the rules that should have been placed in the data tier were not. In other words, we had quite an extensive "to do" list for our next version. This kind of quilt-work programming led us to rethink things at the grass-roots level.

We decided to scrap the version 1.0 design in lieu of a completely new design—one that would support multiple clients, partners to Hutchings Photography. Remember that each client will be supporting its own unique Web sites, and we would probably not get a vote on what or how these sites code. We needed to consider this fact when we created our database.

This fact will, more than likely, apply to you and your design. Because you're building XML Web services that could be consumed by anonymous individuals, you'll need to make your service as friendly as possible. With this new epoch of distributed Web programming, your XML documents must describe all facets of your business and its various transactions. Your reference data must be global, complete, and "politically correct." Maybe in the past, you've cheated and placed some of your business rules into a middle tier (such as ASP pages, COM+ components, and INI files) or into the presentation tier (such as pull-down lists, checkboxes, listboxes, and DHTML script). You cannot rely on your partner building its site the same way, so these types of shortcuts and cheats must be replaced with a more robust and bullet-proof back end.

EXAMPLE With Hutchings Photography's old Web site, we had an ASP script that served up an HTML document where the visitors could choose the category of photograph to search. We had a pull-down (an HTML <SELECT>) control with the values dynamically inserted by the ASP page. The user would pull down the list and see 15 categories. If Hutchings decided to add a new category, the ASP page would pick this up dynamically, and the next visitor would see 16 categories. This worked great for our site. We just had to remember to email each of our handful of partners manually about the new category.

Because we are gearing up this new version to service potentially hundreds of partners, this equates to building and maintaining *all* reference tables in our database. Yes, even the trivial ones—even the ones that in the past were validated in code, by check constraint, or by pull-down list. The reason is that we'll need to provide an XML document with all possible ranges and values to our partners so they can populate their sites. Whether you are using XSD schemas to validate your XML documents or sending over elements that contain the valid choices, you'll need to maintain those lists and rules explicitly somewhere. Partners want to be able to pull their own updates as needed.

Conceptual Modeling

Figure 3.2 shows you what our whiteboard looked like for this project. It's relatively clean compared to some you've probably seen. Look at the scribblings and tell us if this looks like a logical diagram.

No, it looks like an illogical diagram. We see a bunch of objects, verbs, and lines.

Scientists have realized for 30 years that there needs to be another step before the logical modeling process. We've always called it "the whiteboard" or "the napkin," but it's officially referred to as the conceptual model. There's nothing magical about conceptual designs, except that there is now a standardized language and toolset available for use. More on that in a minute.

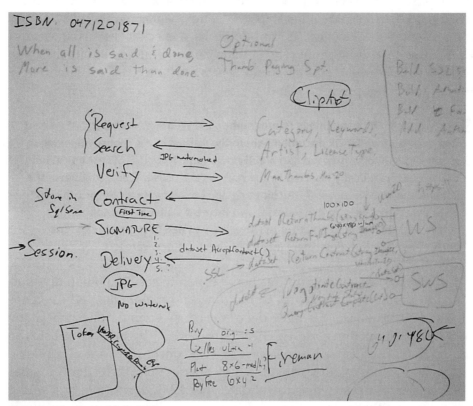

Figure 3.2   Our whiteboard.

TIP We've decided that software developers, database designers, and architects tend to be the largest consumer group of dry-erase "whiteboards." We've visited many software shops, and some of the more progressive ones decorate their walls where the developers are kept with dry-erase material—every surface is a whiteboard. Now, before you go out and plunk down $250 or more on a single 8-foot-by-4-foot whiteboard, consider an alternative. Go to the back of your local home hardware warehouse and ask for shower board. Yes, shower board—the same 8-foot-by-4-foot sheets that a contractor buys and hangs in your bathroom. For about $15, you can buy a sheet, drill a couple of holes, hang it, and then add a plastic trim strip at the bottom to hold your pens.

A conceptual design is a nontechnical, simplistic, whiteboard circle-and-line kind of drawing that everyone can understand. In fact, business folk probably do more circle-and-line drawings than other members of the team. Many developers have these kinds of designs floating around in their skulls. They just make the mistake of sharing them and instead begin at the logical design phase, coding entities, attributes, and relationships, even before the conceptual design is shared. Some developers even go so far as to start right at the physical design—probably because they know that today's tools can reverse engineer back to logical diagrams, if requested.

Reverse Engineering

Reverse engineering is a method of constructing a logical or conceptual model from a physical model. Whether you inherit a database, are analyzing an existing database, or forgot to logically model your database and need some slick handouts for the meeting on Thursday, you're in luck, as most popular tools today will reverse engineer a relational database into a logical model.

Microsoft Visio 2002 (a.k.a. Visio XP) can reverse engineer any relational database for which you have an ODBC driver or OLE DB provider (see Figure 3.3). A logical or conceptual diagram can then be constructed from the underlying database objects: tables, views, and stored procedures. These entities may then be further described by their attributes: data types, keys, indexes, check constraints, and triggers.

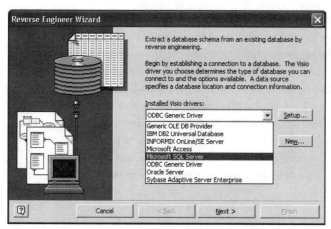

Figure 3.3 Visio's reverse engineering options.

Another option to consider is generating database diagrams directly from SQL Server 2000. We use Microsoft SQL Server 2000 every day. One of the nice features with this version, as well as version 7.0, is the ability to generate readable, detailed database diagrams. The style of the diagrams is similar to that of a logical ER diagram, though you lose a few things with the SQL Server diagrams, such as the separation of logical names and physical names, the extra descriptors, and extra metadata supported by the ER diagrams.

These SQL diagrams are usually satisfactory for small to medium-sized database projects. Compare the diagram generated by SQL Server in Figure 3.4 with that of the previously listed ER diagram in Figure 3.1.

We're not suggesting that you skip logically modeling your database. We just want you know that SQL Server itself has a database diagramming

Customers

Column Name	Condensed Type
CustomerID	nchar(5)
CompanyName	nvarchar(40)
ContactName	nvarchar(30)
ContactTitle	nvarchar(30)
Address	nvarchar(60)
City	nvarchar(15)
Region	nvarchar(15)
PostalCode	nvarchar(10)
Country	nvarchar(15)
Phone	nvarchar(24)
Fax	nvarchar(24)

Orders

Column Name	Condensed Type
OrderID	int
CustomerID	nchar(5)
EmployeeID	int
OrderDate	datetime
RequiredDate	datetime
ShippedDate	datetime
ShipVia	int
Freight	money
ShipName	nvarchar(40)
ShipAddress	nvarchar(60)
ShipCity	nvarchar(15)
ShipRegion	nvarchar(15)
ShipPostalCode	nvarchar(10)
ShipCountry	nvarchar(15)

Order Details

Column Name	Condensed Type
OrderID	int
ProductID	int
UnitPrice	money
Quantity	smallint
Discount	real

Figure 3.4 SQL Server 2000 database diagram.

feature. If you find yourself in sudden possession of a SQL Server database without the accompanying logical diagrams, there may not be a need to reverse engineer into Visio. Refer to SQL Server Books Online for help creating these database diagrams.

Reverse Engineering a Logical Diagram

If your goal is to generate a logical diagram, such as an ER (Entity Relation) diagram from an existing database, then Visio can help. In a new database design project, you probably want to start with a thorough conceptual model and then automatically forward engineer your logical model. There are times when the database already exists and you want simply to infer a logical model from it. One example might be where you are migrating a database from platform A to platform B. Platform B might be a different operating system or DBMS altogether. By reverse engineering the current or legacy system, you can then target just those areas that will change during the migration and, we hope, forward engineer the new physical design with the click of a button—without any custom changes to the DDL script.

You can point Visio at one of several possible databases and versions: MS Access, IBM DB2, INFORMIX, MS SQL Server, Oracle, Sybase, or any generic ODBC driver or generic OLE DB provider. Consult the Visio help for the specific database versions supported as well as the restrictions of the generic drivers and providers. Also, remember that, internally, Visio understands all of these databases, but you must associate the respective Visio driver with an external ODBC driver—especially if you want Visio to reverse engineer or forward engineer for you. See Visio help for more information.

Here are the steps you would follow:

1. Run Visio.

2. Click the File, New, Database, ER Source Model menu options.

3. Click the Database, Reverse Engineer menu options.

4. Select the Visio driver from the list of installed drivers (such as Microsoft SQL Server). You have to do this step only once.

5. Click the Setup button and check the ODBC driver you want to associate with Visio's driver (SQL Server). If you need to, you can create a New DSN by clicking the New button or going through Administrative Tools.

6. Select the data source and click Next. You may be prompted for User ID and password. If you are using Windows integrated security and are logged in with credentials that will access the database, then you can leave the text fields blank and just click the OK button.

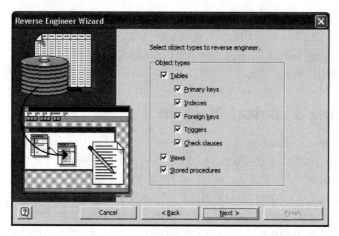

Figure 3.5   SQL Server object types to reverse engineer.

7. Select those types of database objects that you wish to reverse engineer and click Next (see Figure 3.5).

8. Select the actual database objects that you wish to reverse engineer and click Next (see Figure 3.6).

9. If prompted, you should choose to add the shapes to the current page and click Next.

10. Click Finish to begin reverse engineering the database to the ER model.

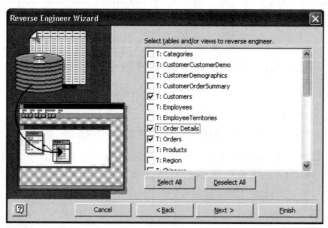

Figure 3.6   SQL Server objects to reverse engineer.

The Output Window

If you followed these steps, you've just reverse engineered a portion of the database. After the process runs, it's a good idea to keep an eye on the Output window. It echoes all of the steps of the engineering operations and informs you of warnings and errors. Here's a sample of what is returned when we reverse engineered the three tables from the Northwind database:

```
Reverse engineering from database 'Northwind' on server 'OMNIBOOK'...
Extracting columns of table 'Customers'.
Extracting columns of table 'Order Details'.
Extracting columns of table 'Orders'.
Extracting check of table 'Customers'.
Extracting check of table 'Order Details'.
Extracting check of table 'Orders'.
Extracting primary key of table 'Customers'.
Extracting primary key of table 'Order Details'.
Extracting primary key of table 'Orders'.
Extracting indexes of table 'Customers'.
Extracting indexes of table 'Order Details'.
Extracting indexes of table 'Orders'.
Extracting foreign keys of table 'Customers'.
Extracting foreign keys of table 'Order Details'.
Extracting foreign keys of table 'Orders'.
Extracting triggers of table 'Customers'.
Extracting triggers of table 'Order Details'.
Extracting triggers of table 'Orders'.
Visio is checking the reverse engineered model ...
'Order Details.OrderID' : Column has same conceptual name as column
'Orders.OrderID', but has a different data type - creating override
datatype.
Fixing up the diagram ...
-------------------------------------------------
Tables reverse engineered : 3; Time taken (in secs) : 0.42
Check Clauses Reverse Engineered : 3; Time Taken (in secs) : 0.16
Primary Keys reverse engineered : 3; Time taken (in secs) : 0.04
Foreign Keys reverse engineered : 2; Time taken (in secs) : 0.21
Indexes reverse engineered : 16; Time taken (in secs) : 0.52
Triggers reverse engineered : 0; Time taken (in secs): 0.06
Total elapsed time(in secs): 1.49
```

Notice that Visio identified an inconsistency with the logical design of Northwind. We highlighted it in boldface. It complained that the OrderID column in the Orders table is not of the same type as the OrderID column in the Order Details table. The two columns are, in fact, of the same data type. They are both four-byte integers. Visio has heartburn with the two columns because the OrderID on the Orders table is an Identity column and thus has the identity constraint transplanted into the schema for the column. The OrderID column for the Order Details table is not an Identity column, so Visio assumed they were not of the same type. Visio *usually* gets it right, but you can still find instances like this one where the warnings can basically be ignored.

> **NOTE** An Identity column in SQL Server is similar to an Autonumber in Microsoft Access or an auto-increment column in other DBMS software. SQL Server allows you to define an Identity on an integer column at the schema level, specifying a seed and an increment value. See SQL Server Books Online for more information.

Changing the Model

What Visio reverse engineers for you is just a starting point. The model will not be very useful as far as logical models go. You should highlight each aspect of the model, one at a time, and update the missing information in the Database Properties window. Be careful when doing this so that you update only the logical names and missing descriptive information—things that won't impact the physical structure of the existing SQL Server database unless, of course, that's your plan.

Remember, you can use this reverse-engineering option to pull down a physical structure into a logical format to update and clarify the design before forward engineering to another, possibly completely different DBMS.

To update the various properties of an entity or relationship, follow these steps:

1. Right-click a single entity or relationship and select Database Properties. You have to do this only once, and then the properties window will show up and stay on the screen (see Figure 3.7).

2. Select the category of property you wish to change, such as the Definition category. The list of categories as well as the properties for each category will be different for entities, relationships, and the other objects in the model.

3. Make the appropriate changes to the properties. Follow the guidance of Visio's online help if you get lost.

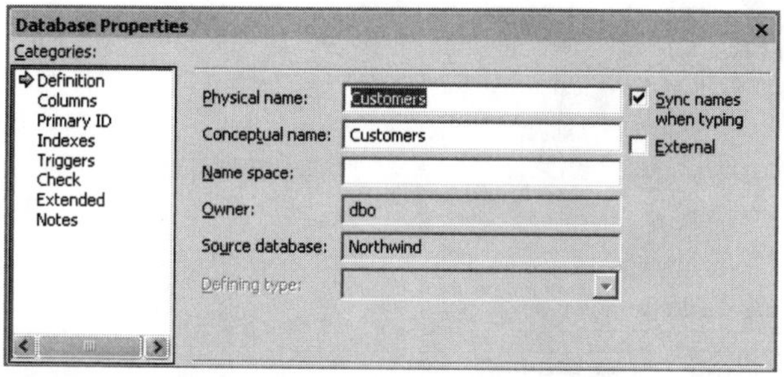

Figure 3.7   The Database Properties window.

Checking the Logical Model for Errors

After you've made updates to the model, or even if you want to see how accurate your shrink-wrapped software's database is, logically speaking, of course, you should opt to check the model for errors. This passive procedure can be run at any time from the Database menu. It's quite fast and provides insight, albeit sometimes very picky and misleading, into the consistency of your model.

The results of the error check are returned to the Output window as simple text messages. Pay special attention to the error messages and give some thought to the warnings as well. In trying to troubleshoot the warnings and errors, you can right-click and select *Go To Source,* which highlights the entity or relationship in the diagram that threw the error or warning. More importantly, you can right-click an error or warning and choose *Get Help for Message,* which opens Visio's help document and takes you to the topic for that error or warning number.

The Verbalizer Window

When you finish making the changes to the various properties, you should also look at the Verbalizer window to see all of the facts surrounding the object in question. Figure 3.8 shows the facts relevant to the Customers entity. If you select a relationship, the Verbalizer window will show all the facts about the cardinality, identifying or nonidentifying nature, and cascading options. Multiple objects can also be selected in the diagram, which will simply cause more facts to appear in the Verbalizer window.

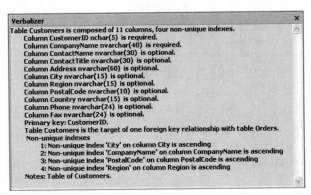

Figure 3.8   The Verbalizer window.

A quick and dirty way to run all of the details about your logical model by your business expert is to highlight all of the entities and relationships in the diagram and view the aggregated results in the Verbalizer window. You could then copy and paste all of those human-readable messages into an email. This is sure to get the business expert's attention, as the facts from a logical diagram are not so human readable. In a bit, we will contrast the readability of these facts with those from a conceptual model.

Visio also provides a nice reporting tool to help with the dissemination of the database table and type information. Look for a Report... menu option under the Database main menu. You can choose between a Table Report (see Figure 3.9) and a Types Report. All reports are fully customizable as to content, grouping, sorting, pagination, headings, and footings. The preview mechanism, which looks similar to that in Microsoft Access, also allows you to save the report in RTF format for easy attachment to an email addressed to your expert.

When the logical model is completed, you can opt to generate a new physical database or update the structure of an existing database. We will cover how to do this, whether from a conceptual or logical model, later in this chapter.

Reverse Engineering a Conceptual Diagram

One of our goals in this chapter is to sell you on the merits of conceptual modeling. We'll discuss the fundamentals of conceptual modeling and Object Role Modeling (ORM) in a bit, but for now we want to present a conceptual diagram. This doesn't mean building one from scratch, but reverse engineering one.

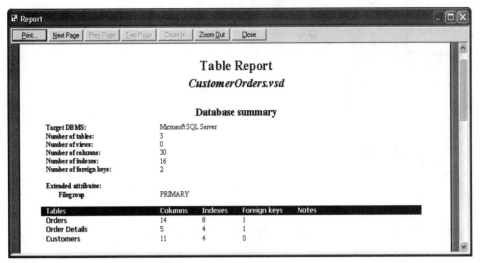

Figure 3.9 Table Report preview.

The quickest way to view and understand conceptual models is to reverse engineer an existing database that you are familiar with. If you are intimate with the inner workings of a particular database system, including its constraints, relationships, rules, and sample data, then you will be able to better understand how conceptual modeling works. If you know the constraints and relationships between a few key tables in your database, you will be able to draw tangents to the conceptual dialect.

Just as with logical models, in the previous section, Visio can reverse engineer directly into a conceptual model. The steps to do so are the same. The only difference is that you start with an ORM Source Model rather than an ER Source Model.

After the reverse engineering is complete, your diagram will be empty, unlike with the ER model. Because conceptual diagrams can become quite large and gangly, Visio lets you decide which objects and facts to drag to the drawing surface.

Once the database is reverse engineered and before you drag anything to the drawing surface, you can see all of the object types realized by the process in the Business Rules window. If this window is not visible at the bottom of Visio, select the Database, View, Business Rules menu options.

The Object Types tab is found within the Business Rules window. Figure 3.10 shows a sample of all of the objects discovered when we reverse engineered Customer, Order, and Order Details. You can see circles with solid borders (Customers, Order Details, and Orders).

Figure 3.10 Object types realized during reverse engineering.

These are the Entity objects in our conceptual diagram, or what SQL Server would call tables. The lighter-colored circles with the dotted-line borders are Value objects, which ER would call attributes and SQL Server would call columns. In the Business Rules window, you see other information for each object, such as the physical data type, size, kind, and reference mode.

You can use the Object Types window as a source to drag and drop onto the drawing surface. If we drag an entity object, such as Customers, it will drop a small ellipsis onto the surface and show CustomerID in parentheses because CustomerID is the reference mode for the object. You can think of a reference mode as the primary key, as SQL Server would call it. If you repeat these steps for Orders and Order Details, you'll end up with three ellipses—whee! (See Figure 3.11.)

This is not a very complicated diagram at this point, so let's add to it. Starting first with the Customers ellipsis, right-click and select Show Relationships. Repeat for the other two objects.

Figure 3.11 Three entity objects.

You just asked Visio to include on the drawing surface all the related Value objects, which we might also refer to as attributes or columns. At this point, things start to get tight and you are probably looking for that zoom control (see Figure 3.12).

This is a perfect example of the size comparison of the tight, compact representation of an ER diagram we saw early in this chapter and of the sprawling representation of a logical ORM diagram. Remember that size isn't everything and it's not fair to judge a model on how well it fits on the printed page. Remember that in a model that is simpler in expression and uses a more natural language, you're bound to give up space.

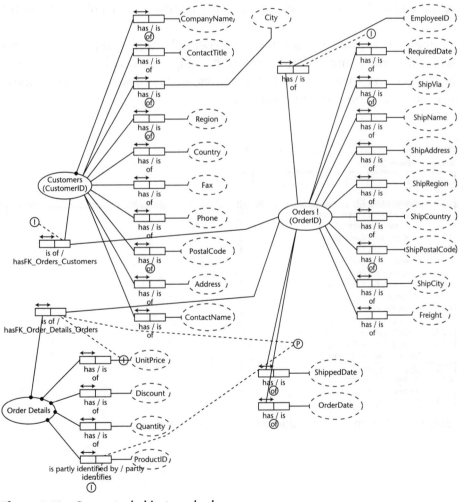

Figure 3.12 Conceptual objects and values.

Probably more important than the entity and value objects that were realized during reverse engineering is the list of fact types that was inferred. Remember, conceptual models are more than just diagramming objects. They're also about illustrating the roles that they play with one another. These roles or interactions come in the form of sentence types, like those listed in Figure 3.13.

Fact types identify two objects, whether they are entities, values, or one of each, and the role they play with each other. If we drag the Customer Has CompanyName fact onto a blank drawing surface, two objects appear, the Customers entity (solid line) and the CompanyName value (dotted line). Figure 3.14 shows what this looks like. Notice the CustomerID again. Remember, that's the reference scheme, or primary key. Reference schemes are not value objects themselves. They are handled internally to the entity object.

Value objects don't use a reference scheme because they are just attributes of an entity and will eventually be mapped to columns of a table. Value object instances are just literal values, such as a string for the name of the customer's company in this case.

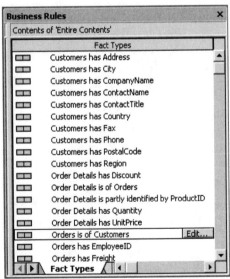

Figure 3.13 Fact types realized during reverse engineering.

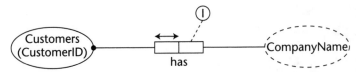

Figure 3.14   The fact type that a customer has a CompanyName.

Notice the small callout with the "I" in the circle. This is known as an Index constraint and is kind of a misnomer, as it's not really a constraint at all, but rather just a notation that there is (or should be) an index created on the physical table. The dotted line shows which role in the predicate will be indexed. It may be that all roles in the predicate are indexed, which would indicate a compound index. We'll cover all constraint types, including Index constraints, later in this chapter.

A third object type in ORM is known as an external object. External objects have been defined in another source model or in another model document in your current source model. An external object allows you to do your definitions once and then link your other diagrams without having to recreate the definitions. This is much like how you would define all of your base classes in one source code file and refer to them from other files in a larger project, especially those being modeled by more than one person.

Changing the Model

Just as with the ER model, what Visio reverse engineered here is just a start. The model will not be very useful as far as conceptual models go. You should highlight each object in the model, one at a time, and update the missing information in the Database Properties window. Be careful when doing this so that you update only the conceptual names and missing descriptive information—things that won't impact the physical structure of the existing SQL Server database unless, of course, that's your plan.

You can update the object and value properties the same way as with the ER models. The categories and appearance of the property page will look a little different because we're specifying conceptual properties here rather

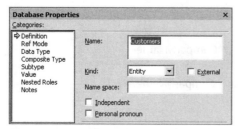

Figure 3.15   The Database Properties window.

than logical properties (see Figure 3.15). Remember that at this level, you want to be very generic and portable. Resist the urge to give your conceptual objects physical names and nonportable data types.

> **TIP**   Visio models support portable data types. *Portable data types* are not specific to a particular database management system, but they are generic to Visio. We highly encourage you to use portable types and avoid selecting a physical data type. When it comes time to forward engineer a database schema, Visio will map the generic, portable data types to the closest data type supported by the DBMS that you are working with. It's also possible under the Database menu to add your own custom data types or change the existing data type mapping. Portable data types offer you the flexibility you need if you are designing a model that will be implemented on more than one type of DBMS or if you are transferring a legacy database from one DBMS to another.

The usefulness and readability of the conceptual model will really spike if you modify the properties of the predicate connecting the two objects. A *predicate* is the role that the two objects play with one another. The predicate is modeled as a series of boxes connecting the two object ellipses. You can make changes to the predicate's definition, readings, examples, constraints, derived, composite types, and notes categories by using the Database Properties window. Together, all of these describe the business rule. Pay particular attention to the Readings, Examples, and Constraints categories because they will directly affect the Verbalizer and Reports that Visio generates. Remember, the Verbalizer and Reports are what your non-technical business types are going to proofread, looking for gaps or overlaps in the business process.

For example, when you reverse engineer a database, you'll end up with the generic "has / is of" reading on a particular fact. It may make more sense, in the case of Customers and CompanyName, to change it to "has / identifies" or whatever human terms will convey better meaning to your experts to help with their analysis.

Checking Conceptual Model for Errors

After you've made updates to your model, or even if you want to see how accurate your shrink-wrapped software's database is, conceptually speaking, you should opt to check the model for errors. This passive procedure can be run at any time from the Database menu. It's fast and provides insight, albeit sometimes picky and misleadingly, into your model.

The results of the error check are returned to the Output window as simple text messages. Pay special attention to the error messages and give some thought to the warnings as well. In trying to troubleshoot the warnings and errors, you can right-click and select Go To Source, which highlights the entity or relationship in the diagram that threw the error or warning. More important, you can right-click an error or warning and choose Get Help for Message, which opens Visio's help document and takes you to the topic for that error or warning number.

The Verbalizer Window

When you finish making the changes to the various properties, look at the Verbalizer window to see all of the facts surrounding the object in question. Figure 3.16 shows the facts relevant to all pieces of the Customers has CompanyName fact. Again, the more items you select in the diagram, the more lines will show in the Verbalizer window.

Compare the readability of these Verbalizer messages with those shown earlier for a logical model. Notice that the messages here are quite different from those we saw earlier in the logical diagram. The statements are almost

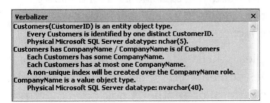

Figure 3.16 The Verbalizer window.

English-like, such as "Each Customers has at most one CompanyName." (Unfortunately, Visio's reverse engineering of Northwind introduced some grungy SQL Server data types into our conceptual model. We should probably clean those up, using portable data types instead, to increase portability to other platforms and also win a few more style points with our experts.)

Keep in mind that your business experts won't understand the ORM diagrams themselves. Your nontechies, however, should not have any trouble reading and understanding the simple messages in the Verbalizer window. If even that is confusing, then we suggest that you take the conceptual model to the next level by providing it with example data to test their rules.

Providing Example Data

Example data is an important piece for ORM models. By adding an honest and thorough sampling of examples to each of your facts, you'll have the backup you need to consider the fact accurate. Be careful, though, because if you dig too deeply with your examples, you may find some holes or some interesting questions about your processes, and you may have to change your design. Hey, that's what this is all about!

In Figure 3.17, we list some sample names for our customers. Notice that we need to specify a realistic value for both the Customer entity object (represented by its reference mode or primary key) and the CompanyName value object. Because the Northwind database uses integers to identify its Customers, we just started at 1 for our examples. We then added Company names to the list. We thought that three was a good number for this fact. Other facts, especially those predicates that have an arity (see accompanying note) higher than binary, would probably need several more examples listed, to get a well-rounded sampling of facts.

NOTE Regarding facts, *arity* refers to the number of objects linked through a particular predicate. The default is binary, meaning two objects in a traditional "has / is of" role. Visio supports up to *nonary* arity, meaning nine objects can be related through that predicate. When specifying example data for a nonary predicate, you'd have nine columns of examples to list and would probably need scores of samples to ensure the fact.

After you add the various examples, you can have Visio analyze the content to tell you if any of the examples you entered violate or do not provide a significant data sample for one constraint or another. Looking at the three examples we provided, one would think that everything would be fine.

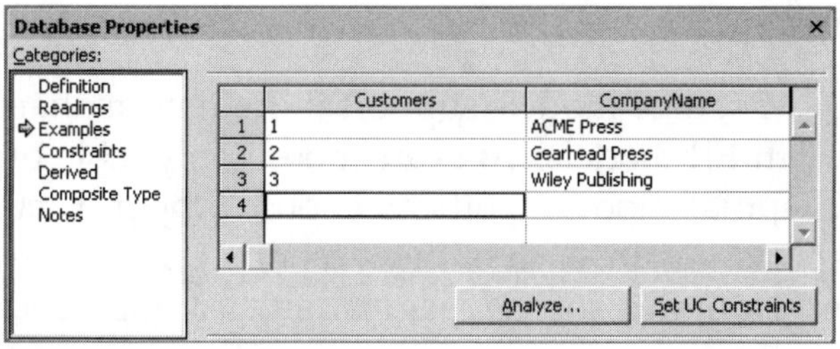

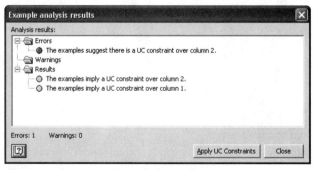

Figure 3.17   Adding examples to our CompanyName fact.

When we clicked Analyze, however, we were shown a glowing red error (the top bullet in Figure 3.18). It seems that ORM saw that we did not have any duplicate CompanyName values in our example lists and was worried that we thought there was a unique constraint over Company-Name when, in fact, there wasn't. This proves how clever the ORM and the Visio team are, to be able to analyze example data to that level. This also illustrates how much thought you need to put into your example data.

At this point, our business expert would need to decide whether we need to add another uniqueness constraint over CompanyName, specifying that we couldn't ever have two customers with the same company name. If our expert disagrees with this assertion, then we should instead simply add a second ACME Press company to our list of examples, which would cause Visio to lighten up and lose the error message.

Figure 3.18   Example analysis results.

Conceptual Model Reports

In Visio 2002, conceptual ORM source models support more reports than do the ER source models. With ER models, you can choose only table or types reports. With the conceptual models, you can choose Object, Fact, Constraint, or Supertype reports. Again, each of these reports can be fine-tuned with regard to content, grouping, sorting, pagination, headings, and footings.

The Object report allows you to print or export a high-level list of the objects in your conceptual diagrams. Figure 3.19 shows the various object type filters you can apply to the report. The default is to include all object types in the report.

The Attributes tab, visible in Figure 3.19, allows you to specify which information is included on the report for each object. The default is to list all attributes, except the Verbalization. Verbalization may be the most important piece of information, especially if this report will end up in the hands of a nontechnical person. In Figure 3.20, we show you a sample of the object type report, including the Verbalization attributes.

Probably more important than the object type report is the fact type report. This report shows all the roles played between the objects, which constitute the bulk of your business rules. You can run the fact type report for all facts in the model, for only certain facts, or by fact arity. The Attributes tab, as with other reports, allows you to select and deselect

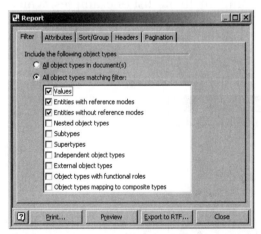

Figure 3.19   Report object type filters.

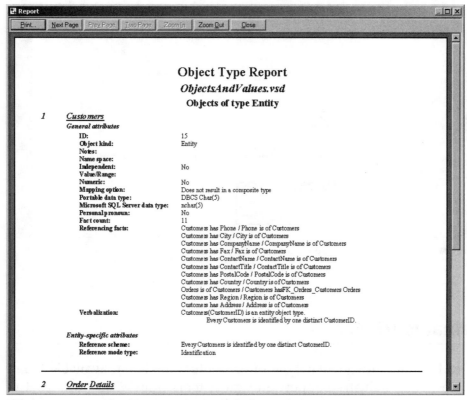

Figure 3.20 Sample object type report, including Verbalization.

which pieces of information are included. By default, a number of attributes are not selected on the object type report: ID, arity, notes, external name space, and external constraints.

Figure 3.21 shows a sample of the fact type report, zoomed in on our Customers has CompanyName fact. You can see that it includes the graphical fact type, readings, constraints, and even the sample data. This report, along with the object type report, is a great final deliverable for the conceptual design phase of a project.

TIP Be sure to check your model for errors before you publish Verbalizer messages or reports with any of your peers.

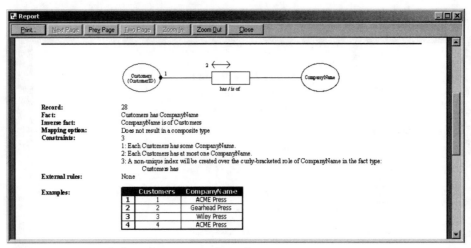

Figure 3.21   Sample fact type report.

What Is ORM?

ORM is the most popular type of conceptual modeling available today. With strong industry support and great tools from Visio (now part of Microsoft), ORM is poised to become the language of choice, much as ER has become the language of choice for logical modeling. As we've already seen, ORM is an approach to describe your entire application domain in simplistic terms. The language of ORM is fact-based and meant to be expressed by people who are not as versed in technology as in the business process.

> **NOTE** When you step into the world of modeling, especially where ORM is prevalent, you will learn many new terms and acronyms. Your application domain, which is the entire application area being modeled, is also known as the universe of discourse (UoD).

The idea of conceptual object-role modeling emerged from Europe in the mid 1970s. Originally, it was known as NIAM (Natural language Information Analysis Method). Many versions and flavors of object-role modeling have sprouted during the last 25 years. We will focus on the Formal Object-Role Modeling Language (FORML) as it's the one supported by Microsoft's Visio for Enterprise Architects (VEA), which is part of Visual Studio .NET Enterprise Architect edition.

NOTE For more information on ORM, including details on its history, case studies, related technologies, periodicals, current research, and many useful documents and resources, you should visit the official site for conceptual data modeling using ORM at www.orm.net. You should also consider *Information Modeling and Relational Databases* by Dr. Terry Halpin (Morgan Kaufmann Publishers, 2001, ISBN 1-55860-672-6).

ORM tools were available before VEA. In fact, VisioModeler is Microsoft's former ORM tool. It is based on InfoModeler version 3.1, so any models built in earlier versions of InfoModeler, such as 2.0 or 3.0, will work in VisioModeler.

VisioModeler drawings, however, are not compatible with InfoModeler, but they will be forward compatible with any of Microsoft's newer ORM tools (such as Visio). Although it is currently an unsupported product, Microsoft has made VisioModeler available for free download. If you'd like to take a look at the software or provide it to your colleagues to get started with ORM, visit Microsoft's download center at www.microsoft .com/downloads and search for the keyword *VisioModeler*. You may have to search All Downloads. The download size is about 25 MB.

The ORM Process

The ORM process is also known as the conceptual schema design procedure (CSDP), which is composed of six steps. These steps, although grueling at times, are important to follow at least in spirit to ensure a solid conceptual foundation to your application. We've simplified the steps a bit to convey the ideas behind the ORM process. There are many more aspects to proper conceptual modeling. A successful modeler should have a foundation in database normalization, mathematics, statistics, and set theory.

Here are the seven (simplified) CSDP steps, which are detailed in separate sections that follow:

1. Transform familiar information examples into elementary facts.
2. Draw the fact types and apply a population check.
3. Check for entity types that should be combined.
4. Add uniqueness constraints.
5. Add mandatory role constraints and check for logical derivations.
6. Add value, set comparison, and subtyping constraints.
7. Add other constraints, and perform final checks.

Step 1: Transform Familiar Information Examples into Elementary Facts

You transform familiar information examples into elementary facts by using natural language and referring to an existing, manual process if possible. The modeler should work directly with a person familiar with the application or process (known as the domain expert). If the expert is unfamiliar to analytical process, he or she may find it easier to start with the output and reports of the system and work backward. The expert must explain things to the modeler in clear, simple descriptions. The modeler's job is to identify the nouns in the discussions and translate them to objects and to identify the verbs in the discussion and translate them to relationships. These will evolve into objects playing roles, which we will define as fact types.

The objects identified during this step are further identified as either entities or values. This transformation from object to value or back again is painless in ORM, unlike in other modeling languages. If you identify an object as a value but later realize that it needs to be described even further, you can right-click and change it to an entity, and nothing skips a beat.

EXAMPLE   A business analyst, Steven, meets with Richard Hutchings to understand and model his business process. Steven has no insight into the business of stock photography, but he is a seasoned analyst and knows the right questions to ask to model a business. Richard has no insight into technology, but he knows his business. Together, they are able to spend a few sessions in front of a whiteboard and identify the objects, roles, and relationships of the business.

During one of these sessions, Richard explains the methods of filing a photographic image in his current filing system. With Steven's understanding of ORM, he guides Richard's explanations and formats the details as facts. Steven makes sure to describe each object relationship in two ways, from the point of view of each object.

Step 2: Draw the Fact Types and Apply a Population Check

Essentially, this step takes all of the brainstorming notes from the prior step and bakes them into an ORM diagram. Using Microsoft VEA, objects and facts are identified using ORM notation, such as the ellipses, lines, and series of boxes, which are predicates. Reference modes are identified and noted in parentheses within the object ellipse.

Use of the Verbalizer is very important during this step. The modeler is able to fine-tune the syntax of the readings so that they make sense to a casual reader. It is important for the expert to be nearby during this step of the modeling process.

Applying the population check simply means listing examples for each fact. It's important to be as thorough as possible with these examples. Try to think of the exception situations and examples that push the envelope of your business rules. At this phase, it may be helpful to include other domain experts to get a grasp of the entire realm of data experienced for each fact. (To avoid analysis warnings, remember to duplicate values that are allowed to be duplicated.)

EXAMPLE **Using the notes from the whiteboard and still having direct access to Richard, the domain expert, Steven launches Microsoft VEA and creates a new ORM source model document. Steven chooses to add content to the document quickly by using the Fact Editor directly. Here, he is able to list the objects, the predicates, and the constraints in one window and then drag and drop the entire fact to the drawing surface. Steven chooses to work directly in Freeform input style, entering in the fact type expression as a properly formatted sentence. As each fact is created, example data is identified. Steven asks some pointed questions, and Richard consults with a few end users for the right answers. This is ideal, as input from all levels ensures a solid system.**

Step 3: Check for Entity Types That Should Be Combined

After your entity objects are discovered and modeled in step 2, it is important to look for areas where objects may be combined and your schema trimmed. This simplifies the model and the resulting physical database. There are no hard and fast rules on when two entity objects may be combined. We recommend that only when an overwhelming majority of the value objects are shared between the two, you consider merging them. Remember, if there are any values that describe only *some* of their associated entities, you're running the risk of designing an inefficient database. Consult your normalization rules for more information on these topics.

If you combine two entities, you will probably need an additional fact type or two to identify the different types. A new fact type will also, more than likely, result in a new value object being added to the model.

EXAMPLE **Looking back over the model, Steven notices that there are two entity objects, Photograph and Artwork, that share many of the same values. Steven asks Richard if the two objects could be combined, possibly into a common entity object like Image. Richard hesitates because in his mind photographs and artwork are not the same thing. Steven knows that, to a database, they are the same and pushes that point.**

Step 4: Add Uniqueness Constraints

When two objects are involved in a role, you need to specify various constraints. One of the most important constraints is uniqueness. These constraints ensure that entries in a role occur there at most once. If no two entity objects have the same name value, for example, you need to establish that uniqueness constraint.

These constraints are depicted in ORM as double-headed arrows (sometimes called bars) over the appropriate box in the predicate. There are several ways to do this in VEA, but the most straightforward way is to use the Fact Editor and then make changes on the Constraints tab.

It is also possible to highlight two or more predicates and establish a uniqueness constraint across all of them. You can do this by highlighting multiple predicates, either by lassoing them in Visio or by clicking the first and shift-clicking the others. With multiple predicates highlighted, right-click any one of them and choose to add a constraint. Select the type of constraint and which parts of the predicate express it.

During this step, it may help to revisit your example data and even introduce more samples, testing the boundaries of the fact. If uniqueness is required, don't violate that in your examples. Conversely, if uniqueness is not required, throw in a duplicate value in the examples to reflect that rule.

EXAMPLE With Richard's guidance, Steven adds uniqueness constraints to the newly combined Image entity object. Each Image will be identified internally to the database by an ImageID as well as identified externally by an ImageNumber. ImageID will be the reference mode of the object, so its uniqueness is guaranteed; just a primary key in the database is guaranteed. The ImageNumber, however, will become a backup primary key and should also be unique. Backup primary keys are also known as Candidate keys.

Steven right-clicks the predicate of the fact, selects Fact Editor, and then goes to the Constraints tab. He then selects Exactly One from the pull-down for the question: Each Image Number identifies how many Image? The diagram is updated to show a second bar over the second box of the predicate, indicating that Image Number is unique for each Image (see Figure 3.22).

Steven asks if the description should be unique. Richard explains that, unlike number and title, an image's description will not be used to fetch single images from the database. Also, two photographs could be described the same way. Richard makes the decision not to enforce unique descriptions. Steven makes the appropriate changes to the Image has an Image Description fact (see Figure 3.23). You see an absence of a bar over the "explains" part of the predicate.

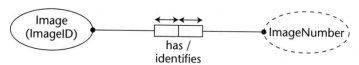

Figure 3.22 Uniqueness constraint on image number.

Step 5: Add Mandatory Role Constraints

A role is mandatory if and only if every object of that type in the database must play that role. If every entity object has a specific value, then that role is considered mandatory. In ORM, this is reflected by a small, solid dot on the end of the relationship lines. In Figure 3.23 you'll see there is only one mandatory dot. It suggests that every image must have a description. Reading the fact the other way, you'll see that it is not mandatory that a given description explain an image. For value objects, this is a bit confusing because we can't really have value objects (columns) floating around in a database without an image record. If the constraint were changed from "zero or more" to "one or more," the mandatory dot would be displayed and the uniqueness constraint would remain the same. This is not required or recommended; the mandatory behavior will be implied by the DBMS anyway because it will end up as a column.

Figure 3.22, however, shows dots on either side of the fact, suggesting that for every image there must be a number and for every number there must be an image. This would be the expected behavior for the uniqueness constraint that we established.

It is also possible to highlight two or more predicates and establish a mandatory role constraint across all of them. You can do this by highlighting multiple predicates, either by lassoing them in Visio or by clicking the first and shift-clicking the others. With multiple predicates highlighted, right-click any one of them and choose to add a constraint. Select the type of constraint and which parts of the predicate express it.

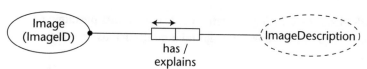

Figure 3.23 No uniqueness constraint for image description.

Again, when establishing mandatory role constraints, it is important that your example data reinforces these behaviors. The rule here is to make a role mandatory if and only if you need to.

EXAMPLE Steven goes through all of the facts in the model and, with Richard's guidance, establishes which roles are mandatory. Steven does not try to be too heavy-handed in assigning the mandatory role constraints. Steven knows that, in the practical world, it is possible to add a constraint later, if the history of data warrants it; if a constraint is in place and a business rule changes, though, it will block the usage of the system by users.

Step 6: Add Value, Set Comparisons and Subtyping Constraints

Value constraints are established when you provide the ORM model with a list of valid values for a given value object. They usually take the form of an enumeration or range. Unlike examples, these values will become the actual business rules enforcing what data may be contained within the database. In VEA, you can specify these values by right-clicking your object, selecting Database Properties, and then selecting the Value category in that window. Numeric ranges, or an enumerated list of character values, can be defined. These constraints are displayed as a note on the diagram.

Set comparison constraints allow the modeler to establish subset, equality, or exclusion constraints between roles. These types of constraints further keep your data in order by enforcing that data from one role sequence must be a subset of another (subset), that one fact must be required if another fact is specified (equality), or that if one fact is specified, another may not be (exclusion).

Subtypes are classifications of a given object type. Photographs and artwork are subtypes of our Image object. Defining subtypes allows us to declare constraints where only a specific subtype will play that role. This solves two problems at once. We are able to maintain our taxonomy within a single, simple object, while still enjoying business rules specific to certain subtypes of that object. Subtyping, as you know from the object-oriented world, also promotes reuse!

EXAMPLE With Richard's blessing, Steven records constraints pertaining to portions of the Hutchings Photography conceptual model, such as the one shown in Figure 3.24.

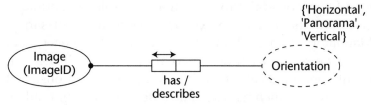

Figure 3.24 Image orientation value constraint.

Step 7: Add Other Constraints and Perform Final Checks

ORM supports a few other constraints as well as the ability to customize some of the constraints we've already covered. Some other constraints include Frequency, Ring, and Index.

Frequency constraints restrict the number of times a particular value (or combination of values) can occur in the population of one or more roles in a given predicate. Frequency constraints can be a specific value, a range of values, or simply a minimum value with no maximum value. If you need to limit the number of times that an object can play a particular role, consider the Frequency constraint. The diagram will be updated with frequency indicators, including the less than or equal to (<=) or greater than or equal to (>=) symbols where applicable. The constraint can be over one or both roles of the predicate.

Ring constraints are used when the same object type must play two roles in a predicate. You can apply a Ring constraint to a pair of roles connected to the same object type, or you can apply a Ring constraint to a pair of roles connected to different object types if the object types are in the same subtype. When you establish a Ring constraint, a ring-shaped symbol will be placed above a role box of the predicate. Ring constraints can be Acyclic, Asymmetric, Antisymmetric, Intransitive, Irreflexive, Symmetric, or a few combinations. A two-letter abbreviation beside the symbol indicates the type of ring constraint. (VEA help provides information on the differences.)

Index constraints are not true conceptual constraints, but simply a way to add hints to your conceptual design to improve performance in a physical database, especially where searches are concerned. ORM Index constraints will be forward engineered as nonunique table indexes. You can apply an Index constraint to one or more roles in one or more predicates as long as all the predicates involved in the index share a single object type.

When you apply an Index constraint to more than one role, a nonunique index is generated for the combination of columns to which the roles map.

Uniqueness, Mandatory, Subset, Equality, Exclusion, Frequency, and Index constraints can be set up as either internal or external. If the constraint applies to only one predicate, then it is internal. If the constraint spans two or more predicates, then it is external. External constraints allow some very creative business rules to be identified and enforced at the conceptual level.

Performing final checks of the model is easy to do by running the Model Error Check option under the Database menu. Attend to any errors or warning messages that appear in the output window before deeming your model concrete.

EXAMPLE The Hutchings Photography model is quite simple and cannot benefit from Frequency or Ring constraints, but Steven does make heavy use of the Index constraints. Knowing that the Hutchings Photography database will be queried more often than it will be written to classifies it as a DSS (Decision Support System) or data warehouse, which means indexes are not only welcome but encouraged.

ORM Forces You to Be an Analyst

While working with ORM, you can't help but look at your business processes and their objects in strange and unique ways. By diagramming all of the objects, an analyst starts to see patterns and redundancies in the entities and values listed. A thorough analysis of a business process will bring to the surface many questions, most of which seem trivial and may annoy the experts providing the answers. If, however, 1 question in 50 makes the domain expert ponder and return with a new or unexpected answer, then it was a successful modeling session.

For example, our modeler might determine that both partner and artist objects share a similar value object for describing their backgrounds. In the first draft of the model, the partner's value object was titled Background and the artist's value object was titled Bio. Both value objects contain the same type and shape of information (lengthy text), and, more important, both objects play the same role—they further describe their related object. Consolidating the Background and Bio value objects into a single object with a more generic name, like Narrative or Description, simplifies the design. This will also cause our analyst to look at other objects to determine if they could benefit by being related to our new Narrative object.

The modeler is enticed to look at every object relationship from all perspectives—how object #1 relates to object #2 as well as how object #2 relates to object #1. You will find, by looking at your relationships from a different point of view, that you can identify areas of redundancy and chances for consolidation. ORM insists on this.

ORM also asks the modeler to be specific about uniqueness and requirements. When you relate two objects together with a predicate, such as "Artist creates Image," you are implored to identify how many artists can create a single image and, inversely, how many images a single artist can create. As a database designer, you can see that we're defining our one-to-many and many-to-many relationships at this stage.

ORM versus ER

Because ORM is the new kid on the block, let's contrast it with the status-quo modeling language, ER. The biggest thing to realize with ORM is that it's not really at the same level as ER. ORM comes in before logical modeling and allows the modeler and the experts to sit down in a constructive and understandable collaboration. We realize that budgets may not allow for a lengthy conceptual modeling phase as well as a lengthy logical modeling phase. We think you should start with ORM and generate the ER diagrams on the fly at the click of a button.

Debates, and even arguments, on modeling tools and approaches can become passionate. Some modelers have invested a substantial portion of their lives in a certain notation and are not quick to try something new. ER notation has a long, rich history and a large base of tools in the marketplace. We are just suggesting that you look at ORM and try some conceptual analysis with it. If you must be sold on ORM over ER, or if you want to know a few areas of comparison, here are a few considerations:

- ER is far from a natural language and is not suited for the initial stages of software design. ER diagrams are great once you have an idea what your entities are. In short, ER diagrams are not a great brainstorming tool. In our opinion, ER diagrams are best derived from existing ORM diagrams. ER diagrams are like the Cliff Notes of a full ORM diagram. Use ORM diagrams for what they are, the ability to describe all facets of your business process in terms of objects and relationships in a standardized, compact form.

- ORM is a simpler, less technical language than ER. Both of them can be used effectively to forward engineer a solid physical design. ORM just starts at a higher level in the process and uses linguistics that are more understandable, thus inviting more input from more people from the project.

- ER diagrams make heavy use of attributes. In ORM, everything is an object, so if you are linking two objects by a fact type that states an "Image is created by Artist," you know that Artist is an object. In ER you might be inclined to create Artist as an attribute (column). This may not seem like much of a problem, but later in your modeling session, you may decide to further describe the Artist object by providing the ability to track name, email address, and narrative information. In ORM, you just create three new value objects and relate them to Artist with appropriate roles. Had this been an ER model, you would have had to go back and express the original Artist attribute to an entity—something that you might forget as you grow your models. In ORM, you do not have to go back, so ORM is more stable.

- Most ER modeling tools work only with binary (two-role) relationships. ORM supports *n*-ary association.

- ER notation cannot express constraints as robustly as ORM, especially when it comes to external (multiple-predicate) constraints.

- ER models typically do not express the concept of domains. With an ORM model, the domains are transparently created as we express our objects and roles. Because we define objects and roles to other objects, in essence, a path or conceptual join is created. These joins are analyzed by ORM at engineering time to construct the domains.

Why Use ORM?

Strictly speaking, an analyst shouldn't use ORM. An experienced modeler should be at the wheel of ORM, creating the models and annotating the facts. The experts and business analysts, however, should be right over the shoulder of the modeler, answering questions and providing insight into the workings of the process. Analysts may have a hard time with the symbolic nature of ORM diagrams. Although conceptual ORM models are simplistic compared to the geekier logical and physical models, the jargon can get in the way of a nontechnical person trying to validate the rules. That's why you should make heavy use of the Verbalizer, examples, and reports.

By starting with ORM, you, your clients, or your business partners can sit down in front of Visio or a whiteboard and really tear into your business processes. Objects, crude relationships, and the ensuing facts can be envisioned quickly using the ORM syntax. More important, you avoid the grungy details of a logical diagram early on. These details, which speak on entities and attributes, are terms that are a bit sophisticated and premature for a conceptual design session. Circles and lines, and nouns and verbs, are what are needed at early brainstorming sessions.

This conceptual design can then be used to generate a formal model as well as a normalized, relational database schema. The conceptual design, however, isn't concerned with the details of the implementation, such as the where or the how.

Visio for Enterprise Architects

Visio for Enterprise Architects (VEA) is installed automatically when you install Visual Studio .NET Enterprise Architect edition. In addition to the features found in Visio 2002 Professional, the EA version adds features geared toward developing enterprise applications with Visual Studio .NET, specifically the abilities to generate database and software models (known as source models) that can then be forward engineered into tangible application components.

If you take two computers side by side and on one of them you install Visio 2002 (XP) Professional edition and on the other computer you install Visual Studio .NET Enterprise Architect edition, both systems have a Visio icon on the Start menu. Upon casual inspection, both installs seem to support the same drawing types and stencils. Both installs support the ORM document type, but these are just the stencils for generating a nice printout to hang on your wall. The VEA version, however, includes an ORM Source Model, which should be selected if you wish to generate logical or physical models from it. Both versions also include the ability to reverse engineer to an ER diagram, but only the VEA version allows you to forward engineer your ER diagram to a physical database model.

The ORM Source Model is different from a standard ORM Model in that it is meant to be added later to a project to build a logical model, which can then be used to generate or update a physical database. You can create an ORM Source Model in one of three different ways:

- Create a new ORM Source Model project that contains your conceptual design.

- Use a reverse-engineered ORM model as a starting point and then refine it.

- Import an existing ORM model, such as VisioModeler, and then refine it.

Engineering a Logical Model from an ORM Model

Once your ORM Source Model is built, you'll have a nice conceptual diagram that you can print for reference, confirmation from the client, or kudos from your peers. Although great benefits, these are probably not the end goals of your effort. The benefit of starting with ORM is that you can roll it forward into a logical design and then again into a physical design. Essentially, this section represents the second of the three steps in the process of baking your ORM model into a tangible database.

Although it is possible to reverse engineer your ORM diagram from a physical database, we've found this to be a slow and somewhat painful process. In our opinion, full "round-trip" engineering is not a viable option, so ensure that your ORM diagram is as complete as possible, checked for errors, and looks good on a report.

Before you can generate a physical model, you'll need to create a standard Database Model Diagram. This document type supports relational notation as well as IDEF1X notation. This template is also used to group one or more source model drawings in a project. The source models in the project can then be merged into a single logical model that can be mapped to a physical database.

TIP Don't get confused by the different templates in VEA. The ORM and ER model templates are source models, meaning that they are the only ones that may be forward engineered into actual database models. They cannot, however, be forward engineered on their own. If you have existing ORM or ER models, you'll need to create a separate, generic Database Model Diagram. This type of diagram is also known as a project because it allows you to keep different source diagrams (ORM and ER), as well as other non-Visio documents, together. Source models do not have forward-engineering options. It's also important to mention that a given source model may contain only a portion of the entire model.

Follow these steps to build a database model from your ORM model:

1. Run Visio for Enterprise Architects (VEA) again.
2. Select File, New, Database, Database Model Diagram from the main menu.
3. Select Database, View, Project from the main menu.
4. In the Project window, right-click the Project node, and select Add Exiting Document.

Figure 3.25   Project window lists source models and other files.

TIP   Be careful not to accidentally select New ORM Source Model and then go on to locate your existing VSD document because you will overwrite it with a blank source model.

5. Locate your ORM source model, and add it to the project. Repeat as necessary until all of the files you wish to associate with the project are listed (see Figure 3.25).

6. Save your Visio document, specifying any of the optional metadata.

7. Select Database, Project, Build from the main menu. The build process will take a few seconds, depending on the size of your source models. Be sure to view the Output window for information, warnings, and errors resulting from the build (see Figure 3.26).

At this point, we have a logical model. Although nothing appears on the drawing surface, if you view the Tables and Views window, you will see several tables (entities) that were just engineered from our ORM source model (see Figure 3.27).

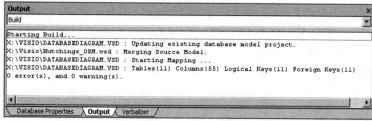

Figure 3.26   Output window echoes information from the build.

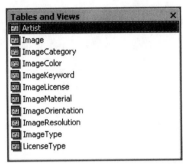

Figure 3.27   Tables forward engineered during build process.

If you wish to generate a logical ER diagram, drag the appropriate tables onto the drawing surface. In Figure 3.28, we have dragged all of our tables onto the drawing surface. Visio arranged them nicely for us, so just some minor tweaking was required to condense the drawing.

We left our tables in the default ER symbol set (IDEF1X) with the default document options intact. We could have gone to the Database, Options, Document menu item and changed the appearance of our document. Here are some of the settings we could have changed:

Symbol set.   IDEF1X (default) or Relational.

Names.   Display conceptual, physical (default), both, or base it on the symbol set.

Tables.   Display keys, display indexes, display nonkeys, display annotations, or display vertical lines.

Data types.   Don't show (default), show physical types, show portable types.

Order.   Display primary key at top (default), display separator line (default), display physical order.

IDEF1X optionality.   Display optionality (default).

Relationships.   Display relationships (default), display crow's feet, display cardinality, display referential actions.

Name display.   Display verb phrase with forward text, display verb phrase with inverse text, display physical name, don't show (default).

At this point, we can continue to work within the database modeling process. Just as with an ER Source Model, this database model allows us to select pieces of the overall model and change the database properties with a right-click. So, we can start adding even more DBMS-oriented details about our model, such as physical data types, default values, indexes, triggers, check constraints, referential actions on relationships, and even extended attributes specific to the database driver we're using.

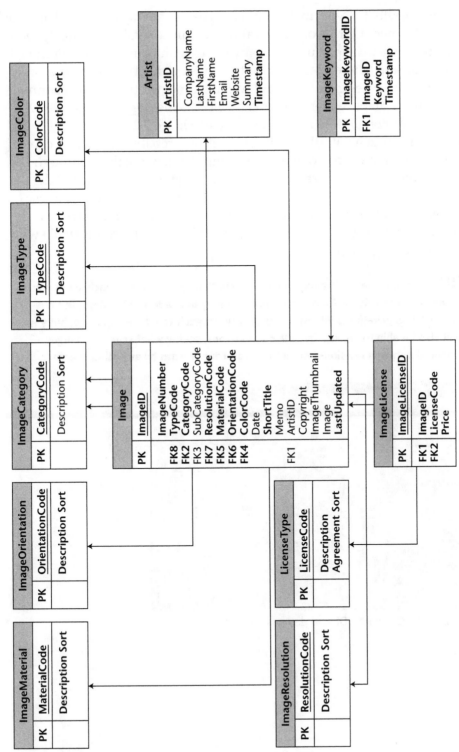

Figure 3.28   ER model engineered from our ORM model.

Remember that if you make any changes, it's always a good habit to recheck the model for errors. Several reports are available for this type of Visio document to help you resolve any issues with your model. This model is your last stop before you generate the physical database, so you want to ensure that your design is solid and well documented before you continue.

From the Database menu, you can select Generate to create the DDL script and, optionally, the new database (see Figure 3.29).

Choosing to generate the DDL by itself is probably the wiser choice. Although Visio has no problem generating the new database through the ODBC driver and this wizard, we feel that a better approach is to take the DDL script and paste it into your query tool (Query Analyzer, in the case of SQL Server) and then execute it there. This gives you a chance to review the DDL, add comments, tweak the code, and become more comfortable with the script during the process.

TIP We recommend checking each DDL script you generate and each script you manually edit to Visual SourceSafe. Doing so may take a few extra steps, but not only will you gain the ability to see exactly when each script was updated, but you will also be able to do side-by-side comparisons, seeing what schema changes occurred between revisions—something you cannot learn by any other means.

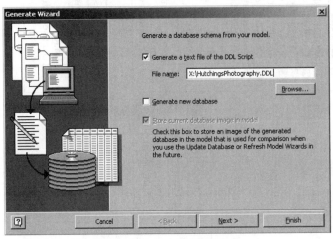

Figure 3.29   Generate DDL and database wizard.

The wizard will continue, asking you to select a Visio driver, the name of the database to generate, the ODBC data source name (with the option to create a new one on the fly), and any security credentials. The wizard will recap the tables that are to be created. You should verify this list.

Next, Visio will physically validate the model. At this point the generic work has been done and a DBMS-specific dialog will appear asking you details about logical filenames, file definitions, and sizes for the database and the transaction log.

When finished, we were presented with the following DDL script:

```
/* This SQL DDL script was generated by Microsoft */
/*    Visio (Release Date: LOCAL BUILD). */
/* Driver Used : Microsoft Visual Studio - Microsoft SQL Server Driver. */
/* Document     : X:\Book2\New\GeneratedER.vsd. */
/* Time Created: March 30, 2002 8:49 AM. */
/* Operation   : From Visio Generate Wizard. */
/* Connected data source : HutchingsPhotography */
/* Connected server      : NEPTUNE */
/* Connected database    : master */
/* Create HutchingsPhotography database. */
use master
go
create database "HutchingsPhotography"
ON PRIMARY
      ( NAME = Hutchings_Photography_Data, FILENAME =
        'x:\HutchingsPhotograph.mdf', SIZE = 5 MB,
        MAXSIZE = UNLIMITED, FILEGROWTH = 256 KB )
LOG ON
      ( NAME = Hutchings_Photography_Log, FILENAME =
        'x:\HutchingsPhotography.ldf', SIZE = 1 MB,
        MAXSIZE = UNLIMITED, FILEGROWTH = 256 KB )
go
use "HutchingsPhotography"
go
/* Create new table "Artist".
*/
/* "Artist" : Table of Artist
*/
create table "Artist" (
   "ArtistID" uniqueidentifier default newid() not null,
```

```
         "CompanyName" varchar(80) null,
         "LastName" varchar(20) null,
         "FirstName" varchar(20) null,
         "Email" varchar(50) null,
         "Web site" varchar(80) null,
         "Summary" text null,
         "Timestamp" timestamp not null) ON 'PRIMARY' TEXTIMAGE_ON 'PRIMARY'
go
alter table "Artist"
     add constraint "PK_Artist" primary key clustered ("ArtistID")
go
/* Create new table " Image"
*/
/* "Image" : Table of Image
*/
create table "Image" (
    "ImageID" uniqueidentifier default newid() not null,
    "ImageNumber" int not null,
    "TypeCode" varchar(20) default ('Photograph') not null,
    "CategoryCode" varchar(20) not null,
    "SubCategoryCode" varchar(20) null,
    "ResolutionCode" varchar(20) not null,
    "MaterialCode" varchar(20) default ('Slide') not null,
    "OrientationCode" varchar(10) default ('Horizontal') not null,
    "ColorCode" varchar(10) default ('Color') not null,
    "Date" varchar(50) null,
    "ShortTitle" varchar(50) not null,
    "Memo" text null,
    "ArtistID" uniqueidentifier null,
    "Copyright" varchar(50) null,
    "ImageThumbnail" image null,
    "Image" image null,
    "LastUpdated" datetime default getdate() not null) ON 'PRIMARY'
    TEXTIMAGE_ON 'PRIMARY')
go
alter table "Image"
     add constraint "PK_Image" primary key clustered ("ImageID")
go
/* other tables DDL snipped from here by author
*/
/* This is the end of the Microsoft Visual
*/
/* Studio generated SQL DDL script.
*/
```

Hutchings Photography ORM Model

By analyzing the original, paper-based system as well as our first attempt at a database-driven Web site, many facets of our database design were already identified. That said, we decided to scrap it and start from scratch—not necessarily because our design was poor, but because we wanted to flex the muscle of ORM and take advantage of all of the engineering features of VEA.

Our original database had the following primary entities:

Artist.   Name, addresses, email address, bio, and so forth of all contributing artists.

Photo.   Title, number, category, artist, and various descriptive fields for the stock photographs.

Category.   Fairly static reference list of the various category taxonomies.

Keyword.   All the searchable keywords for a given photo.

PhotoLicense.   All the applicable licensing modes for a given photo.

License.   Static reference list of the various licensing modes (rights, flat-rate, royalty free, and so forth).

Client.   Reference list of those visitors and customers of the Web site.

Ledger.   An accounting journal of all the transactions of photos licensed.

Our improvements came along three different lines: make it more generic, make it more data driven, and make it more secure. Let's look at each of these issues separately.

Making the system generic meant that we now license artwork, so not everything downloadable from the system is a photographic image—it may be a drum scan of a fine watercolor painting. This change meant adding another reference table for the possible types of image, as well as changing the Photo entity to something more generic.

Making the system more data driven meant that we are now going to be programmatically serving up reference tables to our partner Web sites. How will they know what the various domains are? For example, before we simply had an attribute in our Photo table for resolution, which was basically free-form text. Some people would put in "640x480," and others would enter "low" or even "VGA." Making the database data-driven meant introducing several new look-up tables.

Making the system more secure meant adding entities to support the tighter integration with partners, passing of security tokens, and even auditing all image downloads—thumbnails or otherwise. Hutchings Photography wanted to keep a better eye on the traffic leaving its servers.

Our New Objects

We're a big fan of the Uniqueidentifier data type. The benefits of being able to add new records on the client or the server without the hassle of PK collisions during synchronization, not to mention the benefits of being able to bolt on replication at a later date, outweigh the overhead per record.

We recommended that you shouldn't start bringing in the dirty details of the physical design during conceptual modeling, so why did we bring up the Uniqueidentifier? The reason has to do with database object-naming conventions. There are several conventions out there—most of them are bad or so mainframe-feeling that you'd quiver, so we came up with a few ideas of our own.

When speaking of primary keys, or reference schemes as ORM calls them, we will use either entityID or entityCode, where *entity* is the entity that we're identifying. This is not new, and the odds are that you do something similar; however, we differentiate between ID and Code, where ID is a Uniqueidentifier data type and Code is a more readable and understandable natural key, often a short char or varchar. Our thinking is that we tend to make our more frequently updated, higher-trafficked OLTP tables Uniqueidentifier based and our static reference tables more readable. For example, if we have our Artist entity, where each artist is identified by a 16-byte Uniqueidentifier, we'll call that attribute ArtistID. If, however, we have our License entity, where each licensing mode is identified by a character string like Flat or Rights, we'll name that attribute LicenseCode. This way, we can look at our design and know immediately which entities have Uniqueidentifier keys (and are expected to change often) and which entities have more readable keys (and are more static in nature).

> **NOTE** To keep this chapter more tutorial, we're not modeling our database. We're also not walking through the entire brainstorming process of ORM, starting with all objects and then tediously identifying the relationships as well

as which objects are values. If you'd like to trundle through all of our documentation and models, you can visit our companion Web site at http://code.hutchingsphoto.com.

Our new database is composed of the following primary entities, shown with their corresponding reference modes and a short description:

Artist (ArtistID). Master table of all photographers and artists.

Audit (AuditID). Security-related table tracking date, time, and visitor who requests thumbnails or images.

Image (ImageID). Master table of all photographs and artwork, including thumbnails and images.

ImageCategory (CategoryCode). Reference table of image category codes.

ImageColor (ColorCode). Reference table of image color codes.

ImageKeyword (ImageKeywordID). Child table of keywords applicable to a particular image.

ImageLicense (ImageLicenseID). Child table of license modes applicable to a particular image.

ImageMaterial (MaterialCode). Reference table of image material codes.

ImageOrientation (OrientationCode). Reference table of image orientation codes.

ImageResolution (ResolutionCode). Reference table of image resolution codes.

ImageType (TypeCode). Reference table of image type codes.

LicenseType (LicenseCode). Reference table of image licensing codes.

Partner (PartnerID). Master table of all registered partners.

SecurityToken (TokenID). Security-related table storing issued tokens, expiration, and notes.

System. Utility table storing system-wide settings.

Transactions. Master table that reinforces the audit table, shows license acceptance, and indicates delivery.

Summary

Logical modeling should be a mandatory requirement for all database projects. Fortunately, it seems to be mandatory for all *successful* projects. The more time you put into a logical design, the more inconsistencies, anomalies, redundancies, and potential problems you will discover early in the database design session. As we all know, the earlier you discover bugs in a project, the cheaper it is to fix them in terms of both time and budget.

Remember the old adage "on time, on budget, bug free—choose two"? Well, all database projects can be bug free without jeopardizing time or budget through a lengthy analytical and modeling process. More important, modelers should be required to have a background in psychology so that they can strategically catch and keep the interest of the business experts while those experts ask all of their seemingly dull and repetitive questions.

Conceptual modeling fills this niche nicely. Conceptual modeling is at a level above traditional logical modeling in that it is a little slower paced and more verbose in a readable language, supports example codes, and (when implemented using VEA) offers many wonderful reports—all pluses for a nontechnical business analyst.

The technical modeler enjoys some new benefits, too. By analyzing and taking notes at the atomic level of your business, as you do with ORM, rather than at the molecular level, as you do with traditional ER, the really interesting questions can be asked, new patterns can be witnessed, and redundancies can be avoided. By reviewing the meaningful text and topical examples, you can see the ways in which your atoms (business objects) fit together to form your molecules (entities) and thus provide the structure for your application domain.

ORM modeling will feel different from the traditional ER or UML diagrams to which you may have grown accustomed. We think that it's kind of fun, but we admit that it's a bit challenging to stay focused at that atomic level all the time. We find that we always want to jump up to the molecular level or higher within our ORM diagrams and start thinking in terms of entities, attributes, data types, indexes, and triggers. But by jumping to these technical details too early in a conceptual design, your efforts may become counter-productive and nonportable, and you may run the risk of losing your business experts' attention.

Visual Studio Enterprise Architect edition makes it easy to forward engineer your existing ORM diagrams, even those created by analysts simply running Visio 2002 Professional edition. By creating a Database Model Diagram as a project, you are able to associate one or more existing ORM models and then build the logical model or continue to build the physical model—finally, with all of those gooey technical details!

CHAPTER

4

Designing a SQL Database

We hope that we drove home the importance of analysis and conceptual design in the previous chapter. We're going to assume at this point that we have a solid database schema that is robust enough to describe and hold our business data, while at the same time being strict enough to maintain our business rules.

By using Object Role Modeling (ORM), we were forced to consider all aspects of the Hutchings Photography database from multiple points of view. By spending the hours that we did in front of Visio Enterprise Architect, and even more hours with our domain experts, we are confident that our logical designs are accurate. Our office walls are now covered with many printouts, some ORM and some Entity Relationship (ER), including lists of verbalized messages and example data for reassurance that our models are correct. All of this documentation is important, either for consulting modelers (to ensure that they have completed their contractual obligation) or for staff modelers.

Some aspects of the database design cannot be modeled with the tools provided in Visio. While ORM does a great job orchestrating the construction of database tables, columns, relationships, and constraints, it won't engineer additional triggers, stored procedures, and functions to further support the business model. We consider these kinds of objects to be bolt-on features that the tools missed.

For Hutchings Photography to deploy its database so that it is ready for prime time and will support a high-volume, publicly callable Web service, we need to ensure our database has some of the following features:

- Strong security model
- High-performance code
- High-performance server
- Customizable views of the data

This list of features is the same for just about any Web- or Windows-based application that uses a database. Web service applications are really no different. The only noticeable difference might be that we are storing all of our reference data in small tables rather than enforcing them through triggers or constraints. We discussed this aspect in the last chapter and stated that it's required so that we can easily construct a single XML document that our partners can download and that describes all of our reference tables.

This list of features made shopping for a database server easy. Because we were upgrading our previous application, which used SQL Server 7.0, the obvious choice was the current version, SQL Server 2000. Fortunately, SQL Server 2000 is strong in the areas in which we are most interested. The next section will show you the features that caught our eye.

Features of SQL Server 2000

SQL Server 2000 includes a convoy of new features and options. Our application is a high-performance, Web-based application that uses XML and advanced database objects, communicates using XML Web services, and needs periodic data mining, so we'll make use of most of the new features and options of SQL Server 2000. Let's begin with a discussion of XML support.

XML Support

The .NET Framework natively speaks and understands XML. Additionally, SQL Server can speak and understand XML on its own. Although not required for a .NET application, this feature can be useful for testing or for any situation when you need to quickly generate an XML file relative to your database query.

Primarily, the XML support offered in SQL Server 2000 is to enable you to send and receive data in XML format. XML data can be received from

SQL Server via the SELECT or OPENXML statement or by defining XML views. These views can be accessed via XPath queries, which retrieve the results from the database and return them as XML documents. Interfacing with this XML functionality of SQL Server 2000 can be performed using classic ADO, ADO.NET, or HTTP access protocols.

Microsoft continues to provide XML support for SQL Server 2000 in the form of the Web Services Toolkit, available at www.microsoft.com/sql/downloads. These downloads are separate from the product and its updates, and they deliver tools, code, samples, and white papers for building SQL Server XML-enabled applications, specifically XML Web services. Included with the toolkit is Microsoft's flagship product, SQLXML. As of this writing, the current version is 3.0. SQLXML 3.0 extends the built-in XML capabilities of SQL Server 2000 with, among other things, the ability to create and host Web services using only IIS and SQL Server.

SQLXML 3.0 also includes extensions to the .NET Framework to allow C# and Visual Basic .NET applications to interact with the SQLXML capabilities of the toolkit. Here is a snippet of a C# application code using the new Microsoft.Data.SqlXml namespace and classes:

```
using System;
using Microsoft.Data.SqlXml;
class HutchingsTest
{
    static string HutchingsConnString =
        "Provider=SQLOLEDB;Server=Omnibook;" +
        "Database=Hutchings;Trusted_Connection = True;"
    public static int PartnerTest()
    {
        Stream strm;
        SqlXmlParameter p;
        SqlXmlCommand cmd = new SqlXmlCommand(HutchingsConnString);
        cmd.ClientSideXml = true;
        cmd.CommandText = "exec ws_ReturnPartner For XML Auto";
        p = cmd.CreateParameter();
        p.Value = "ACME";
        strm = cmd.ExecuteStream();
        StreamReader sw = new StreamReader(strm);
        Console.WriteLine(sw.ReadToEnd());
        return 0;
    }
    public static int Main(String[] args)
    {
        PartnerTest();
        return 0;
    }
}
```

The simplest way to view XML data right from SQL Server 2000 is to use the FOR XML clause on your SQL SELECT statements. By doing so, you can quickly generate or emit XML from a traditional SQL SELECT statement. For example, here is a traditional SELECT statement:

```
SELECT LicenseCode, Description, Modifier FROM LicenseType
```

This statement returns something similar to the following:

```
LicenseCode Description                                            Modifier
----------- ------------------------------------------------------ -------
Buyout      Buyout - client is sent the original                        20
Flat        Flat Rate - client receives 800 x 600 res.                   5
Free        Royalty Free - client receives 640 x 480 res.               10
Rights      Rights Protected - client receives ultra - high res.         1
```

Here is the same SELECT statement returned as XML from SQL Server 2000, using the FOR XML RAW clause. The Raw switch transforms each row in the result set into an XML element with a generic *row* identifier. Each column that is not NULL gets mapped as an attribute.

```
SELECT LicenseCode, Description, Modifier FROM LicenseType FOR XML RAW
```

This statement returns the following:

```
<row LicenseCode="Buyout" Description="Buyout - client is sent the
original" Modifier="20"/><row LicenseCode="Flat" Description="Flat Rate
- client receives 800 x 600 res." Modifier="5"/><row LicenseCode="Free"
Description="Royalty Free - client receives 640 x 480 res."
Modifier="10"/><row LicenseCode="Rights" Description="Rights Protected -
client receives ultra - high res." Modifier="1"/>
```

Here is the same SELECT statement returned as XML from SQL Server 2000, using the FOR XML AUTO clause. The Auto switch is a good choice for a quick and dirty dump of your data as XML. It returns the results in a simple, nested XML tree. If multiple tables are referenced, each table will be an XML element. (You'll notice that columns are mapped to attributes. This is the default behavior, but it can be overridden.)

```
SELECT LicenseCode, Description, Modifier FROM LicenseType FOR XML AUTO
```

This statement returns the following:

```
<LicenseType LicenseCode="Buyout" Description="Buyout - client is sent
the original" Modifier="20"/><LicenseType LicenseCode="Flat"
Description="Flat Rate - client receives 800 x 600 res."
Modifier="5"/><LicenseType LicenseCode="Free" Description="Royalty Free
- client receives 640 x 480 res." Modifier="10"/><LicenseType
LicenseCode="Rights" Description="Rights Protected - client receives
ultra - high res." Modifier="1"/>
```

Finally, here is the same SELECT statement returned as XML from SQL Server 2000 using the FOR XML EXPLICIT clause. The Explicit switch gives you the most control but requires you to provide XML hints in your SELECT statement. Consult SQL Server 2000 Books Online for all of the details.

```
SELECT 1          as Tag,
       NULL       as Parent,
       LicenseCode as [LicenseCode!1!Code],
       Description as [LicenseCode!1!Description],
       Modifier   as [LicenseCode!1!Modifier]
FROM LicenseType FOR XML EXPLICIT
```

This code returns the following:

```
<LicenseCode Code="Buyout" Description="Buyout - client is sent the
original" Modifier="20"/><LicenseCode Code="Flat" Description="Flat Rate
- client receives 800 x 600 res." Modifier="5"/><LicenseCode Code="Free"
Description="Royalty Free - client receives 640 x 480 res."
Modifier="10"/><LicenseCode Code="Rights" Description="Rights Protected
- client receives ultra - high res." Modifier="1"/>
```

You can further alter the XML returned from the previous examples by appending XMLDATA and ELEMENTS keywords to the FOR XML clause. The XMLDATA switch forces SQL Server to include the schema for the data elements being returned. The ELEMENTS switch forces SQL Server to return the data in element normal form (data as elements) rather than attribute normal form (data as attributes).

```
SELECT LicenseCode, Description, Modifier FROM LicenseType
   FOR XML AUTO, XMLDATA, ELEMENTS
```

This code returns the following:

```
<Schema name="Schema3" xmlns="urn:schemas-microsoft-com:xml-data"
xmlns:dt="urn:schemas-microsoft-com:datatypes">
<ElementType name="LicenseType" content="eltOnly" model="closed"
```

```
order="many"><element type="LicenseCode"/><element
type="Description"/><element type="Modifier"/></ElementType><ElementType
name="LicenseCode" content="textOnly" model="closed"
dt:type="string"/><ElementType name="Description" content="textOnly"
model="closed" dt:type="string"/><ElementType name="Modifier"
content="textOnly" model="closed" dt:type="ui1"/></Schema><LicenseType
xmlns="x-
schema:#Schema3"><LicenseCode>Buyout</LicenseCode><Description>Buyout -
client is sent the
original</Description><Modifier>20</Modifier></LicenseType><LicenseType
xmlns="x-
schema:#Schema3"><LicenseCode>Flat</LicenseCode><Description>Flat Rate -
client receives 800 x 600
res.</Description><Modifier>5</Modifier></LicenseType><LicenseType
xmlns="x-
schema:#Schema3"><LicenseCode>Free</LicenseCode><Description>Royalty
Free - client receives 640 x 480
res.</Description><Modifier>10</Modifier></LicenseType><LicenseType
xmlns="x-
schema:#Schema3"><LicenseCode>Rights</LicenseCode><Description>Rights
Protected - client receives ultra - high
res.</Description><Modifier>1</Modifier></LicenseType>
```

> **NOTE** If you're an XML aficionado, you'll notice that the XML returned doesn't have the XML directive (<?xml version="1.0"?>) or the root node, both required for a well-formed XML document. You would need to add them, either from a client application or manually with a text editor, before deploying the document to the world.

User-Defined Functions

In SQL Server 2000, Microsoft finally gave developers the ability to write their own, albeit limited, user-defined functions (UDFs). SQL Server has always had dozens of system functions and variables that provide functionality, but it was never enough. We could always build our own stored procedures, but they were bulky and difficult to call inline with other stored procedures or trigger code. We needed the ability to build our own functions, which could be referenced inline with a SELECT statement, stored procedure, trigger, or even DEFAULT constraint.

Of the three types of UDFs in SQL Server 2000 (scalar functions, inline table-valued functions, and multistatement, table-valued functions), we are most excited about scalar functions. Granted, there are a number of operations that you cannot perform inside a scalar function, but enough high-level programming can be encapsulated inside a UDF to make it a very interesting feature. SQL Server 2000 Books Online documents well the operations *not* allowed inside a UDF; but essentially, you cannot call a stored procedure or any function that returns *nondeterministic* values, which are functions that will not return the same values every time, such as NewID().

One UDF that we created in SQL Server 2000 could have been easily implemented in C# or Visual Basic .NET. It is a function that looks up an Artist by ArtistID and returns a friendly name. Because Artists can have last names, first names, and optionally company names, we wanted to build a function that would format the output correctly regardless of how the data was provided for the Artist. Here is the source code of our Artist-Name scalar function:

```
CREATE FUNCTION ArtistName ( @ArtistID uniqueidentifier )
RETURNS varchar(130)
AS
BEGIN
    -- declare working variables
    DECLARE @CompanyName varchar(80)
    DECLARE @LastName    varchar(20)
    DECLARE @FirstName   varchar(20)
    DECLARE @ReturnName  varchar(130)
    -- lookup artist
    SELECT  @CompanyName = CompanyName,
            @LastName    = LastName,
            @FirstName   = FirstName
    FROM    Artist
    WHERE   ArtistID     = @ArtistID
    -- format the artist's name
    IF @LastName IS NULL
        IF @CompanyName IS NULL
            SET @ReturnName = NULL
        ELSE
            SET @ReturnName = @CompanyName
    ELSE
        BEGIN
            SET @ReturnName = @LastName
            IF @FirstName IS NOT NULL
                SET @ReturnName = @ReturnName + ', ' + @FirstName
            IF @CompanyName IS NOT NULL
                SET @ReturnName = @ReturnName + ' (' + @CompanyName + ')'
        END
    -- return the scalar value
    RETURN (@ReturnName)
END
```

We can call this handy function from stored procedures, views, triggers, or default constraints. Here's an example of what it looks like when we test it. The first artist has a company name. The second artist has no company name. The third artist never provided Hutchings Photography with his full name—which is a great test of our function.

```
SELECT dbo.ArtistName('A82FBD2F-6486-48F8-BC12-396F2CF6D215')
------------------------------------------------------------
Hutchings, Richard (Hutchings Photography)
SELECT dbo.ArtistName('2933C186-5761-41D6-8695-B1C622683B43')
------------------------------------------------------------
Jordan, David
SELECT dbo.ArtistName('7B5204C0-17E5-4002-A1C1-7AAECCF879D8')
------------------------------------------------------------
Christo
```

Notice that the ArtistName function handles the nice formatting of the name, regardless of how much information the artist provides. It could be updated to handle titles and other salutations. This type of formatting function is nice for queries or reports.

NOTE When calling user-defined functions, you need to prefix the function name with its owner credentials, even if the owner is dbo. This is a bit different from referencing other dbo objects in SQL Server.

INSTEAD OF Triggers

Triggers are a great place to put code when you want to ensure that some action takes place when data is inserted, updated, or deleted from a particular table. They can perform everything from business rule enforcement to denormalization to manual replication of data. The sample code that Visio for Enterprise Architects generates could and probably should be placed into triggers where appropriate. VEA stops short of actually creating the triggers for you, however. Its goal was to simply recommend the appropriate code and allow you to use it within triggers or stored procedures as you see fit.

With triggers, you have access to two special tables: Inserted and Deleted. These tables hold the actual data that is about to be inserted or deleted, respectively. In the case of an update trigger, both of these tables are used, one to hold the look of the data before the change (Deleted table) and the other to hold the new data that will persist (Inserted table). This is how triggers have operated for many versions of SQL Server.

So why do we need INSTEAD OF triggers? INSTEAD OF triggers fire in place of the triggering action. If you specify an INSTEAD OF update trigger when you attempt to insert a new record, the special inserted and deleted tables are populated, but the operation halts before the base tables are updated. The INSTEAD OF triggers execute before any other constraints, so they can perform special preprocessing actions as well. This is interesting behavior and opens the door to some new and creative approaches to business rule enforcement.

We use INSTEAD OF triggers a bit differently, however. Many databases that we design must implement some level of auditing. Managers and clients want their databases secure and don't mind spending the extra time to track who changed what and when. What better way to track all of the changes to a table than by echoing the old data along with additional pieces of information to a separate, denormalized database?

For example, if we want to be very careful about our Partner table, we could build insert, update, and delete triggers that copy the old and new values to a mirrored database, appending with that data the date, time, user, and IP address of who made the change. Once you implement this kind of auditing system and then provide an interface with which the user or manager can peek at who changed the data, you'll have hit a home run. While the trigger code should not be very sophisticated, the problem we ran into was a show-stopper.

Regular SQL Server triggers do not support text, ntext, or image data. This is a big deal if your database has large text or image columns (BLOBs). This describes our database designs of the past as well as the current Hutchings Photography design. If you try to reference a column with a data type of text, ntext, or image inside the Inserted or Deleted tables, you'll get an error.

With SQL Server 2000, we can now use INSTEAD OF triggers because they support the text, ntext, and image data types in those two special tables. Our trigger code can now access the old text or image data and echo it to our auditing database. This was a deal breaker in SQL Server 7.0, which required us to redesign our databases a few times. We had hoped that Microsoft would fix this bug in SQL Server 2000, but it gave us INSTEAD OF triggers instead.

NOTE If you're interested in seeing the auditing code that we implemented on the Partner table, visit http://code.hutchingsphoto.com and look for the download. For more information, look up "Using text, ntext, and image Data in INSTEAD OF Triggers" in SQL Server 2000 Books Online.

Cascading Referential Integrity

Many of us expected Microsoft to provide us with the ability to check a box and have the SQL engine cascade updates and deletes to related tables in SQL Server 7.0. After all, Microsoft Access and Microsoft Visual FoxPro have had that ability for many versions. We finally get this feature in SQL Server 2000.

By mentioning an ON DELETE or ON UPDATE clause when creating a FOREIGN KEY constraint, SQL Server 2000 handles the updates and deletes automatically when a parent primary key is changed or the parent row is deleted. In the past, SQL Server would just prevent you from doing this, but it wouldn't offer you any code to help cascade the updates or deletes through the child table. Granted, the trigger code was not very sophisticated to write, but it was a pain to have to write it in different triggers for several different tables.

Here is a snippet of our DDL script to create the FOREIGN KEY constraint on the artist table:

```
ALTER TABLE [dbo].[Image] ADD
    CONSTRAINT [FK_Artist_Image] FOREIGN KEY ( [ArtistID] )
        REFERENCES [dbo].[Artist] ( [ArtistID] )
        ON DELETE CASCADE  ON UPDATE CASCADE
```

NOTE Use cascading triggers diplomatically because they cause a lot of data to be altered or disappear altogether if you make the wrong change. With our preceding example, it's not that we expect to be deleting all content for a particular artist or for a particular category, but we want that option. We made sure the Hutchings Photography user interfaces do not allow for an entire category to be deleted, but we reserve that option for the managers and IT staff.

Multiple Instances of SQL Server

On the surface, this doesn't seem like a particularly interesting feature, and for most people who install SQL Server 2000, it's not. Many shops just install the software on the default instance on port 1433 and start assembling databases. That's great. If you have multiple databases, you can segregate security accordingly per database by making only select individuals database owners, readers, writers, and so forth. Customers of the server or division in your company can spin up their own database and the other camps won't be allowed in. Only system-level administrators will have access to all the databases.

So what happens when database owners need system administrator privileges to do their jobs? With prior versions of SQL Server, they had to enable multiple people to be system administrators, giving out passwords and then asking those folks to stay out of any databases that didn't belong to them. Worse yet, the one overworked system administrator had to schlep his or her password around the company and do the typing for the folks that didn't have that level of clearance. Either of these solutions is a bad solution and sometimes leads to another full purchase of SQL Server to install on a separate server for another group.

SQL Server 2000 solved this problem by allowing multiple instances to be installed on the same machine. It basically requires a second, complete install to add another instance. You'll have to name the instance and provide a separate port number. After that, it will appear, for all intents and purposes, as a separate server.

So why is this interesting to Hutchings Photography? Hutchings Photography is in the business of online stock image licensing; it is also in the business of making money. Already, one partner has come forward wanting to use the Hutchings Photography Web service for its own business—basically setting up a competitive system with Hutchings' help. A licensing arrangement was worked out, and the idea of creating another database on the existing SQL Server was discussed.

As previously mentioned, this is a bad idea because the other firm's database administrator wants complete control of his or her company's database, and Hutchings Photography definitely doesn't want a stranger in its site. Spinning up a second instance of SQL Server 2000 solved this problem. Because Windows 2000 local and domain administrators are automatically system administrators in SQL Server, Hutchings can never be shut out of the other system in case of emergencies or other security situations.

Access via HTTP

Our business model doesn't include a requirement for our partners or their clients to contact our SQL Server directly. SQL Server 2000 still provides us with an option to help us with testing or remote troubleshooting. HTTP access can be set up for our SQL Server in just a few, easy steps; then the queries can be sent using HTTP, in a couple of different formats.

If this sounds like a security concern, it is. HTTP access directly to a SQL Server shouldn't be installed just because it looks interesting. If you are installing it just to evaluate it, remember to remove it when you are finished. You should install this access only over a tight security foundation, both on the IIS server and the SQL Server. One such restriction you might consider is to limit the IP addresses that are allowed to visit the site to your intranet or a limited extranet of known partners. Hutchings Photography, as well as you and your applications, will maintain more control and security of its data when accessing through a layer of code, such as the .NET Framework rather than through HTTP.

Most of this step is handled through a wizard. From the Microsoft SQL Server program group, select Configure SQL XML Support in IIS. This brings up a Microsoft Management Console (MMC) application, allowing you to create or edit existing virtual directories for SQL Server 2000, as illustrated in Figure 4.1.

The wizard then walks you through several screens of settings, where you will specify the virtual directory name and physical path, both seen in Figure 4.2. Keep in mind that a virtual directory points to exactly one database. If you want one directory to bridge two or more databases, then you'll need to create the appropriate stored procedures or views in the background to support this. You must also specify security credentials, SQL server, and the database to which to connect. These options are found on the corresponding tabs.

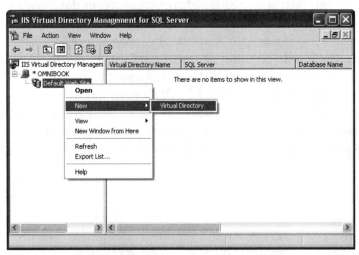

Figure 4.1   Creating a new virtual directory for SQL Server.

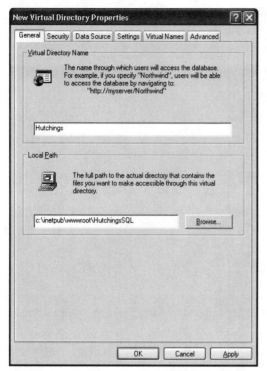

Figure 4.2   Setting the virtual directory name and physical path.

Deciding the type and extent of access to your SQL Server database is done via the Settings tab (Figure 4.3). Give some thought before you start enabling the types of access here. By default, only template queries are enabled. Template queries are valid XML documents that consist of one or more SQL queries.

Probably the simplest and most basic type of query to allow is the URL query. URL queries allow you to specify a SQL query directly in the URL. This is a security concern, but we will show you how these types of queries can be useful, especially in an environment where database developers or testers don't have access to the appropriate SQL tools.

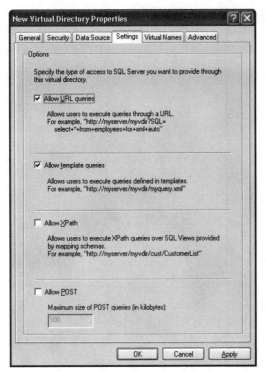

Figure 4.3 Specifying the type of access to SQL Server.

Also available on the Settings tab are the abilities to enable XPath queries and POST data back to the database. SQL Server's XPath query support is a subset of the full W3C XPath language to query. SQL Server Books Online provides further details.

Here is an example of an XPath query specified on in a URL query:

```
http://MyHost/hutchings/schema/MySchema.xml/Artist[@LastName="Smith"]?
root=root
```

Learning XPath will be very beneficial to database developers, as it has been for XML programmers. XPath allows specifying some powerful queries using a very abbreviated syntax.

Notice that in the preceding example we appended "?root=root" on the end of the query. This is required for the XML being returned to be valid, by having a root node. It's funny that you can specify this option here in HTTP queries, but you cannot specify it in the FOR XML clause of a SELECT statement.

We execute a standard SQL SELECT statement via the URL, like this:

```
http://myHost/Hutchings?sql=SELECT+*+FROM+License+FOR+XML+RAW&root=ROOT
```

We will receive nicely formatted XML, like this:

```
<?xml version="1.0" encoding="utf-8" ?>
<ROOT>
<row LicenseCode="Buyout" Description="Buyout - client is sent the
original" Modifier="20"/>
<row LicenseCode="Flat" Description="Flat Rate - client receives 800 x
600 res." Modifier="5"/>
<row LicenseCode="Free" Description="Royalty Free - client receives 640
x 480 res." Modifier="10"/>
<row LicenseCode="Rights" Description="Rights Protected - client
receives ultra - high res." Modifier="1"/>
</ROOT>
```

By allowing POST queries, you are opening the door to allow HTML forms to post information directly to SQL Server. The standard input mechanism of an HTML form can be used to capture user input and be passed as a SQL statement.

If you are familiar with HTML, then you may know about the TEXTAREA element. You can use the TEXTAREA element in HTML to construct a template, which is then sent to the SQL Server during the HTTP POST operation.

A sample HTML document to POST changes back to SQL Server might look something like this:

```
<html>
<body>
<form name="Partner"
      action="http://myHost/Hutchings/Template/UpdatePartner.XML"
      method="POST">
<input type=hidden name="contenttype" value="text/xml">
<textarea name="partnerdata" cols=50 rows=5>
   &lt;root&gt;
      &lt;Partner pid=&quot;1&quot; name=&quot;ACME Photos&quot; /&gt;
      &lt;Partner pid=&quot;2&quot; name=&quot;Penguin Photos&quot; /&gt;
   &lt;/root&gt;
</textarea>
<br><input type=Submit value="Submit">
</form>
</body>
</html>
```

Analysis Services

SQL Server 2000 includes new and improved Online Analytical Processing (OLAP) services. They have been renamed to Analysis Services and include some new data mining capabilities. Data mining can be executed against your database or OLAP cubes to identify interesting data and patterns and to mate these observations with predictions.

SQL Server's analysis services provide new user interface wizards, dialog boxes, and editors, which help you quickly perform data mining tasks like building data mining models. Beyond the built-in interfaces, Microsoft has also included these extensions to the data mining capabilities:

MDX.   Although not .NET code, the Multidimensional Expressions (MDX) language provides low-level programmatic access to multidimensional objects and data.

ADO MD.   The ActiveX Data Objects Multidimensional language supports these services.

PivotTable Service.   This enables clients, such as Excel 2002, to interact with the data mining services and access offline cubes.

Before being able to access any of these services, tools, or APIs, the Analysis Services must be installed. This is not performed as part of a typical install. We should also point out that, although some of the Analysis Services are supported by the Standard and Personal editions of SQL Server, you really need to have the full Enterprise Edition, especially when you want to define your own OLAP partitions, to enjoy HTTP OLAP support, to work with very large dimensions, for real-time OLAP, or for distributed partitioned cubes. The data mining services, however, are available in all editions of SQL Server, except for the Desktop Engine and CE editions

It is not recommended that you install or run analyses on a production server or on a server that should be spending the majority of its clock cycles on serving clients in other ways such as backup and restore or replication of data to a separate server for analysis.

As Hutchings Photography amasses data from the visitors of the Web site, we can use the OLAP features in SQL Server 2000 to analyze the images being requested, looking for trends. For example, after September 11, we had many requests for photos of police, firefighters, and the New York City area. If, for some reason, the humans at Hutchings Photography had missed this trend, the OLAP Analysis Services and custom data mining clients would have been able to identify the fact. With little coding, the categories and keywords being searched could be analyzed and then, by listening to the statistics, Hutchings could scan and upload more images to offer promotions and even decrease prices accordingly. Data mining can also be used to identify potential cases of fraud.

> **NOTE** Microsoft has updated Books Online for SQL Server 2000. You should download and install them separately, as well as any service packs for SQL Server. To find these downloads, visit www.microsoft.com/sql/downloads.

Creating a Database Structure from Our Model

Using Visio for Enterprise Architects, we were able to create our Object Role Modeling (ORM) source models for our database. As part of the final steps in Visio, we were able to associate our source models with a database diagram project, supply additional logical details, and then generate the Data Definition Language (DDL) code for SQL Server 2000, which we then used to generate the database and all its objects.

Here are those steps again, at a high level:

1. Use proper ORM techniques and follow the conceptual schema design procedure (CSDP) design process to create an ORM source model.
2. Validate and check the ORM model for errors.
3. Create a database model in Visio, and include the ORM source models.
4. Validate and check the database model for errors.
5. Generate a new database (or at least the DDL) from the database model.

As mentioned, when you click the Generate option on the Database menu, you'll be presented with Visio's Generate Wizard. With this wizard, you can generate the DDL script and, optionally, the database itself. You also have the option to store the current database schema in your Visio model to support Updating and Refreshing of the model as changes are made. Models should be updated when you, or Visio, detect any changes to the underlying database and you want to incorporate those changes into your model. This is especially important when you are about to update the database structure from your model and want to be sure that the database hasn't changed in the background.

When refreshing a model, the wizard can detect the following types of database object changes from SQL Server 2000:

Table.   Detects any check constraints, triggers, extended attributes, or table types that have changed and detects whether the table was deleted. The wizard does not, however, detect newly added tables.

Column.   Detects any added or removed columns as well as changes in name, data type, nullability, status, collection type, check constraint, or extended attributes.

View.   Detects any changes to the definition but does not detect newly added views.

Primary key.   Detects any new or removed primary keys as well as changes to names or definitions of existing primary keys.

Relationship.   Detects any new or removed relationships (foreign key constraints) as well as changes to names or definitions (columns, cardinality, or referential integrity).

Index.   Detects any new or removed indexes as well as changes to columns, collation, extended attributes, or uniqueness.

TIP Although we found the Visio 2002 online help to be generally useless, there are a few good topics on refreshing and updating your models and how to keep the model synchronized with your database. In the Visio help, type "model and database synchronization" into the Answer Wizard for a page of helpful information.

As part of the Generate Database step, Visio starts to ask us some of the physical database questions. Figure 4.4 shows a screen that pops up asking about the logical name, physical path and name, and sizes of both the data file and log file to be built. These questions are necessary for the DDL script to create the database itself initially. If your database already exists, but without any objects inside, you can always remove or comment out the CREATE DATABASE statement in the script.

Good naming conventions suggest that you name your files Database_Data.mdf and Database_Log.ldf, where *Database* is the name of your database. Figure 4.4 shows our database file and our physical path. We have left the other settings at their defaults because 3 MB is large enough for an empty database structure such as ours. We also opted to leave the Max size to be UNLIMITED so as not to govern the growth of the database. Because only Hutchings Photography staff will be adding large amounts of data (the images), they'll be able to keep an eye on the hard drive and know when it's time for action.

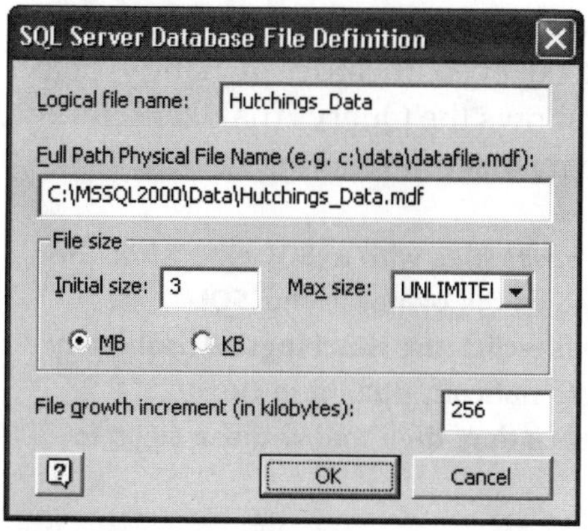

Figure 4.4 Specifying the database and transaction log files.

After specifying these filenames, Visio completes the generation of the DDL script. Here is a section of the script, focusing on the creation of the database itself. This is also the area where you could delete, comment out, or change to suit your needs.

```
/* Create Hutchings database. */
use master
go
create database "Hutchings"
ON PRIMARY
    ( NAME = Hutchings_Data,
      FILENAME = 'C:\MSSQL2000\Data\Hutchings_Data.mdf',
      SIZE = 3 MB, MAXSIZE = UNLIMITED, FILEGROWTH = 256 KB )
LOG ON
    ( NAME = Hutchings_Log,
      FILENAME = 'C:\MSSQL2000\Data\Hutchings_Log.ldf',
      SIZE = 1 MB, MAXSIZE = UNLIMITED, FILEGROWTH = 256 KB )
go
```

NOTE At the Web site for this book at http://code.hutchingsphoto.com, you will find the full models and DDL script generated for our database. Included in this chapter are abbreviated models and scripts.

Executing the DDL

Open the DDL script in the Windows Notepad, or if you have the SQL Server 2000 tools installed, open the script in Query Analyzer. Query Analyzer is the utility for writing and testing SQL scripts to execute them against a SQL

Server database. The advantages over Notepad include syntax color coding and syntax verification. SQL Server 2000 even includes a handy object browser tree and a debugger. Figure 4.5 shows the Query Analyzer window with a portion of the DDL script and the results of executing it.

TIP Although Query Analyzer opens and saves files with a .SQL extension, the product doesn't register itself with Windows as the owner of the .SQL extension. This means that you cannot double-click the HutchingsDDL.sql query file, or any .SQL file for that matter, and automatically open it in Query Analyzer. If you would like to have this association, then follow these steps to configure Windows yourself:

1. Go to My Computer or Windows Explorer.

2. Click Tools - Folder Options.

3. Click the File Types tab.

4. Locate the SQL extension (if you don't have a SQL extension, you can quickly create the entry by clicking the New button).

5. Click the Advanced button.

6. Click New to add a new action.

7. Name the action Open.

8. Name the application (use your path and be sure to include the quotes) "C:\Program Files\Microsoft SQL Server\80\Tools\Binn\isqlw.exe" "%1".

9. Click OK.

10. Make the Open action the Default action by clicking the button.

11. Click OK.

After you load the DDL script into Query Analyzer, you should review and verify all of the object names and details. This is the step where the rubber meets the road. Once you run the script, memory and disk space will be allocated, and the physical database will be built. This is your last chance to make *easy* changes.

TIP Any changes you make to the DDL script should be made manually back to your database diagram and even your ORM diagram. In theory, Visio supports reverse engineering and the ability to synchronize and update your database diagram from the physical database, but we think you should do it manually instead, as we've seen a few discrepancies with the automatic approach.

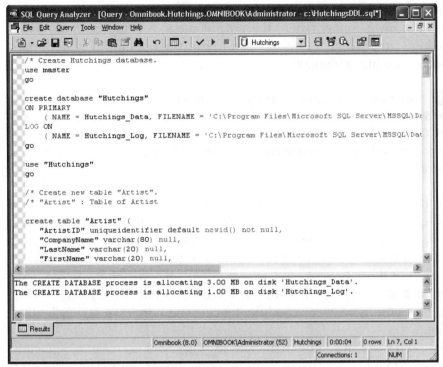

Figure 4.5   Using SQL Server 2000 Query Analyzer.

Then you should ask Query Analyzer to parse the script and check for syntactical and contextual errors. When you click the blue check mark button or press Ctrl-F5, you will parse the entire script looking for errors in the SQL syntax, referencing objects, and other procedural errors. This action will not run the script.

Here is one such error that Query Analyzer noticed:

```
Server: Msg 911, Level 16, State 1, Line 2
Could not locate entry in sysdatabases for database 'Hutchings'. No
entry found with that name. Make sure that the name is entered
correctly.
```

This error won't actually be realized when the script is run. SQL Server's parser simply got upset because in the script, we were referencing a database that didn't yet exist. If you look at the first few lines of the script, however, you'll see that the database gets created before the line of code that was in error. Because we separated our commands into batches using the GO statement, the parser was unable to follow the continuity.

Clicking the green triangle or pressing F5 executes the script. Keep an eye on the lower pane, where the output messages and date are listed, including errors. This window is used to capture the output of both parsing and executing statements.

> **TIP** Execution and parse errors are listed in the output window in red, such as the "Server: Msg 911, Level 16, State 1, Line 2" message mentioned in the main text. There will be an accompanying message in black. In Query Analyzer, you can double-click the red error message to take you to the point in the script that caused the error.

For the command-line types that are reading this book, we want to mention the OSQL utility. OSQL is documented in SQL Server 2000 Books Online. Essentially, it is the command-line version of the ISQLW program (Query Analyzer). OSQL is great for ad hoc, interactive execution of Transact-SQL (T-SQL) statements and scripts. What's better is that you can batch many calls to OSQL into a traditional Windows batch file (.bat) or command file (.cmd) and even schedule it, using the Windows Task Scheduler service.

OSQL can work in an interactive mode, where the users enter SQL statements in a manner consistent with a command prompt. The results are echoed back in the same command prompt window. What's handier, in our opinion, is to submit an OSQL *job*, which is just a SQL script file, such as the DDL script produced by Visio. Remember, these script files are just text files that contain a series of valid T-SQL statements executed one at a time.

> **NOTE** The OSQL utility is similar to an older utility called ISQL. ISQL is a deprecated utility, but it still ships with, and gets installed by, SQL Server 2000. Where ISQL uses the older, slower DB-Library technology, OSQL uses newer, ODBC technology. While neither utility makes use of .NET, either utility will work to execute your script. Also, don't confuse ISQL with ISQLW. ISQLW is Query Analyzer, includes the GUI, and doesn't use deprecated technology.

As with any well-behaved command-line utility, OSQL can inform you of its usage and syntax by running OSQL /? at the command prompt. By default, SQL Server 2000 adds the folder to its tools to your PATH variable, so our PATH looks likes this:

```
PATH=C:\WINNT\system32;C:\WINNT;C:\Program Files\Microsoft SQL Server\
80\Tools\Binn\;C:\Program Files\Microsoft BizTalk Server\
```

If you run the Visual Studio command prompt, which is found under Start, Programs, Microsoft Visual Studio .NET, Visual Studio .NET Tools, Visual Studio .NET Command Prompt, then your PATH will be appended to include many other wonderful folders, most of which handle command-line compilation and manipulation of the .NET Framework. Typing SET at the .NET command prompt also shows you many wonderful environmental settings (dozens more than using the standard command prompt), which are useful for command-line compilation of .NET languages.

Here is what our PATH looks like when we run the special .NET command prompt:

```
PATH=C:\Program Files\Microsoft Visual Studio
.NET\Common7\IDE;C:\Program Files\Microsoft Visual Studio
.NET\VC7\BIN;C:\Program Files\Microsoft Visual Studio
.NET\Common7\Tools;C:\Program Files\Microsoft Visual Studio
.NET\Common7\Tools\bin;C:\Program Files\Microsoft Visual Studio .NET\
FrameworkSDK\bin;C:\WINNT\Microsoft.NET\Framework\v1.0.3705;C:\WINNT\
system32; C:\WINNT\system32;C:\WINNT;C:\Program Files\Microsoft SQL
Server\80\Tools\Binn\;C:\Program Files\Microsoft BizTalk Server\
```

Figure 4.6 shows the results of executing OSQL /? from a command prompt. By combining several of the commands on the command line, we can specify the server, the credentials, the input file, and an output file:

```
OSQL -SOmnibook -E -iHutchingsDDL.sql -I -n -oHutchingsResults.txt
```

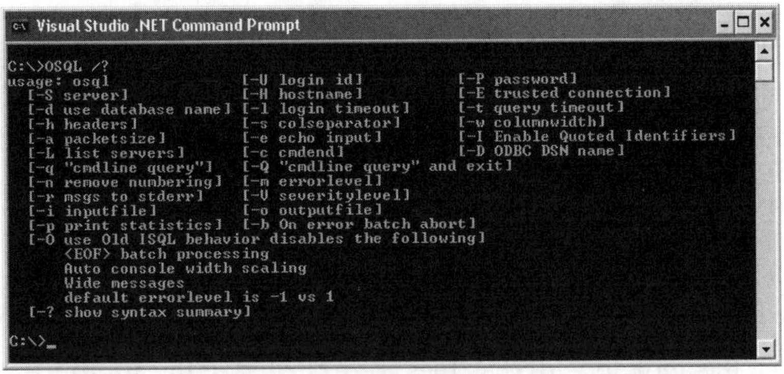

Figure 4.6 Usage syntax of the OSQL command-line utility.

Here's a brief description of each switch used in our OSQL example:

-S.   To name the server. You can also use (local) here, for the local SQL Server.

-E.   To use trusted security. When logged in as an administrator to develop code, you should use this switch; otherwise, you must use -U and -P to pass a standard security credential.

-i.   To specify the name of the input file, the DDL script generated by Visio.

-I.   To tell OSQL that Visio has delimited the object names with double quotes. Normally, they are seen as string delimiters (like an apostrophe) by OSQL. This parameter is important.

-n.   To suppress the line numbers in the output. Otherwise, the output is very busy.

-o.   To specify the name of the output file. If you omit this, the results will be echoed to the command window (a.k.a. standard out or stdout).

After executing the previous OSQL statement, the database and all of its objects are created. The only messages returned and captured in our text file were these:

```
The CREATE DATABASE process is allocating 3.00 MB on disk
'Hutchings_Data'.
The CREATE DATABASE process is allocating 1.00 MB on disk
'Hutchings_Log'.
```

Verifying the Physical Design

Whether you use Query Analyzer (QA), which sports a nice GUI, or OSQL, which is very fast and batch executable, or have Visio for Enterprise Architects build it for you, your database will be built. Once that step is accomplished, you should verify the physical design. Assuming your models were sound, the physical design should be just as sound, but you should still do some checking before testing it with your application. Here are a few ways in which to verify your physical design:

- Verify that the .mdf and .ldf disk files were created in the appropriate SQL Server folder.

- From Enterprise Manager (EM), expand the appropriate database trees and verify the objects.

- From QA, verify that the Hutchings database appears in the Object Browser (press F8).

- From the QA Object Browser, expand and verify the user tables, columns, indexes, triggers, and so forth.

- From QA, run `Execute sp_helpdb Hutchings` to verify files, sizes, usage, and options.

- From QA, run `DBCC CHECKDB ('Hutchings')`.

DBCC is SQL Server's Database Console Command (or Consistency Checker) and is a collection of utility statements that do a number of things, primarily to check the physical and logical consistency of a database. The DBCC commands are cataloged into maintenance, status, validation, and miscellaneous statements. See SQL Server Books Online for a complete list of the DBCC statements.

One statement that you can run right away is DBCC CHECKDB, which checks the allocation and structural integrity of each object in the database. For example, when we run `DBCC CHECKDB ('Hutchings')`, we are presented with this output:

```
DBCC results for 'Hutchings'.
DBCC results for 'sysobjects'.
There are 63 rows in 1 pages for object 'sysobjects'.
DBCC results for 'sysindexes'.
There are 45 rows in 3 pages for object 'sysindexes'.
DBCC results for 'syscolumns'.
There are 311 rows in 5 pages for object 'syscolumns'.
DBCC results for 'systypes'.
There are 26 rows in 1 pages for object 'systypes'.
DBCC results for 'syscomments'.
There are 101 rows in 4 pages for object 'syscomments'.
< snipped out other system tables >
DBCC results for 'Image'.
There are 0 rows in 0 pages for object 'Image'.
DBCC results for 'ImageCategory'.
There are 0 rows in 0 pages for object 'ImageCategory'.
DBCC results for 'ImageColor'.
There are 0 rows in 0 pages for object 'ImageColor'.
DBCC results for 'ImageKeyword'.
There are 0 rows in 0 pages for object 'ImageKeyword'.
DBCC results for 'ImageLicense'.
There are 0 rows in 0 pages for object 'ImageLicense'.
DBCC results for 'ImageMaterial'.
There are 0 rows in 0 pages for object 'ImageMaterial'.
DBCC results for 'ImageOrientation'.
There are 0 rows in 0 pages for object 'ImageOrientation'.
DBCC results for 'ImageResolution'.
```

```
There are 0 rows in 0 pages for object 'ImageResolution'.
< snipped out other user tables >
CHECKDB found 0 allocation errors and 0 consistency errors in database
'Hutchings'.
DBCC execution completed. If DBCC printed error messages, contact your
system administrator.
```

As you can see from our results, there isn't any data, let alone any problems with our tables. DBCC CHECKDB will check each table to make sure that the index and data pages are correctly linked, the indexes are in their proper sorted order, all pointers are consistent, the data on each page is reasonable, and all page offsets are reasonable. You can see that this is a fairly exhaustive test. Any errors indicate the presence of some potentially critical problems, which your DBA should address immediately.

SQL Server Enterprise Manager (EM)

From Enterprise Manager, you can also graphically and hierarchically see your database and all of its constituent objects. Using the Microsoft Management Console, you can drill down into your SQL Server and locate your newly created database. (You may have to hit the Refresh button if the database doesn't appear in the list.) After locating the database in the list, you'll be able to highlight the tables node in the tree and then see the tables themselves in the right-hand pane (see Figure 4.7).

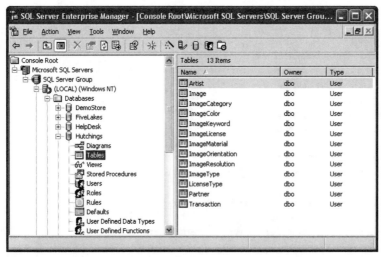

Figure 4.7   Verifying your database using Enterprise Manager.

You can right-click each table and select Properties. This will let you see some of the schema for each table. The schema is abbreviated and really shows only the name, data type, size, nullability, and default values of each column of the table. You can see much more information quickly, however, by generating a database diagram. We showed you a sample database diagram in the previous chapter. Here's how easy it is to create one:

1. Within Enterprise Manager (EM), locate and expand the appropriate SQL Server.

2. Locate and expand the appropriate database.

3. Right-click the Diagrams node and select New Database Diagram.

4. After the wizard launches, click Next.

5. Highlight all available tables and click the Add button, then click Next.

6. Review the table listing, click Finish, and wait for the diagram to generate.

7. With all of the tables still selected, right-click any of them and select Table View—Standard.

8. With all of the tables still selected, right-click any of them and select Arrange Selection.

9. Use the Zoom button on the toolbar (magnifying glass icon) to find the optimal resolution.

10. With all of the tables still selected, right-click any of them and select Autosize Selected Tables.

11. Right-click anywhere on the background and choose Show Relationship Labels.

You can also choose to show page breaks, add optional text annotations to the diagram, and select a custom Table View to show even more table and column properties. Figure 4.8 shows a portion of our sample diagram that we created in about 45 seconds.

By this point in your database design life cycle, you've probably got more models, diagrams, printouts, and posters than you know what to do with, so we don't want to stress this feature as a documentation tool. As we've said before, SQL Server database diagrams are a quick way to generate a nice diagram after the fact.

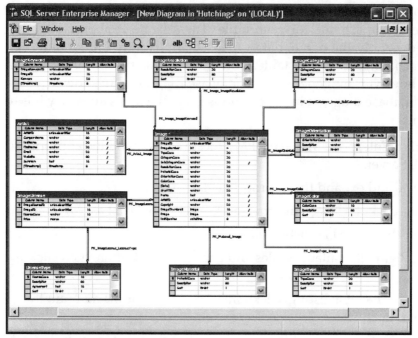

Figure 4.8 Sample database diagram generated by SQL Server.

What's more important is the ability to add, edit, and delete columns from tables and the tables themselves. By right-clicking a table, such as our Image table, we can go to Properties and then make changes to the important, behind-the-scenes aspects of our database. Figure 4.9 shows you the Properties page.

Looking at the various tabs in Figure 4.9, you'll see that you can change properties on many different levels. Here is a quick list of the tabs and what properties you can tweak on each tab:

Tables.   Change the table's name, owner, Identity column, RowID column, filegroups, and description.

Columns.   Change data types, description, sizes, nullability, default, identity, and other properties.

Relationships.   Add, edit, or remove relations between the current table and another, with special behaviors.

Indexes/Keys.   Add, edit, or remove indexes and related behaviors, such as unique, fill factor, and clustered.

Check Constraints.   Add, edit, or remove SQL snippets that serve to enforce business rules in the table.

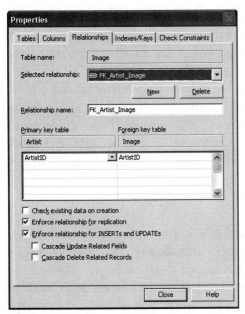

Figure 4.9 Table Properties page.

Adding Objects

Our original Object Role Modeling (ORM) models and subsequent database models can describe our database only so far. We would say that implementing ORM through Visio gets us about 90 percent there. A true ORM expert, using subtypes and many of the advanced constraint features of ORM, could probably bring that number closer to 95 percent.

From our ORM baseline, we want to add some of our own database objects to enforce our special business rules, increase performance, and tighten security. The next few pages highlight areas of improvement to our design that can be done only at the physical level.

Stored Procedures

Stored procedures are simply compiled T-SQL scripts that perform discrete units of work. They are very useful for two reasons. First, they are fast. SQL Server compiles these procedures into executable code that runs as fast (arguably) as any other compiled language. Stored procedures are also fast for another reason—they exist on the same server as the data itself, so zero network traffic is required to shuttle information to a piece of running code. Middleware components, although fast because they're running in the .NET Framework or are natively compiled code, still have to cope with the fact that the data must be fetched and brought to their tier to make any kind of decisions. The fastest compiled program out there becomes the slowest if it must go to the wire for data.

Second, stored procedures are secure. By creating smart stored procedures and then assigning appropriate security permissions to all roles in your application, you can literally shut off access to the base tables. With the base tables unreachable, except by a very tightly controlled DBO or SA password, all access must be performed through your stored procedures. The procedures can then be extremely guided in their execution, with tight business rule enforcement, role authentication, and auditing implemented right in the T-SQL code.

For Hutchings Photography, we used stored procedures for the requesting of thumbnails, watermarked images, and finally the quality images themselves. We will focus on the returning of thumbnails as an example of where a stored procedure can improve performance. We plan to offer our partners the ability to return thumbnails by one of several different methods:

By ID.   Given an ImageID (a GUID), return the thumbnail.

By number.   Given an Image Number (an integer), return the thumbnail.

By title.   Given the title or a title mask, return the thumbnail or thumbnails.

By combination.   Given a category, license code, or one or more keywords, return the thumbnails.

The first two methods will return 0 or 1 thumbnailed images. The last two methods will return 0 or more images. As you will see in later chapters, we will implement these as four separate Web methods. For simplicity's sake, however, we implemented them as a single stored procedure. We dissect our ws_ReturnThumbs stored procedure over the next few pages.

First, here is the preamble to the procedure, where we list our parameters and declare our variables to be used in the stored procedure. Notice that all of our parameters, which are those eight variables declared before the AS, are all set to NULL if no argument is supplied. We then declare a few variables to be used for the body of the stored procedure, including a couple of rather larger varchars, which you will see in use later.

```
CREATE PROCEDURE ws_ReturnThumbs
   @ImageID      varchar(40)   = NULL,
   @ImageNumber  int           = NULL,
```

```
    @Title          varchar(50)    = NULL,
    @Category       varchar(20)    = NULL,
    @SubCategory    varchar(20)    = NULL,
    @LicenseCode    varchar(10)    = NULL,
    @Keywords       varchar(1000)  = NULL,
    @ReturnImage    bit            = 0
AS
    DECLARE         @ErrorMsg      varchar(80)
    DECLARE         @ImageUID      uniqueidentifier
    DECLARE         @Event         varchar(2000)
    DECLARE         @SQL           nvarchar(1000)
    DECLARE         @Temp          varchar(250)
    DECLARE         @Keyword       varchar(50)
```

Scalable applications, such as our Web service, should not use temporary tables, or at least minimally use temporary tables, because SQL Server has to manage that storage area in TempDB by potentially hundreds of simultaneous sessions. Our temporary table, however, made it possible for one stored procedure to handle so many different Web methods calls.

```
-- Create Temporary Table
CREATE TABLE #TempImage (ImageID uniqueidentifier)
```

Our single stored procedure handles each of the four Web methods separately. First, we handle the returnThumbByID method, which passes a Uniqueidentifier (GUID) value into SQL Server. This section of T-SQL should be fairly self-documenting. Notice that we make sure that the @ImageID, which is typed as a string, has a length of 36 and matches the pattern or mask of a Uniqueidentifier, which is the gnarly looking LIKE statement that follows. (We are especially proud of this code, by the way!)

We are doing this level of validation because our Web service cannot guarantee that the partner will validate or even format the parameters before calling our code. Once we are sure that the ID is a Uniqueidentifier, we convert it and then see if it applies to a valid image in the database.

If the ImageID is still valid at this point, we stick it into our temporary table for later in the script and then audit the request. The auditing of requests is a cornerstone to both our security and commerce model. Remember that requesting thumbnailed and watermarked images can be done anonymously, and not until a pristine image is requested do we care who requested it. Later, our security model may be improved and we will track more metrics about the requests.

```
-- Validate ImageID for Length
IF LEN(@ImageID) <> 36
BEGIN
    SET @ErrorMsg = 'Invalid Image ID: ' + @ImageID
```

```
        GOTO MyError
END
-- Validate ImageID for Format
IF @ImageID NOT LIKE '[0-9A-F][0-9A-F][0-9A-F][0-9A-F][0-9A-F]
    [0-9A-F][0-9A-F][0-9A-F]-[0-9A-F][0-9A-F][0-9A-F]
    [0-9A-F]-[0-9A-F][0-9A-F][0-9A-F][0-9A-F]-[0-9A-F]
    [0-9A-F][0-9A-F][0-9A-F]-[0-9A-F][0-9A-F][0-9A-F]
    [0-9A-F][0-9A-F][0-9A-F][0-9A-F][0-9A-F][0-9A-F]
    [0-9A-F][0-9A-F][0-9A-F]'
BEGIN
    SET @ErrorMsg = 'Invalid Image ID: ' + @ImageID
    GOTO MyError
END
-- Convert to Uniqueidentifier
SET @ImageUID = CONVERT(uniqueidentifier,@ImageID)
-- Validate ImageID for Existence
IF NOT EXISTS (SELECT 'x' FROM [Image] WHERE ImageID = @ImageUID)
BEGIN
    SET @ErrorMsg = 'Invalid Image ID: ' + @ImageID
    GOTO MyError
END
-- Populate temporary table
INSERT #TempImage (ImageID)
    SELECT  ImageID
    FROM    Image I
    WHERE   ImageID = @ImageUID
-- Audit the request
SELECT  @Event = '"' + ShortTitle + '", Image Number: ' +
        CONVERT(varchar(10),ImageNumber)
FROM    Image
WHERE   ImageID = @ImageUID
INSERT  Audit (EventType,Event,ImageID) VALUES
        ('Thumbnail Requested',@Event,@ImageUID)
```

The next two sections of our stored procedure are similar to the previous one, so we won't discuss them in detail. They handle the returnThumb-ByNumber and returnThumbByTitle Web methods. The final Web method is the most complicated one as far as our T-SQL code is concerned because it can be based on one of several combinations or parameters, including a list of one or more comma-separated keywords.

```
-- First, validate the category
IF @Category IS NOT NULL
BEGIN
  SET @SQL = 'CategoryCode = ''' + @Category + ''''
  IF @SubCategory IS NOT NULL
    SET @SQL = @SQL + ' AND SubCategoryCode = ''' + @SubCategory + ''''
END
```

```
    -- Next, the License Type
IF @LicenseCode IS NOT NULL
   IF @SQL IS NULL
      SET @SQL = 'EXISTS (SELECT ''X'' FROM ImageLicense WHERE
         ImageID = I.ImageID AND LicenseCode = ''' +@LicenseCode + ''')'
   ELSE
      SET @SQL = @SQL + ' AND EXISTS (SELECT ''X'' FROM ImageLicense
         WHERE ImageID = I.ImageID AND
         LicenseCode = ''' +@LicenseCode + ''')'
-- No keywords, then we're finished
IF @Keywords IS NULL
   BEGIN
      SET @Event = @SQL
      SET @SQL =N'SELECT I.ImageID FROM Image I WHERE ' + @SQL
      INSERT #TempImage EXECUTE sp_executesql @sql
      -- Audit the request
      IF @@RowCount > 0
         INSERT Audit (EventType,Event) VALUES
            ('Thumbnails Requested','Looking for "' + @Event + '"')
   END
```

The code for looping through the keywords is a bit ugly. We could have written a nice user-defined function to help with this, but we figured that this would be the only time, and the way we append each keyword discovered in the comma-separated list to the WHERE clause of the SQL statement is unique.

Notice that we are dynamically building a SQL statement with a custom WHERE clause with all of our keywords listed as separate AND clauses. Our thinking was that if a partner sends over a request with three keywords, such as "Island," "Suntan," and "Snorkel," we should try to help identify the exact image that he or she is looking for rather than return masses of images. A partner who wants to see all images with these keywords can execute three separate queries.

Rather than use the EXECUTE() function from T-SQL versions of days gone past, we use the sp_executesql system stored procedure, which is new in SQL 2000 and is quite an improvement. With the sp_executesql stored procedure, you can substitute parameters from call to call, which makes it more versatile. SQL Server will also generate execution plans that are more likely to be reused, which makes it more efficient. For the specifics, look up "Using sp_executesql" in SQL Server 2000 Books Online.

What makes it possible for stored procedure 1 (which follows) to successfully interact with stored procedure 2 (the dynamic one being called by sp_executesql) is this line of code:

```
INSERT #TempImage EXECUTE sp_executesql @sql
```

Notice that we are doing a couple of interesting things with this line. We are inserting into our temporary table the results of executing our dynamic SELECT statement after passing it to our sp_executesql system stored procedure. Normally, two stored procedures run in separate processes and have a difficult time passing table data back and forth, so many SQL programmers use global temporary tables, which are a transactional and performance nightmare.

Here is the snippet of the stored procedure that handles the bulk of the Web service requests—requests for thumbnails by category and keyword:

```
-- Fix the Keywords (remove any delimitters and spaces)
SET @Keywords = REPLACE(@Keywords,'''','')
SET @Keywords = REPLACE(@Keywords,' ','')
-- Loop through all the keywords and build subqueries
SET @Temp = @Keywords
WHILE CHARINDEX(',',@TEMP) > 0
BEGIN
  -- Parse out the keyword
  SET @Keyword = LEFT(@Temp,CHARINDEX(',',@Temp)-1)
  -- Add clause to SQL statement
  IF @SQL IS NULL
    SET @SQL = 'EXISTS (SELECT ''X'' FROM ImageKeyword
      WHERE ImageID = I.ImageID AND Keyword = ''' +@Keyword + ''')'
  ELSE
    SET @SQL = @SQL + ' AND EXISTS (SELECT ''X'' FROM ImageKeyword
      WHERE ImageID = I.ImageID AND Keyword = ''' +@Keyword + ''')'
  -- Trim the keywords string and continue
  SET @Temp = RIGHT(@Temp,LEN(@Temp)-CHARINDEX(',',@Temp))
END
-- Add final clause to SQL statement
IF @SQL IS NULL
  SET @SQL = 'EXISTS (SELECT ''X'' FROM ImageKeyword
    WHERE ImageID = I.ImageID AND Keyword = ''' +@Temp + ''')'
ELSE
  SET @SQL = @SQL + ' AND EXISTS (SELECT ''X'' FROM ImageKeyword
    WHERE ImageID = I.ImageID AND Keyword = ''' +@Temp + ''')'
-- Dynamically Execute the statement
SET @Event = @SQL
SET @SQL =N'SELECT I.ImageID FROM Image I WHERE ' + @SQL
INSERT #TempImage EXECUTE sp_executesql @sql
-- Audit the request
IF @@RowCount > 0
  INSERT Audit (EventType,Event) VALUES
    ('Thumbnails Requested','Looking for "' + @Event + '"')
END
```

Next, if the appropriate Web method code ran and we ended up with image IDs in our temporary table, we will return two recordsets. The first one will contain the bulk of the metadata and the image thumbnails themselves.

The second recordset will tell the partner which image is available under which licensing mode, if the partner wants to display that information at this point. (Most partners will wait until the watermarked image is returned and displayed before sharing the types of licensing modes available. We return the licensing information for that Web method as well.)

```
-- Return recordset #1 (image thumbnail information)
SELECT I.ImageID,
       I.ImageNumber,
       I.ShortTitle,
       I.Memo,
       I.TypeCode,
       I.CategoryCode,
       I.SubCategoryCode,
       I.ResolutionCode,
       I.MaterialCode,
       I.OrientationCode,
       I.ColorCode,
       I.Date,
       A.ArtistID,
       A.CompanyName  as ArtistCompany,
       A.LastName     as ArtistLastName,
       A.FirstName    as ArtistFirstName,
       A.Email      as ArtistEmail,
       A.Website    as ArtistWebsite,
       A.Summary    as ArtistSummary,
       I.Copyright,
       I.ImageThumbnail
  FROM Image I
       LEFT OUTER JOIN Artist A   ON I.ArtistID = A.ArtistID
       INNER JOIN #TempImage T  ON T.ImageID = I.ImageID
-- Return recordset #2 (licensing information)
SELECT IL.ImageID,
       IL.LicenseCode,
       IL.Price
  FROM ImageLicense IL
       INNER JOIN #TempImage T  ON T.ImageID = IL.ImageID
```

As you will see in the Web service construction chapter, we will be returning an ADO.NET DataSet object from our C# code, which gets coerced into an XML document. This format easily and logically supports two separate recordsets. The XML programmer on the partner's end can easily pull out just the thumbnail data, just the licensing data, or both.

Finally, we must clean up our stored procedure, such as dropping our temporary table. Using temporary tables can reduce stored procedure performance, especially if you do not drop them as soon as possible. Although handling multiple job steps is made possible by temporary tables, you want to follow a strict list of dos and don'ts. That list is found in SQL Server

2000 Books Online under the Transact-SQL Tips topic. Here is our cleanup and error-handling code:

```
   -- Cleanup
   DROP TABLE #TempImage
   RETURN 0
MyError:
   -- Cleanup
   DROP TABLE #TempImage
   -- Raise a SQL Server error with a severity of 12
   RAISERROR (@ErrorMsg,12, 1)
   RETURN -1
GO
```

Database Care and Feeding

We hope that your business has IT staff whose duties include database administrator. If you're lucky, you've got a full-time, educated, and certified database administrator (DBA) on the payroll who can handle the support of your SQL Server. Otherwise, the database programmers or domain administrators have to wear this hat.

A DBA's duties include everything from performing backups to tuning the server. Some shops consider it a part of the DBA's duties to write stored procedures and triggers and to tweak the database schema. Other shops don't want their DBAs near the schemas—just to keep the server running optimally. Regardless of the extent of a DBA's duties, if the DBA is not you, then you may have to sharpen your negotiation skills to get your database implemented. We've even met DBAs who were oddly reminiscent of the Black Knight from Monty Python and the Holy Grail—it's their turf and not yours.

On the other hand, if you become the de facto DBA, then you can probably use a few pointers on maintaining and troubleshooting a SQL Server database. The Database Maintenance Plan wizard and the SQL Profiler are two important features of SQL Server to master. They allow you to protect your data and troubleshoot your database.

Database Maintenance Plans

Maintenance plans are sets of scheduled jobs that are easy to set up and ensure that your database and transaction logs are optimized and backed up. Additionally, indexes can be rebuilt, statistics updated, exhaustive tests run, and a number of notifications issued. We call Maintenance Plans and the Maintenance Plan Wizard a DBA in a Box.

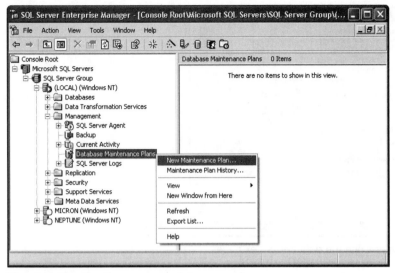

Figure 4.10   Creating a new maintenance plan.

Database Maintenance Plans are best created using the wizard. The wizard can be launched like any other wizard in SQL Server, by selecting the Tools, Wizards, [menu option] from inside Enterprise Manager. We like to expand the list of Database Maintenance Plans, however, allowing us to see what we've already set up. Figure 4.10 shows how to run the wizard from the Database Maintenance Plans node of the tree.

The wizard walks you through an interview, asking you all of the relevant questions about which databases you want to maintain under the plan. You can choose to create a maintenance plan for system or user databases. For our implementation, we chose to create a single maintenance plan for just the Hutchings database.

Figure 4.11 shows the first question of interest, which is how to optimize the database. Specifically, the wizard wants to know if you would like it to periodically reorganize the data and index pages as they are physically arranged on disk. This can be thought of as running defrag for your database. We consider it to be a good idea as long as your database isn't so large that it won't complete before the more important backups are made. You can also opt to remove unused space from the database files (.mdf or .ndf). These options ensure that the database pages will contain an equally distributed amount of data and free space to allow future growth to be faster.

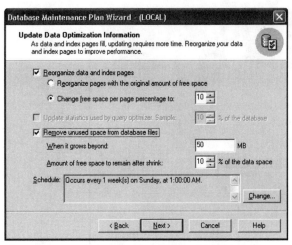

Figure 4.11 Optimizing the data and index pages.

Figure 4.12 shows the next question, which is whether the maintenance plan should check for database and index integrity. This step, by the way, will simply execute the DBCC CHECKDB Transact SQL statement that we've already mentioned. Any integrity problems will get reported. Time permitting, we recommend that you choose to include indexes and attempt to repair any minor problems with them that may be discovered. You should also perform these tests before backup so that any problems will abort the backup step. This is important because life may have you go off and forget about the maintenance plans for a few weeks or months, and by the time you get back and discover the corrupted database, all of your backups are toast. We're speaking from experience on this one.

The next step begins the crucial backup questions. Figure 4.13 shows the wizard asking whether you want to back up and verify the database and the destination to back up. The database backup option causes the entire database to be backed up. This is known as a Full Database backup, as opposed to a differential or file/filegroup backup.

Once you have chosen to back up the database, you'll need to tell the wizard where to back up. By default, the wizard will back up to this disk folder:

```
C:\Program Files\Microsoft SQL Server\MSSQL\BACKUP
```

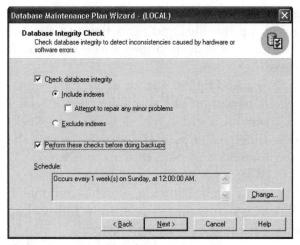

Figure 4.12   Checking database integrity.

You can change this path to another one on the SQL Server. It can also be on a network file share, but you'll need to make sure that the SQLSERVER-AGENT service runs under a Windows account that has permission to write to the remote share. You might consider a domain account if this is what you're trying to accomplish.

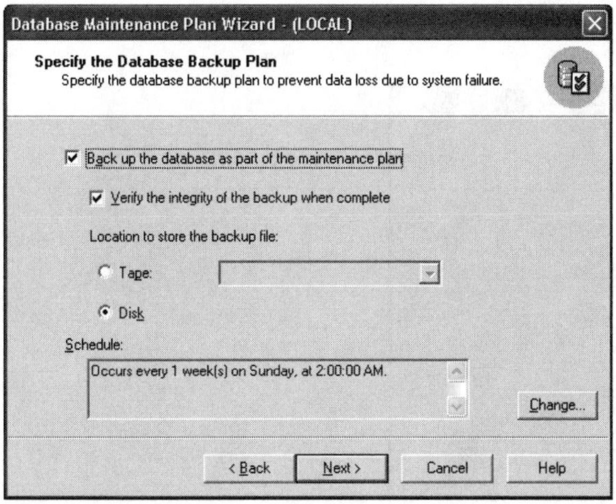

Figure 4.13   Backing up the database.

Another approach is to back up to the local folder and then have a second job or backup software pick up the files and send them to another computer or to tape. Preferably, these final destinations are off site, in case something catastrophic happens.

Figure 4.14 shows the questions asked by the wizard about the destination folder. You can also have SQL Server build a subfolder for your database for organization. It's nice to enable a sliding window of a few weeks so that SQL Server will delete older backups and conserve space. The default is 4 weeks, but we recommend bumping this up to 8 weeks, 12 weeks, or more, if you've got the disk space.

The next steps cover backing up the transaction log, which is optional. If your database is small enough, you may want to perform a full backup every night. This is certainly the easiest to back up and restore.

If, however, your database is larger, then it may be impractical to do a full backup every night, so then a good plan is to run the full backup on the weekend, with just transaction log backups every night. Transaction log backups are smaller because they back up only the recorded changes to the database since the last transaction log backup. The downside to this approach is that when it comes time to restore, you'll have to start with your last full backup and then restore all transaction log backups made after that. The transaction log backup steps are identical to the last two that we've covered for database backups.

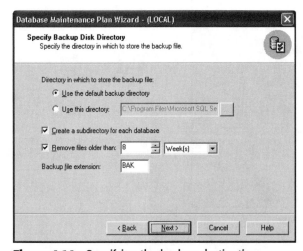

Figure 4.14 Specifying the backup destination.

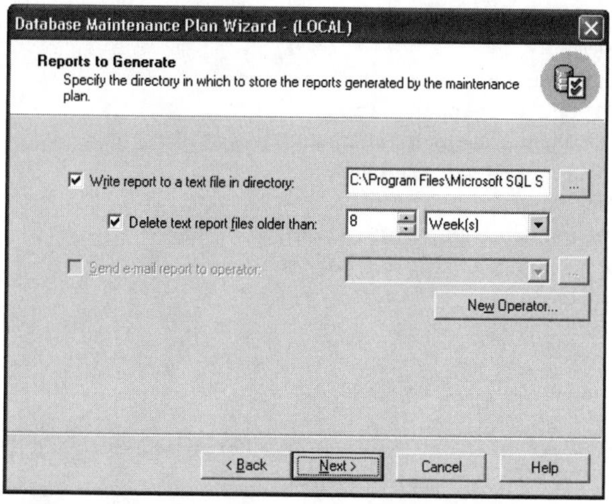

Figure 4.15   Generating maintenance plan reports.

Figure 4.15 shows the step where you can specify where to generate reports and how long to keep them. These reports will contain details of the steps executed and any error information. The report filenames are such that the date and time the job ran are appended to the plan, such as:

```
HutchingsMaintenancePlanA_200207071210.txt
```

If SQL Mail has been successfully installed, SQL Server can email the report to the operator. This is handy because you can quickly review last night's maintenance activity when you arrive at your inbox the next morning.

The final step of the wizard allows you to persist the maintenance report as rows in the sysdbmaintplan_history table in the MSDB database. This table is queried by Enterprise Manager when you show job history and allows you to build your own custom queries. You can choose to limit the table to a certain number of rows (the default is 1000) before it starts recycling. You can also choose to persist this information to a remote server instead of or in addition to your local SQL Server. When finished, you can review all of the information that the wizard captured.

```
DATABASES
   Hutchings
SERVERS
   (local)
OPTIMIZATIONS
```

```
        Occurs every 1 week(s) on Sunday, at 1:00:00 AM.
        Perform the following actions:
            Reorganize data and index pages, changing the free
            space to 10 percent of the original space.
            Shrink database when it grows beyond 50 MB.
            Leave 10 percent of data space as free space.
    INTEGRITY CHECKS
        Occurs every 1 week(s) on Sunday, at 12:00:00 AM.
        Perform integrity checks before backing up database.
        Perform the following actions:
            Check database
    COMPLETE BACKUP
        Occurs every 1 week(s) on Sunday, at 2:00:00 AM.
        Backup media: Disk
        Backup destination: C:\Program Files\Microsoft SQL Server\MSSQL\BACKUP
        Delete backup files which are older than 8 Week(s).
        Verify the backup after completion.
        Create a subdirectory for each database, to store the backup files.
    TRANSACTION LOG BACKUP
        Occurs every 1 week(s) on Monday, Tuesday, Wednesday,
            Thursday, Friday, Saturday, at 12:00:00 AM.
        Backup media: Disk
        Store backup files in the default SQL Server Backup directory.
        Verify the backup after completion.
    Reports will be generated and stored in directory:
        C:\Program Files\Microsoft SQL Server\MSSQL\LOG\
```

You should save this maintenance plan, giving it a friendly name. We called ours HutchingsMaintenancePlanA. After the wizard has created the job, you'll see it listed under the Database Maintenance Plans node under the Management folder for that SQL Server.

Interestingly, SQL Server implements these maintenance plans with multiple SQL Server Agent jobs. If you expand the SQL Server Agent folder and then highlight the Jobs node, you'll see several new jobs added. Our maintenance plan created the following jobs:

- DB Backup Job for DB Maintenance Plan 'HutchingsMaintenancePlanA'
- Integrity Checks Job for DB Maintenance Plan 'HutchingsMaintenancePlanA'
- Optimizations Job for DB Maintenance Plan 'HutchingsMaintenancePlanA'
- Transaction Log Backup Job for DB Maintenance Plan 'HutchingsMaintenancePlanA'

These jobs are not listed in the order of execution, but rather alphabetically. You need to right-click and go into Properties to view or adjust the schedule. We won't cover all of the possible ways you can edit these jobs, but keep in mind that you can tweak your maintenance plans, schedules, and notifications in this way.

Each of these jobs has only one step, which farms out all of the maintenance work to a system stored procedure, so customizing the step will require some in-depth knowledge of these stored procedures. For example, here is the stored procedure called to support the DB Backup Job:

```
EXECUTE master.dbo.xp_sqlmaint N'-PlanID 2EB863F6-2DED-4D15-9AE9-
DBC05AEA4DB1 -Rpt "C:\Program Files\Microsoft SQL
Server\MSSQL\LOG\HutchingsMaintenancePlan4.txt" -DelTxtRpt 8WEEKS -
WriteHistory  -VrfyBackup -BkUpOnlyIfClean -CkDB  -BkUpMedia DISK -
BkUpDB "C:\Program Files\Microsoft SQL Server\MSSQL\BACKUP" -DelBkUps
8WEEKS -CrBkSubDir -BkExt "BAK"'
```

Once you spend 5 or 10 minutes setting up a maintenance plan, it will run faithfully and without interaction as long as your SQL Server is up. Notification of errors to your inbox or pager is beneficial so that you have to spend your time with only the exceptional situations, not the drudgery.

SQL Profiler

Another important tool to understand is SQL Profiler. In those cases where you are troubleshooting SQL queries and other commands being executed from the Web service or another client application, SQL Profiler shows you the who, when, where, and what.

For example, suppose that a partner contacts Hutchings Photography to say that no images are being returned for a fairly straightforward query. You can go back and forth asking a lot of time-consuming questions, such as what options are being selected and what buttons are being clicked. Short of watching over the remote user's shoulder, you never really know for sure what is being sent.

There are tools and APIs for watching (or sniffing) the low-level IP and HTTP traffic being sent to your Web site and Web service, but that might capture a bit too much information. SQL Profiler will capture just the traffic between the client application (our .NET Web service code) and the SQL Server in question. By looking at which stored procedure is being called and what parameters are being passed, you can narrow the troubleshooting's scope.

SQL Profiler has another, different purpose from troubleshooting. SQL Profiler and the Index Tuning wizard can be used together to help analyze queries and determine which indexes need to be created, altered, or dropped. As you may already know, having the right balance of indexes for a database and its workload can be a complicated decision-making process. The choice between narrow indexes (those with few columns) and wide indexes (those with many columns to cover more queries) can be a difficult one to make. Because there are no simple rules to follow, all you can do is start with a good guess as to the type and number of indexes, then time will tell. The Index Tuning wizard can be used to automate this task. Results captured by the SQL Profiler can be fed to the wizard and analyzed, making index recommendations. For more information, look up the Index Tuning wizard in SQL Server 2000 Books Online.

SQL Profiler can be launched as a separate application from the SQL Server program group, which initially displays an empty window. You must begin a new trace or open an existing one. For ad hoc troubleshooting, we typically create a new trace and then discard it at the end of the session. For a shortcut, you can just click the left-most toolbar button to create a new trace.

SQL Profiler must first know which SQL Server you want to watch. The Connect to SQL Server dialog box is the standard one you've seen in Query Analyzer. Provide your user credentials, if necessary. Figure 4.16 shows the properties on the General tab that you can specify when creating a new trace. Your options of saving to file or saving to table are in addition to viewing them on the screen.

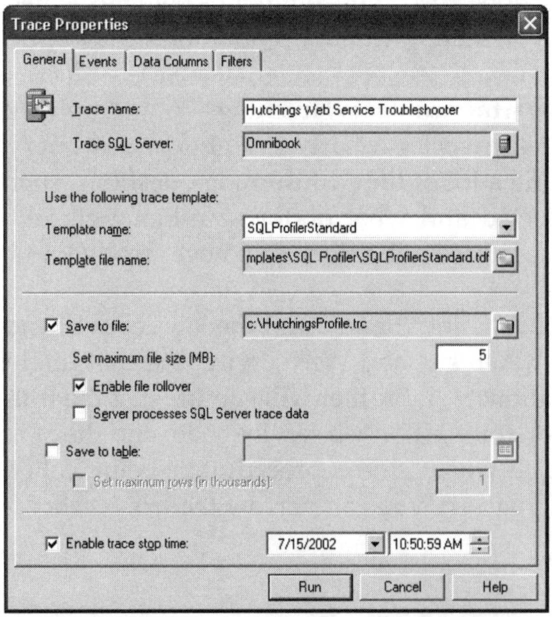

Figure 4.16   Creating a new SQL Profiler trace.

In addition, you can choose when to trace. These are known as the events. By default, SQL Profiler tracks only when someone performs a login or logout to the SQL Server, executes Remote Procedure Call (RPC), and executes Transact SQL statement. That last one will catch most of the traffic you are interested in. You may want to explore some of the dozens of other events that you can watch.

The next tab allows you to select what to trace. By default, SQL Profiler collects only these data items: EventClass, TextData, ApplicationName, NTUserName, LoginName, CPU, Reads, Writes, Duration, ClientProcess-ID, SPID, and StartTime. These are the primary data items that you'll be interested in.

Filters, as the name implies, allow you to specify the criteria for determining which events to capture. Your choices include watching for a specific database, user, CPU, application name, time, hostname, index, login name, object, permission, and so forth. For example, if you are interested only in capturing the traffic from the Hutchings Web service .NET application, you could set the ApplicationName filter to "LIKE Hutchings".

Figure 4.17 shows a sample trace captured for us when we ran it on our Windows 2000 Server. When you highlight a specific event, SQL Profiler expands the TextData column into the pane at the bottom so that you can see larger statements easier.

In essence, that's all that SQL Profiler does. You can tweak what gets captured and when it gets captured, but it's basically just a great sniffing utility to help you understand what statements are getting executed against your SQL Server. See SQL Server 2000 Books Online for more help configuring SQL Profiler.

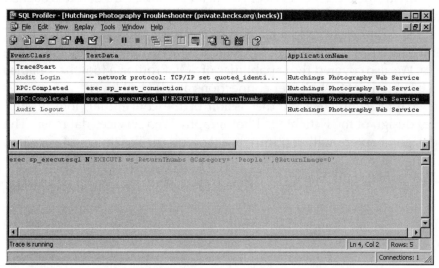

Figure 4.17 Sample trace on Windows 2000 server.

Summary

SQL Server 2000 is the cornerstone to a successful .NET Web service—especially one as data intensive as that of Hutchings Photography. While SQL Server has many built-in XML features, not including all of those added with the downloadable Web Services Toolkit (SQLXML 3.0), we intend to use SQL Server for what it does best—maintain relational data in a secure, high-performance environment.

By starting with our ORM model, Visio was able to compile all of our hard work and designs into a SQL Server-friendly DDL script. We were then able to take that script, make any subtle or documentation changes to it that we deemed necessary, parse it, and then run it. In a matter of seconds, our normalized database was constructed, along with all the appropriate objects and sample T-SQL code, compliments of Visio.

After our database was created came the steps necessary to validate the physical design. Validation included making sure, from many angles, that the database was built correctly. Once we were comfortable that the physical database was solid with no anomalies, we were able to extend the physical design, adding custom stored procedures, functions, and triggers. While Visio recommended many snippets of code to support our business rules, it was important for us to identify areas of optimization and improved security that neither Visio nor ORM could foresee. We looked at some of the new features of SQL Server 2000 here, such as using inline scalar functions.

Proper database maintenance and troubleshooting skills are important to a successful database deployment. When your database is the back end for a highly trafficked Web service, you need to make sure that it is backed up and optimized often. If any problems are discovered, the DBA needs to be notified in a timely manner. The Database Maintenance Plan Wizard was introduced as an easy way to create and schedule such maintenance services. We also covered the capabilities of SQL Profiler, a tool that enables you to troubleshoot SQL Server connections at a logical level.

This chapter completes the discussion of the conceptual, logical, and physical design of the Hutchings Photography Web services database. The next design chapters will continue to take you up the layers of services, describing our data access components in the next chapter and finally our XML Web service and its code in Chapter 6.

CHAPTER 5

Building ADO.NET Components

ADO.NET is a part of the .NET Framework that allows access to data sources and the manipulation of the data received from those sources. For those familiar with ADO, this may seem like the next iterative release. In many ways, it is. You still use a set of classes in ADO.NET to retrieve and manipulate data, and in many cases those classes have similar or identical names to those found in classic ADO. Much, however, has changed. In fact, the changes have been huge.

The overall focus of ADO.NET has shifted from maintaining a connection to the data source to disconnected access to the data source. This is a fundamental shift in the way data is accessed. In the past many developers have relied on database locking to maintain the integrity of the data. In a disconnected environment, though, data concurrency becomes a major issue.

The disconnected aspect of ADO.NET is one of its key features and is behind much of the hype of .NET. Through the disconnected classes we can build an in-memory relational database with all the associated tables, relationships, and constraints. In addition, there is sufficient XML metadata describing the data that updates can be easily made back to the data source.

One of the most important things to realize when first learning to deal with the disconnected objects is that they are independent of any data source implementation. Most readers will have likely dealt with data access technologies that were tightly coupled to their providers. Even previous versions of ADO, independent though they were of the data sources themselves, were tightly coupled to COM+ and OLE DB. ADO.NET, on the other hand, maintains all of its metadata internally as XML and can be used to represent a wide variety of different types of data stores, including spreadsheet models, relational models, and many textual models. Its internal representation is a relational model, and it works best when provided with data in regular structures.

The Internet has become a patchwork of different types of Web and database servers. With the possibility of so many volatile links, sluggish routes, and rickety hardware between your database and your client, you could easily classify everything as unstable. Your data, however, still needs to be shared and processed—sometimes at each tier of the application. The modern distributed application cannot bask in the safety that current hardware and Microsoft products will be running on each tier. Reality brings the realization that there may be as many platforms and vendor software as tiers in your application. Threading your data through this heterogeneous haystack requires a standard that transcends a Microsoft technology. We call it XML for short.

ADO.NET is built on an XML foundation. ADO.NET enjoys a solid disconnected behavior by being able to persist data to XML as a stream or file and then deserializing it into meaningful objects on the receiving end. Because the intermediate form is XML, any client or technology that understands XML can transform it into a number of meaningful structures. Since the XML blitz of the last few years, it is safe to assume that an XML parser is available for just about any platform.

As expected, ADO.NET supports traditional connected scenarios as well. ADO.NET can easily handle single- or two-tier .NET database applications, mating Visual Basic windows client applications or C# ASP.NET Web applications with data that lives in Access, SQL Server, Oracle, or any other ODBC or OLE DB data providers. ADO.NET continues to serve the needs of any LAN or WAN .NET applications, which benefit from a persistent connection to their data source, just as MDAC ADO has done in the past.

ADO.NET shines, however, when allowing data to be manipulated when it is not permanently connected to a data source. MDAC ADO has supported disconnected recordsets in the past, but ADO.NET has achieved enlightenment. If ADO.NET had a charter or list of design goals it would include data sharing, standardization, performance, scalability, and readability.

The ADO.NET Object Model

The full ADO.NET object model is too large to depict here. For a full explanation, we recommend *Programming ADO.NET,* written by Steven Borg and Richard Hundhausen (John Wiley & Sons, 2002).

The ADO.NET model divides neatly into two segments: the segment that deals with pure data manipulation, regardless of source, and the segment that deals directly with data sources.

The first segment contains the DataSet, DataTable, and other objects that carry no information about their source. These objects are pure .NET. They speak only XML and can be used by any .NET language or environment. They are completely disconnected from the data source. They don't even speak SQL.

The second segment gets down and dirty with the data source. It has to speak not only .NET, but also the language of the data source with which it communicates. The .NET Data Providers live on this level. Some speak OLE DB, translating to .NET for the DataSet objects. Another speaks Tabular Data Stream (TDS), translating from SQL Server to .NET. Both of those data providers also speak SQL.

Thanks to this stratification, the data manipulation in the DataSet remains pure across all platforms and data sources, effectively shielded from the complexities of diverse data sources (including data sources that don't speak SQL at all). The .NET Data Providers dirty their hands in the muck of different data source protocols, retrieving data from the sources, and translating it into the .NET language for use by the DataSet and DataTable objects. (See Figure 5.1.)

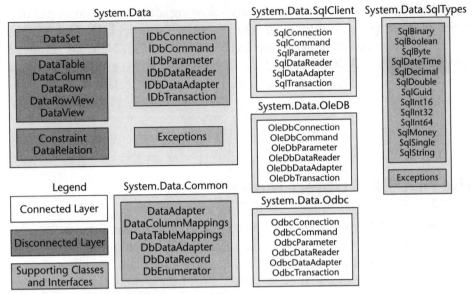

Figure 5.1 The ADO.NET namespace has many layers.

Some ADO.NET Classes

The following sections detail the ADO.NET classes that we believe will be of most interest to you.

Connection

The Connection class represents a unique connection to a data source. A Connection manages all the communication between your ADO.NET application and the data source. This could be a network connection to a remote database server or a file handle to an ISAM (Indexed Sequential Access Method) file on a local drive, such as a dBase, Paradox, Excel, or ASCII text file. Connections are opened after specifying the Connection-String information, which includes the location of the data source, any security credentials required to open it, and possibly the name of the provider or driver to use. Connections can also manage explicit transactions. (See Figure 5.2.)

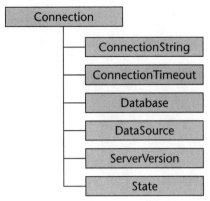

Figure 5.2   The ADO.NET Connection Object Model is relatively simple.

Command

The Command class, in its various implementations throughout ADO.NET, represents a SQL statement or stored procedure to execute against a given connection. The executing statement may return results to the client, or it may perform specific insert, update, or delete operations. For a look at the object model of the Command object, see Figure 5.3. Most ADO.NET commands support these three modes of execution:

ExecuteNonQuery.   For action queries, like updates, where no results are returned.

ExecuteReader.   For queries that return results for read-only, forward-only access to the data source.

ExecuteScalar.   For queries that return a single value, such as an average price.

Parameter

The Parameter class, as with MDAC ADO, serves the Command object. The parameters collection can contain one or more parameter objects, which match the parameters of the SQL command or stored procedure being executed. Because stored procedures can return information via output parameters and return values, the direction of each parameter object is important. (See Figure 5.4.)

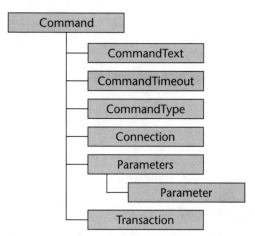

Figure 5.3   The Command Object Model executes commands against a database.

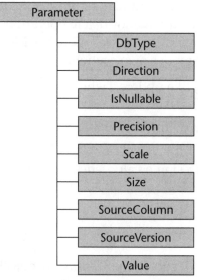

Figure 5.4   The Parameter Object Model is used when passing parameters to a stored procedure.

DataSet

You can think of a DataSet, the flagship of ADO.NET, as an in-memory view of your database. The DataSet is a collection of client-side, static, batch optimistic, disconnected recordsets (known as DataTable objects in ADO.NET). But it is more than just a number of MDAC ADO recordsets. The DataSet class can contain any number of sets of data: tables, stored procedures, SQL queries, or views. The DataSet can track any relationships between these tables as well as all schema information. In fact, a DataSet can represent your entire database. Because the DataSet can encapsulate so much information and persist it using XML, it becomes an ideal means of transport for a .NET Web service.

The DataSet class contains collections of DataTable and DataRelation classes. The DataTable, in turn, provides DataRow, DataColumn, and Constraint classes. With these five classes, ADO.NET provides enough information to reconstruct your database schema in memory. The DataTable class provides the Rows collection, which is a collection of DataRow objects. DataRows are where you interact with your data. To support conflict resolution, these DataRows can maintain several different versions of data: Default, Original, Current, and Proposed. (See Figure 5.5.)

Having the DataRelations established for two or more DataTables provides referential integrity in memory. It also enables you to use ADO.NET's programming model to navigate between related tables. Given a DataRow, you may call the GetChildRows or GetParentRow methods to return related DataRows.

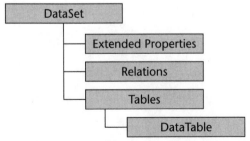

Figure 5.5   The DataSet is the key object in ADO.NET.

DataTable

Similar to the MDAC ADO Recordset class in functionality, the ADO.NET DataTable represents a single table of in-memory data. You can create DataTables as standalone objects or refer to them as part of a robust hierarchy within a DataSet object. DataTable's beefy object model allows it to hold all its necessary schema information: columns, constraints, keys, row data, and relations. (See Figure 5.6.)

DataAdapter

The DataAdapter provides an interface between a data source and the .NET framework data handling objects, such as the DataSet. The DataAdapter both retrieves data from a data source, populating a DataSet with data and constraints, and resolves updates, additions, and deletions back to the data source. The DataAdapter depends on a Connection object to provide the connection to the data source and Command objects to retrieve data from and resolve changes to the data source. (See Figure 5.7.)

NOTE You can think of the DataAdapter as a proxy or broker that reconciles data between the DataTable in the DataSet and the data in the data source.

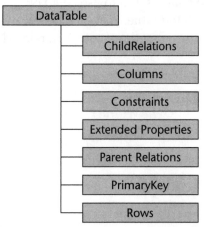

Figure 5.6 The DataTable is contained inside a DataSet.

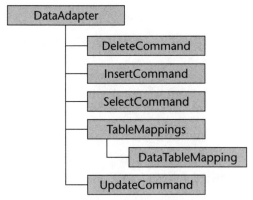

Figure 5.7 A DataAdapter is used to connect a DataSet to a database.

A DataAdapter abstracts the specifics of the data source from the DataSet. This abstraction means that manipulation in your application is identical regardless of the data source. You can learn one set of classes and members regardless of the data source.

DataReader

The DataReader provides read-only, forward-only access to a data source. Because it maintains only one record in memory at a time, there is minimal resource impact. Because there is no need to create a DataSet object (or other data structures found in the System.Data namespace) and the DataReader is always fully connected to the database, it is much faster than other forms of data access. It can be an excellent choice for populating read-only controls, printing reports, or providing data for Web pages; however, be aware that once a DataReader has been opened, the connection it is using cannot be used by any other object and the connection to the data source is maintained until the DataReader's Close method is called. Although this may not impact your data source, it may force you to instantiate a second Connection object to interact with your DataReader. (See Figure 5.8.)

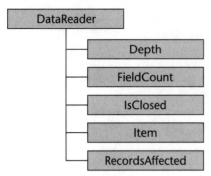

Figure 5.8   A DataReader is a fast, read-only, forward-only way to access a database.

ADO.NET Data Providers

The concept of a data provider roughly translates to the idea of an OLE DB provider from the MDAC ADO world. The data provider is the collection of classes built specifically for communicating with one type of data source. With regards to System.Data.Odbc and System.Data.OleDb, these are generic mechanisms, which use COM Interop to communicate with legacy drivers and providers.

The Holy Grail, however, lies in using custom data providers that target a specific data source, such as System.Data.SqlClient. Targeted data providers are engineered for optimal communication to a specific data source, even going so far as communicating with the server using its native protocols. Microsoft and other database vendors are on board to provide these data providers as soon as possible.

OLE DB .NET Data Provider (System.Data.OleDb)

OLE DB is only a few years old and has already proven itself very valuable and powerful. Microsoft and several other database vendors have provided OLE DB providers primarily because the COM interfaces allow a much richer access to their data stores than the traditional, rigid ODBC APIs allowed, though Microsoft's MSDAORA provider remains a workable way of connecting to Oracle 7 and, to some degree, Oracle 8 databases.

You may use the OLE DB .NET Data Provider to access SQL Server 7.0 or 2000, but life is better (and faster) if you use System.Data.SqlClient, which uses managed code and speaks directly to the server in its native tongue, which is Tabular Data Stream (TDS). TDS allows SQL Server and its clients to communicate regardless of the operating system, server release, or network protocols. If you need to communicate with SQL Server 6.5, you need to use System.Data.OleDb.

Keep in mind that OLE DB providers use COM and thus are not managed code. Using System.Data.OleDb requires the "expensive" COM Interoperability Services.

Some other compatibility notes:

- The MSDAORA OLE DB provider has not yet been tested with Oracle 9.0.

- The OLE DB .Net Data Provider does not currently support the generic OLE DB Provider for ODBC (MSDASQL). If you need to access ODBC data sources, you should consider using a native provider or the ODBC .Net Data Provider directly.

- The OLE DB .Net Data Provider does not currently support the OLE DB Provider for Data Shaping (MSDADS). If you need to shape your data hierarchically, you should consider streaming it out to XML and transforming it appropriately.

- The OLE DB Data Provider does not support the OLE DB 2.5 interface. Thus you cannot use the MS OLE DB Provider for Exchange, the MS OLE DB Provider for Internet publishing, or any other provider exposing the OLE DB 2.5 interface.

SQL Server .NET Data Provider (System.Data.SqlClient)

This is the only targeted .Net Data Provider available as of this writing. This data provider is also the only one of the three that runs 100-percent managed code, with no Interop required. System.Data.SqlClient has been customized for the extra features and idiosyncrasies of SQL Server. The primary classes, SQLDataReader, SQLDataAdapter, and SQLCommand, have all been tailored to directly access SQL Server's formats.

It is also considerably faster to use this provider over one of the other two. For this reason alone, you should use the SQL Server .NET managed provider to communicate with SQL Server.

NOTE Microsoft has hinted that there will be a SQL Server server-side .NET Namespace—(perhaps System.Data.SqlServer?). We can only speculate that this could be something useful like the existing SQL Distributed Management Objects (SQL-DMO), which allow full administration of SQL Server through a robust API.

Introduction to the Hutchings Data Layer

To provide significant functionality for the XML Web services that Hutchings Photography requires, we must be careful in creating the structure of the Data Layer. Not only will this later interact directly with the SQL Server database, but it will define the structure of the data that is sent to the Web service consumers.

A great deal of the optimization of the data access has already been taken care of internally to the SQL Server data source through the use of proper indices and stored procedures. This takes some of the burden of creating the data layer because we can simply use the stored procedures that were so carefully crafted. This is true of any sophisticated relational database we may be using, whether that is Oracle, SQL Server, or any other of the myriad high-quality database systems available.

This doesn't mean, though, that we can completely ignore performance issues in the data layer. By architecting carefully and ensuring that we're using good design patterns, we'll keep our performance as high as possible. One of the major concerns for any heavily accessed Web service is scalability. Luckily, as we've mentioned earlier, ADO.NET and the .NET Framework are designed for building highly scalable applications.

Last, we'll need to take a quick look at the hardware and software platforms on which our solution will run. Arguably, other than having the performance benefits of .NET, these platforms are the most important pieces of our overall architecture, especially for performance and security.

Because XML Web services can be served and consumed from any platform, we could use any OS and machine type to serve them. Because Visual Studio .NET and the .NET Framework are such good technologies and both speed and simplify our development greatly, we will use them to implement and serve the Hutchings Photography XML Web services.

NOTE The Mono project by Ximian Software is an attempt to create an Open Source implementation of the .NET Framework that will run on the Linux operating system. If this project is successful, look for the Apache Web server to be extended to support the serving of XML Web services created using .NET. Although there are compelling reasons to use the Windows operating system to serve Web pages and Web services, a successful Linux port would significantly broaden the appeal of using .NET to create both Web applications and Web services.

Because of prior investment in hardware, Hutchings Photography already has a server dedicated to SQL Server 2000 and another Web server dedicated to its current Web site. Both servers run Windows 2000 Server with the latest service packs and security patches.

We haven't yet stressed the choice of a Web server platform. Because ASP.NET will be hosting our Web services and ASP.NET requires IIS 5.0 or above, this is a relatively simple choice. We need to be sure, though, that we're running IIS with the latest security patches and updates. Although .NET was designed with security in mind and has so far proven to be very tight, our Web services will also depend on the rest of the systems involved. IIS has been shown as a popular target for hackers for a variety of reasons, so we need to be very security conscious.

For reasons covered in the last chapter, we'll use SQL Server 2000 as our database. Once again, SQL Server was chosen for its speed, low total cost of ownership, and security. Because we'll be hitting SQL Server only through the stored procedures, we're greatly increasing our level of security. And because there will be no direct queries of SQL Server through the Web, we're protecting ourselves from attacks such as SQL injection.

The .NET Framework and ADO.NET

Using the .NET Framework and ASP.NET as a Web server platform provides an extraordinary leap in functionality, programmer productivity, site security, and performance. It also allows us to use ADO.NET and the rest of the .NET Base Class Library.

Two of the first decisions we need to make are the transport protocols and the data format that we'll use to return data to the consumers of our Web services. Because we're dealing with XML Web services, the obvious choices are SOAP riding on HTTP for the transport protocols and XML as the data format. Although these protocols are the most common, neither is set in stone. In fact, the XML-P protocol being developed by the W3C specifically states that HTTP is not the only protocol that will support object access through the Internet. Because our primary goal is the construction of XML Web services that can easily punch through firewalls and travel freely throughout the Internet, we'll focus on SOAP riding on HTTP and XML.

Design of the Data Layer

Now that we've discussed hardware, software, and protocols, it's time to get down to architecting the actual data layer. The goal of Hutchings Photography is to wholesale the images that are currently in its archive. Our data layer needs to support this goal. In Chapter 2, the business requirements were explained. What is left to do now is the construction of the data objects so that they support those requirements. For instance, we want to be sure that the data format we return to a consumer is expressive enough to contain the information required to automate the sale, under various types of licenses, of the photos. We also want to be extensible as our business grows and develops and as new business opportunities present themselves.

One of the key objects in ADO.NET is the DataSet. The DataSet is a sophisticated object that can represent a large variety of different scenarios and yet is as conceptually simple as a relational database. It is also widely supported throughout the user interface classes of the .NET Framework. In addition, it is automatically serialized as a W3C standard XML document. This makes it an excellent selection for providing the data structure that Hutchings Photography can fill with a wide variety of data, both textual and binary.

By default, all binary data in a dataset is serialized using Base64 encoding. Another encoding is certainly possible, but we would need to encode the binary data first and then attach it to the proper column of the DataSet. Because Base64 is a well-known and well-supported encoding scheme, we'll use the default encoding provided by the DataSet's XML serialization. In addition, this means that if the consumer of our Web service is using .NET, the binary objects (images, in our case) are automatically deserialized into an array of bytes on the distant end, simplifying their life. Non-.NET consumers will have to deserialize using the Base64 encoding, but they would have had to deserialize regardless of the serialization used.

> **NOTE** In our situation, to serialize to a different standard, simply read the array of bytes stored in the DataColumn that contains our image data into a byte array and then run that byte array through another encoder. The resulting text can then be inserted into a sufficiently large DataColumn.

Last, the DataSet is, by default, serialized with complete schema information, making it a robust mechanism for all consumers because they can validate the returned XML. Because of these significant advantages, we'll use the DataSet object as our primary data structure for sending both our metadata and image payload to the Web service consumer.

DataSets

The design of the DataSet objects involves some of the more complicated required pieces. We want to be sure that we design them to be robust enough to support all the requirements we have, yet simple enough to be easily consumed, even by non-Microsoft consumers.

Basically, we want to return the data that was architected in the stored procedures built earlier. But we need to make sure that we clean the data up so that it has a consistent look across all the various XML Web services we're providing. Plus, as we'll see when we look at the DataAdapters we're using, we'll see that they don't automatically provide us with very friendly DataTable objects; however, they do return the DataSet in an XML format that will likely be common in the near future. Rather than pretty up the XML and put it all into a more human-readable form, we'll leave the XML in its current form. There is one very good reason for this: Because XML is so easily transformed into other formats, it is likely that other platforms such as Linux will develop a set of standard XSL transforms that will transform this rather ugly DataSet format into something useful to the consumer. If we try to make the format "friendlier," it will invalidate any attempt to change it later with a standard transform.

The purpose behind the ReturnThumbs Web service is to simply return a number of thumbnails that fit some passed criteria along with sufficient metadata so that decisions on how to display them can be made by the Web service consumer. Hutchings Photography envisions that most individuals will want to call this method first in order to present a series of thumbnails to an individual who will select which ones are of most interest. Then other calls, returning a full watermarked image, and negotiation for prices can take place.

The information returned for each image is as follows:

ImageID. This is the Hutchings ID for the image, which is a GUID.

ImageNumber. This is a friendly candidate key that is more easily jotted down by people browsing the thumbnails.

ShortTitle. The ShortTitle is a very brief title describing in broad terms what the image is about.

Memo. The Memo field is a longer description of the image.

TypeCode. The TypeCode is the type of image on file. For example, it could be *Photograph, Illustration,* or *Artwork.*

CategoryCode. This code describes the broad category the image fits into, such as *Employment* or *Nature.*

SubCategoryCode. This code categorizes the image more specifically than the category code. For instance, the SubCategoryCode might be the code for *Dog* under a CategoryCode representing *Pets.*

ResolutionCode. This code provides information on how detailed the image is. Some images are at a higher resolution than others.

MaterialCode. MaterialCode describes the type of material the image will be provided on if the actual image is requested from Hutchings Photography.

OrientationCode. The OrientationCode can be Horizontal, Vertical, or Panorama, which describes the orientation of the image.

ColorCode. ColorCode describes the color format of the image—for example, *Color* or *B&W* for a color photograph or black-and-white image, respectively.

Date. The Date is when the image was created. For photographs it is the day the photo shoot occurred. This is a textual field rather than a Date field, which means that the date may be returned in any number of formats.

ArtistID. This is the Hutchings ArtistID number. Because this is a GUID it is virtually unreadable by a human; however, it can be used for automated searches of the database.

ArtistCompany. This is the company that employed the artist at the time of the photo shoot. This may also simply be the name of the artist, if self-employed.

ArtistLastName. This field contains the last name of the artist.

ArtistFirstName. This field contains the first name of the artist.

ArtistEmail. This field contains the email address of the artist. This may or may not be provided, depending on availability of the email address and the policies of the company hiring the artist. This may be an email address of the artist's company or possibly Hutchings Photography itself, depending on the image.

ArtistWebSite. This is the URL of the artist's Web site, if any. As with ArtistEmail, this may also be the Web site of the artist's company or Hutchings Photography—or an empty string.

ArtistSummary. This is a short biography of the artist.

Copyright. This is the copyright of the image itself. It is also the text of the watermark that is printed on the image when a watermarked image is provided to a consumer and the copyright information that must be included in the actual use of the image under the standard licensing agreements.

ImageThumbnail. This is the actual bytestream that contains the thumbnail of the final image. As part of a DataSet object, this is the binary bytestream; however, it is serialized as a Base64 encoded textual encoding of the binary stream. This means that if you are using .NET to consume the Web service, you will have to deal with only the binary bytestream because it will automatically be deserialized when it is assigned to a DataSet object. If you are using a different consumer, though, you will need to handle the unencoding yourself.

In addition, a table providing information on the different licensing options, including price, for each photo is also included. This is important because some companies may wish to sort the images by available licensing or price. This information is as follows:

ImageID. Once again, this is the ImageID, as GUID, to which the licensing types apply.

LicenseCode. This code represents one type of licensing that is available for this image. Be aware that there may be many rows with the same ImageID, but differing LicenseCode values. Together, they provide a unique identifier for the row.

Price. This is the price, in U.S. currency, of the image under the license indicated by this row.

DataAdapters

In ADO.NET the only objects with direct knowledge about the data source are the Connection, Command, and DataAdapter objects. Of these, the DataAdapter is the most configurable and has the most influence on the structure of the DataSet that it feeds. Because of this impact on the DataSet we'll look most closely at these objects.

Through the judicious creation of our stored procedures in Chapter 4, we're able to have a one-to-one correspondence between the stored procedures and our Select, Insert, Update, and Delete commands associated with our DataAdapters. This simplifies the creation of our DataSet objects greatly.

> **NOTE** It is generally a good idea to have a one-to-one correspondence between a DataAdapter and a table (or view) in the DataSet. This allows a convenient way to both retrieve and update data from the data store. It's not necessary that each DataAdapter map to one table in the DataSet, however, because the Update command of each adapter is generally smart enough to pass only the appropriate data to the store. Still, developers often find it convenient to have the DataSet look something like the schema of the data store because this can simplify development and reduce confusion.

The first DataAdapter we'll cover is the one tied to our requirement to provide a group of thumbnails based on a query. This DataAdapter will support the creation of our response to the RequestThumbnail() Web service.

Building the Data Layer

Now that we have the basic architecture of the DataSet adapters designed, let's get to work on actually creating the required objects. Because the majority of developers working with XML Web services and the .NET Framework will be using Visual Studio .NET, we'll focus initially on creating all of our objects using the tools and wizards available in the graphical IDE.

The first thing we need to build is the connection to the data source; then we need to build the data adapters that will feed our data set. We can then create the DataSet that will hold all of the data and connect the DataTable objects inside the DataSet.

Graphically Building the DataAdapters

To build the DataAdapters, we'll use the great features available in the Visual Studio .NET IDE. To begin, we need to create a Connection to our Hutchings Photo database. To do this, we'll use the Server Explorer (see Figure 5.9).

To view the Server Explorer, you can select View, Server Explorer or press Ctrl-Alt-S. Now, by right-clicking the Data Connections item, you can select Add Connection... and step through the wizard (see Figure 5.10).

Figure 5.9   The Server Explorer is used to access server resources.

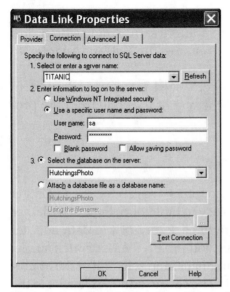

Figure 5.10   The Add New Data Connection wizard adds a new connection to a database.

Once you've stepped through the wizard, you've established a relation to the HutchingsPhoto database and should test the connection. When it succeeds, you're ready to add the data adapters.

Now, if you expand the HutchingsPhoto database and then the Stored Procedures, you'll see all the stored procedures created in Chapter 4. If you drag a stored procedure from the Server Explorer to the Design Palette, you end up with a SqlCommand object, and not a SqlDataAdapter object, because a Sql-Command is perfect for calling a Stored Procedure. You will automatically get the proper SqlCommand when you add your SqlDataAdapter.

To add the SqlDataAdapter to the project, select the Data tab from the Toolbox. (To activate the Toolbox, select it from the View menu or press Ctrl-Alt-X.) Now drag a SqlDataAdapter from the Toolbox to the Design Palette. This will automatically fire up the Data Adapter Configuration wizard. Walk through the wizard, being sure to select Use Existing Stored Procedures and the ws_ReturnThumbs stored procedure as the data adapter's Select command. Because this DataAdapter will be used only to select data from the database, you need to add only this single stored procedure. When the wizard is completed, rename the SqlDataAdapter to daRequestThumbnails.

The remaining stored procedures are converted into DataAdapters in much the same way. You can download the rest of the code from the project's Web site.

Graphically Building the First DataSet

Now that we've added the required data adapters, we can focus on creating the DataSet. The DataSet is actually fairly easy to build once the DataAdapter objects are built. To build the DataSet, right-click any of the data adapter objects and select Generate DataSet.... This will fire up the Generate DataSet wizard. Name the DataSet dsRequestThumbnails, and select all of the appropriate data adapter objects. (See Figure 5.11.) Be sure to add the DataSet to the designer. (Because you may have named your DataAdapters differently, the tables listed in Figure 5.11 may not necessarily match yours.)

Once the DataSet is generated we need to make sure we have established all the required relationships between the DataTables that have been added to the DataSet.

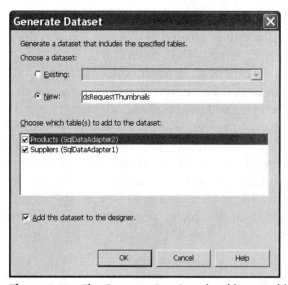

Figure 5.11 The Generate DataSet wizard is a graphical way to build a DataSet object.

Using the Schema Editor

Right-click the DsRequestThumbnails DataSet, and select View Schema.... This opens the DataSet in the graphical view. You'll see the DataTable objects as separate tables. By clicking the XML tab at the bottom, you can see the DataSet schema in its XML view. (We love this!) Click DataSet again because we'll be working in the graphical view. (See Figure 5.12.)

Select parent column in the Supplier table, and drag it to child column in the Product table. This creates a relation between the two tables. (See Figure 5.13.) (We use the Northwind database to demonstrate this concept because we have not yet built a relationship in any of our returned data. You will likely use it if you choose to duplicate the entire Hutchings Photography Web service functionality.)

Creating Nested Relations

Once you have a relationship, you can set the Nested property to True. This ensures that when the DataSet is serialized to XML, the child data is nested beneath its parent data.

Polishing the DataSet

As discussed earlier, we can make the DataSet look considerably more human readable. We choose not to do that here because the majority of the consumers of our data will be .NET platforms (and will thus not need to worry about the actual XML) or will be on other major platforms (which will likely have prebuilt XSL Transforms to convert the raw DataSet XML into something useful for them). Any modification of our XML structure then becomes, at best, a waste of energy and, at worst, something that will prevent a consumer from easily consuming our Web service data with prebuilt tools.

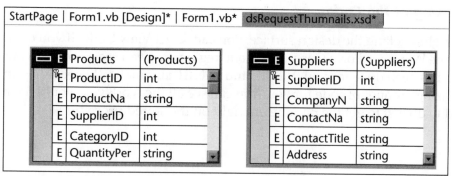

Figure 5.12   You can design a DataSet schema graphically.

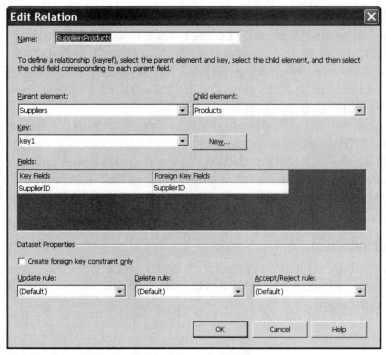

Figure 5.13 You can edit a Relation graphically.

What the Other DataSet Objects Look Like

The other DataSet objects look similar to the one we just built, but they are dependent on different stored procedures. Please see our Web site, where you can download the complete code.

Looking at the Code

By right-clicking the design surface, you can select View Code. If you open up the Windows Form Generated Code region, you can see all of the work that has been done for you. Visual Studio .NET automatically generates an amazing amount of code for you. You can see all the work you would have had to do just to get the parameters right on the stored procedures!

```
private void InitializeComponent()
{
    this.daReturnThumbs = new _
        System.Data.SqlClient.SqlDataAdapter();
    this.sqlSelectCommand1 = new _
        System.Data.SqlClient.SqlCommand();
    this.sqlConnectionImages = new _
        System.Data.SqlClient.SqlConnection();
    //
    // daReturnThumbs
    //
    this.daReturnThumbs.SelectCommand = this.sqlSelectCommand1;
    //
    // sqlSelectCommand1
    //
    this.sqlSelectCommand1.CommandText = "[ws_ReturnThumbs]";
    this.sqlSelectCommand1.CommandType = _
        System.Data.CommandType.StoredProcedure;
    this.sqlSelectCommand1.Connection = this._
        sqlConnectionImages;
    this.sqlSelectCommand1.Parameters.Add(new _
        System.Data.SqlClient.SqlParameter("@RETURN_VALUE", _
        System.Data.SqlDbType.Int, 4, _
        System.Data.ParameterDirection.ReturnValue, false, _
        ((System.Byte)(10)), ((System.Byte)(0)), "", _
        System.Data.DataRowVersion.Current, null));
    this.sqlSelectCommand1.Parameters.Add(new _
        System.Data.SqlClient.SqlParameter("@ImageID", _
        System.Data.SqlDbType.VarChar, 40));
    this.sqlSelectCommand1.Parameters.Add(new _
        System.Data.SqlClient.SqlParameter( _
        "@ImageNumber", System.Data.SqlDbType.Int, _
        4, System.Data.ParameterDirection.Input, _
        false, ((System.Byte)(10)), ((System.Byte)(0)), _
        "", System.Data.DataRowVersion.Current, null));
    this.sqlSelectCommand1.Parameters.Add(new _
        System.Data.SqlClient.SqlParameter("@Title", _
        System.Data.SqlDbType.VarChar, 50));
    this.sqlSelectCommand1.Parameters.Add(new _
        System.Data.SqlClient.SqlParameter("@Category", _
        System.Data.SqlDbType.VarChar, 20));
    this.sqlSelectCommand1.Parameters.Add(new _
        System.Data.SqlClient.SqlParameter("@SubCategory", _
```

```
       System.Data.SqlDbType.VarChar, 20));
this.sqlSelectCommand1.Parameters.Add(new _
   System.Data.SqlClient.SqlParameter( _
   "@LicenseCode", System.Data.SqlDbType.VarChar, _
   10));
this.sqlSelectCommand1.Parameters.Add(new _
   System.Data.SqlClient.SqlParameter("@Keywords", _
      System.Data.SqlDbType.VarChar, 1000));
this.sqlSelectCommand1.Parameters.Add(new _
   System.Data.SqlClient.SqlParameter( _
   "@ReturnImage", System.Data.SqlDbType.Bit, 1));
//
// sqlConnectionImages
//
this.sqlConnectionImages.ConnectionString = "data " +
   "source=TITANIC;initial catalog=Images;" +
   "persist security info=False;user id=sa" +
   ";workstation id=TITANIC;packet size=4096";
```

Building Our WebData Component from Scratch

Because we are sadists, we're subjecting you to a more difficult (and more enlightening) method of building our data access component—by building it from scratch. Often, a blend of automated and manually built code is best. Drag and drop all the data access stuff, then grab all of that automatically built code, and paste it into a new form or component where you want to fully optimize it.

The code that follows can be read from the top down. We'll add some commenting for explanation.

The first thing to do is declare all of the namespaces that we'll use. The Imports statements are all listed before the class declaration.

```
Imports System.Data.SqlClient
Imports System.Data
Imports System.IO
Imports System.Drawing
Imports System.Drawing.Imaging
```

Then we provide the class declaration and the variables that we'll use. You will need to change the value of the connection string to ensure that it works on your machine. The following code declares a class called WebData, which provides all of our data access.

```
Public Class WebData
  ' Connection Strings - please change for tighter security,
```

```
' and your settings
Private Const CONNECT_STRING_LOCAL As String = _
     "Server=titanic;Database=Images;Application " +
     "Name=Hutchings Photography Web Service;" +
     "User ID=sa;Password=;"
Private Const DEFAULTCOPYRIGHT As String = _
     "Copyright (c) HutchingsPhotography.com"
Private Const DEFAULTWIDTH As Integer = 640
Private Const DEFAULTHEIGHT As Integer = 480
Private CONNECTSTR As String
```

The next code passage provides some useful functions that will help us deal with the images we'll use.

```
' Private supportive routines
' Convert a string parameter to numeric, 0 if empty or invalid
Private Function ParmToInt(ByVal strParm As String) As Integer
If strParm = "" Or Not IsNumeric(strParm) Then
ParmToInt = 0
Else
ParmToInt = CInt(strParm)
End If
End Function
' Given a byte array, resize it to the specified height/width
' plus ability to default to thumb from the database
Private Function ResizeThumb(ByVal OriginalImage As Byte(), _
ByVal DefaultThumb As Byte(), _
ByVal intHeight As Integer, _
ByVal intWidth As Integer) As Byte()
Dim myImage, myResizedImage As System.Drawing.Image
Dim myMemoryStream As MemoryStream
' Validate sizes
If intHeight = 0 And intWidth = 0 Then
ResizeThumb = DefaultThumb
Else
Try
' Convert to an Image object
myMemoryStream = New MemoryStream(OriginalImage)
myImage = myImage.FromStream(myMemoryStream)
' Compute sizes, if necessary
If intHeight = 0 Then
intHeight = myImage.Height / _
(myImage.Width / intWidth)
ElseIf intWidth = 0 Then
intWidth = myImage.Width / _
(myImage.Height / intHeight)
End If
' Resize
myResizedImage = myImage.GetThumbnailImage( _
```

```
intWidth, intHeight, Nothing, Nothing)
' Convert back to Byte Array
myMemoryStream = New MemoryStream()
myResizedImage.Save(myMemoryStream, ImageFormat.Jpeg)
ResizeThumb = myMemoryStream.ToArray
Catch ex As Exception
' Any error and just return back the orignal thumbnail
ResizeThumb = DefaultThumb
End Try
End If
End Function
' Given a byte array, resize it to the specified height/width
Private Function ResizeImage(ByVal OriginalImage As Byte(), _
ByVal intHeight As Integer, _
ByVal intWidth As Integer) As Byte()
Dim myImage, myResizedImage As System.Drawing.Image
Dim myMemoryStream As MemoryStream
Try
' Convert to an Image object
myMemoryStream = New MemoryStream(OriginalImage)
myImage = myImage.FromStream(myMemoryStream)
' If size not specified, go with default or less
If intHeight = 0 And intWidth = 0 Then
If myImage.Height > DEFAULTHEIGHT Or _
myImage.Width > DEFAULTWIDTH Then
If (DEFAULTHEIGHT - myImage.Height) > _
(DEFAULTWIDTH - myImage.Width) Then
intWidth = DEFAULTWIDTH
Else
intHeight = DEFAULTHEIGHT
End If
Else
intHeight = myImage.Height
intWidth = myImage.Width
End If
End If
' Compute sizes for aspect ratio
If intHeight = 0 Then
intHeight = myImage.Height / (myImage.Width / intWidth)
ElseIf intWidth = 0 Then
intWidth = myImage.Width / (myImage.Height / intHeight)
End If
' Resize if necessary
If intHeight = myImage.Height And intWidth = _
myImage.Width Then
myResizedImage = myImage
Else
myResizedImage = myImage.GetThumbnailImage( _
intWidth, intHeight, Nothing, Nothing)
End If
```

```vb
' Convert back to Byte Array
myMemoryStream = New MemoryStream()
myResizedImage.Save(myMemoryStream, ImageFormat.Jpeg)
ResizeImage = myMemoryStream.ToArray
Catch ex As Exception
' Any error and just return back the orignal thumbnail
ResizeImage = OriginalImage
End Try
End Function
' Given a byte array and a string, convert to image, watermark,
' and then convert back to a byte array
Public Function Watermark(ByVal OriginalImage As Byte(), _
ByVal strWatermark As String) As Byte()
Dim myLightBrush As New SolidBrush(Color.White)
Dim myDarkBrush As New SolidBrush(Color.Black)
Dim myGraphics As System.Drawing.Graphics
Dim XPos, YPos, myFontSize As Integer
Dim myImage As System.Drawing.Image
Dim myMemoryStream As MemoryStream
Dim myStringFont As Font
Dim myTextSize As SizeF
' Determine Watermark
If strWatermark = "" Then strWatermark = DEFAULTCOPYRIGHT
' Convert to an Image object
myMemoryStream = New MemoryStream(OriginalImage)
myImage = myImage.FromStream(myMemoryStream)
' Create a Graphics object
myGraphics = Graphics.FromImage(myImage)
' Start with a very large font and reduce by 1 pixel until it fits
myFontSize = 500
Do
myFontSize = myFontSize - 1
If myFontSize = 0 Then Exit Do
' Determine size of new font
myStringFont = New Font("Verdana", myFontSize, _
FontStyle.Regular, GraphicsUnit.Pixel)
myTextSize = myGraphics.MeasureString(strWatermark, _
myStringFont)
' Loop until it fits
Loop Until (myTextSize.Height < myImage.Height And _
myTextSize.Width < myImage.Width)
' Valid Font Size?
If myFontSize > 0 Then
' Center the watermark
XPos = (myImage.Width - myTextSize.Width) / 2
YPos = (myImage.Height - myTextSize.Height) / 2
' Draw the String with a shadowed effect
myGraphics.DrawString(strWatermark, myStringFont, _
myDarkBrush, XPos - 2, YPos - 2)
myGraphics.DrawString(strWatermark, myStringFont, _
```

```
                       myLightBrush, XPos, YPos)
myGraphics.DrawString(strWatermark, myStringFont, _
myDarkBrush, XPos + 2, YPos + 2)
End If
' Convert back to Byte Array
myMemoryStream = New MemoryStream()
myImage.Save(myMemoryStream, ImageFormat.Jpeg)
' Return the image
Watermark = myMemoryStream.ToArray
End Function
' Resize all Thumbnail elements from Image and then
' remove Image column
Private Sub ProcessAllThumbSizes(ByRef tblData As DataTable, _
ByVal intHeight As Integer, _
ByVal intWidth As Integer)
Dim myRow As DataRow
' DataTable empty?
If tblData.Rows.Count < 1 Then
Exit Sub
End If
' Resize Thumbnails, if necessary
If intWidth > 0 Or intHeight > 0 Then
For Each myRow In tblData.Rows
myRow.Item("ImageThumbNail") = _
ResizeThumb(myRow.Item("Image"), _
myRow.Item("ImageThumbNail"), intHeight, intWidth)
Next
' Remove the Image column if it exists (only used
' for resizing)
If tblData.Columns.Contains("Image") Then
tblData.Columns.Remove("Image")
End If
End If
' Save Thumbnail #1 to disk for testing
If UCase(System.Environment.MachineName) = "NEPTUNE" Then
Dim myMemoryStream As MemoryStream
Dim myImage As System.Drawing.Image
Dim myByteArray As Byte()
myByteArray = tblData.Rows(0).Item("ImageThumbnail")
myMemoryStream = New MemoryStream(myByteArray)
myImage = myImage.FromStream(myMemoryStream)
myImage.Save("x:\ResizedThumb.jpg")
End If
End Sub
' Resize all Image elements
Private Sub ProcessAllImageSizes(ByRef tblData As DataTable, _
ByVal intHeight As Integer, _
ByVal intWidth As Integer)
Dim myRow As DataRow
' DataTable empty?
```

```
      If tblData.Rows.Count < 1 Then
      Exit Sub
      End If
      ' Resize Images, if necessary
      For Each myRow In tblData.Rows
      myRow.Item("Image") = ResizeImage( _
      myRow.Item("Image"), intHeight, intWidth)
      Next
      ' Save Image #1 to disk for testing
      If UCase(System.Environment.MachineName) = "NEPTUNE" Then
      Dim myMemoryStream As MemoryStream
      Dim myImage As System.Drawing.Image
      Dim myByteArray As Byte()
      myByteArray = tblData.Rows(0).Item("Image")
      myMemoryStream = New MemoryStream(myByteArray)
      myImage = myImage.FromStream(myMemoryStream)
      myImage.Save("x:\ResizedImage.jpg")
      End If
      End Sub
      ' Watermark all Image elements (should only be 1, however)
      Private Sub ProcessAllWatermarks(ByRef tblData As DataTable)
      Dim myRow As DataRow
      ' Dataset empty?
      If tblData.Rows.Count < 1 Then
      Exit Sub
      End If
      ' Watermark each image
      For Each myRow In tblData.Rows
      myRow.Item("Image") = Watermark( _
      myRow.Item("Image"), myRow.Item("Copyright"))
      Next
      ' Save Image #1 to disk for testing
      If UCase(System.Environment.MachineName) = "NEPTUNE" Then
      Dim myMemoryStream As MemoryStream
      Dim myImage As System.Drawing.Image
      Dim myByteArray As Byte()
      myByteArray = tblData.Rows(0).Item("Image")
      myMemoryStream = New MemoryStream(myByteArray)
      myImage = myImage.FromStream(myMemoryStream)
      myImage.Save("x:\Watermark.jpg")
      End If
      End Sub
      ' Utility Function to turn a simple error message into
      ' a DataSet object
      Private Function ExceptionDataset(ByVal ex As Exception, _
      Optional ByVal strMsg As String = "") As DataSet
      Dim dsError As New DataSet("Custom")
      Dim rowError As DataRow
      ' Populate DataSet with a single table, two columns
      dsError.Tables.Add("Error")
```

```
dsError.Tables("Error").Columns.Add("Message", _
System.Type.GetType("System.String"))
dsError.Tables("Error").Columns.Add("Source", _
System.Type.GetType("System.String"))
dsError.Tables("Error").Columns.Add("Additional", _
System.Type.GetType("System.String"))
' Add error information
rowError = dsError.Tables("Error").NewRow()
rowError("Message") = ex.Message
rowError("Source") = ex.Source
rowError("Additional") = strMsg
dsError.Tables("Error").Rows.Add(rowError)
' Done
ExceptionDataset = dsError
End Function
```

Now we get into some of the more interesting stuff. The first thing we'll do is look at the constructor for the class. You may not need the constructor on your machine, but because the authors run multiple computers (which you might do as well), we needed it badly.

```
' Class Initialization
Public Sub New()
' Determine which connection string to use
If UCase(System.Environment.MachineName) = "TITANIC" Then
CONNECTSTR = CONNECT_STRING_LOCAL
Else
' CONNECTSTR = (our shared SQL Server - No, we're not
' going to publicly declare its location)
End If
End Sub
```

Now, we're finally ready for some of the important code. We'll implement only the methods used in the ReturnThumbs Web service.

```
' Start implementing the Web Methods
Public Function ReturnThumbsByID(ByVal ImageID As String, _
ByVal strThumbHeight As String, _
ByVal strThumbWidth As String) As DataSet
Dim conImage As New SqlConnection(CONNECTSTR)
Dim adpImage As New SqlDataAdapter()
Dim intThumbHeight As Integer
Dim intThumbWidth As Integer
Dim dsThumbs As DataSet
Dim ImageGUID As Guid
' Exception Handling
Try
ImageGUID = New Guid(ImageID)
intThumbHeight = ParmToInt(strThumbHeight)
intThumbWidth = ParmToInt(strThumbWidth)
```

```vb
' Open Connection
conImage.Open()
' Initialize the Data Adapter - return image if resizing
If intThumbHeight = 0 And intThumbWidth = 0 Then
adpImage.SelectCommand = New SqlCommand( _
"EXECUTE ws_ReturnThumbs @ImageID='" + _
ImageGUID.ToString + "',@ReturnImage=0", _
conImage)
Else
adpImage.SelectCommand = New SqlCommand( _
"EXECUTE ws_ReturnThumbs @ImageID='" + _
ImageGUID.ToString + "',@ReturnImage=1", _
conImage)
End If
' Fill the DataSet
dsThumbs = New DataSet("Thumbs")
adpImage.Fill(dsThumbs, "Thumbs")
ProcessAllThumbSizes(dsThumbs.Tables("Thumbs"), _
intThumbHeight, intThumbWidth)
' Accept the changes (To not return a complicated diffgram)
dsThumbs.AcceptChanges()
Catch ex As Exception
conImage = Nothing
ReturnThumbsByID = ExceptionDataset(ex)
Exit Function
Finally
If Not conImage Is Nothing Then conImage.Close()
conImage = Nothing
End Try
' Return
ReturnThumbsByID = dsThumbs
End Function
Public Function ReturnThumbsByNumber(ByVal ImageNumber As String, _
ByVal strThumbHeight As String, _
ByVal strThumbWidth As String) As DataSet
Dim conImage As New SqlConnection(CONNECTSTR)
Dim adpImage As New SqlDataAdapter()
Dim ImageNumberInt As Integer
Dim intThumbHeight As Integer
Dim intThumbWidth As Integer
Dim dsThumbs As DataSet
' Exception Handling
Try
ImageNumberInt = CLng(ImageNumber)
intThumbHeight = ParmToInt(strThumbHeight)
intThumbWidth = ParmToInt(strThumbWidth)
' Open Connection
conImage.Open()
' Initialize the Data Adapter - return image if resizing
If intThumbHeight = 0 And intThumbWidth = 0 Then
adpImage.SelectCommand = New SqlCommand( _
"EXECUTE ws_ReturnThumbs @ImageNumber='" + _
```

```
ImageNumberInt.ToString + "', _
@ReturnImage=0", conImage)
Else
adpImage.SelectCommand = New SqlCommand( _
"EXECUTE ws_ReturnThumbs @ImageNumber='" + _
ImageNumberInt.ToString + "',@ReturnImage=1", _
conImage)
End If
' Fill the DataSet
dsThumbs = New DataSet("Thumbs")
adpImage.Fill(dsThumbs, "Thumbs")
ProcessAllThumbSizes(dsThumbs.Tables("Thumbs"), _
intThumbHeight, intThumbWidth)
' Accept the changes (To not return a complicated diffgram)
dsThumbs.AcceptChanges()
Catch ex As Exception
conImage = Nothing
ReturnThumbsByNumber = ExceptionDataset(ex)
Exit Function
Finally
If Not conImage Is Nothing Then conImage.Close()
conImage = Nothing
End Try
' Return
ReturnThumbsByNumber = dsThumbs
End Function
Public Function ReturnThumbsByTitle(ByVal ImageTitle As String, _
ByVal strThumbHeight As String, _
ByVal strThumbWidth As String) As DataSet
Dim conImage As New SqlConnection(CONNECTSTR)
Dim adpImage As New SqlDataAdapter()
Dim intThumbHeight As Integer
Dim intThumbWidth As Integer
Dim dsThumbs As DataSet
' Exception Handling
Try
intThumbHeight = ParmToInt(strThumbHeight)
intThumbWidth = ParmToInt(strThumbWidth)
' Open Connection
conImage.Open()
' Initialize the Data Adapter - return image if resizing
If intThumbHeight = 0 And intThumbWidth = 0 Then
adpImage.SelectCommand = New SqlCommand( _
"EXECUTE ws_ReturnThumbs @Title='" + ImageTitle + _
"',@ReturnImage=0", conImage)
Else
adpImage.SelectCommand = New SqlCommand( _
"EXECUTE ws_ReturnThumbs @Title='" + ImageTitle + _
"',@ReturnImage=1", conImage)
End If
' Fill the DataSet
dsThumbs = New DataSet("Thumbs")
```

```vb
    adpImage.Fill(dsThumbs, "Thumbs")
    ProcessAllThumbSizes(dsThumbs.Tables("Thumbs"), _
    intThumbHeight, intThumbWidth)
    ' Accept the changes (To not return a complicated diffgram)
    dsThumbs.AcceptChanges()
Catch ex As Exception
    conImage = Nothing
    ReturnThumbsByTitle = ExceptionDataset(ex)
    Exit Function
Finally
    If Not conImage Is Nothing Then conImage.Close()
    conImage = Nothing
End Try
    ' Return
    ReturnThumbsByTitle = dsThumbs
End Function
Public Function ReturnThumbs(ByVal Category As String, _
ByVal SubCategory As String, _
ByVal LicenseCode As String, _
ByVal Keywords As String, _
ByVal strThumbHeight As String, _
ByVal strThumbWidth As String) As DataSet
Dim conImage As New SqlConnection(CONNECTSTR)
Dim adpImage As New SqlDataAdapter()
Dim strArgs As String
Dim intThumbHeight As Integer
Dim intThumbWidth As Integer
Dim dsThumbs As DataSet
' Exception Handling
Try
intThumbHeight = ParmToInt(strThumbHeight)
intThumbWidth = ParmToInt(strThumbWidth)
' Open Connection
conImage.Open()
' Build Argument List
If Category <> "" Then
strArgs = strArgs + IIf(strArgs = "", "", ",") + _
"@Category='" + Category + "'"
End If
If SubCategory <> "" Then
strArgs = strArgs + IIf(strArgs = "", "", ",") + _
"@SubCategory='" + SubCategory + "'"
End If
If LicenseCode <> "" Then
strArgs = strArgs + IIf(strArgs = "", "", ",") + _
"@LicenseCode='" + LicenseCode + "'"
End If
If Keywords <> "" Then
strArgs = strArgs + IIf(strArgs = "", "", ",") + _
"@Keywords='" + Keywords + "'"
End If
' Initialize the Data Adapter - return image if resizing
```

```
If intThumbHeight = 0 And intThumbWidth = 0 Then
adpImage.SelectCommand = New SqlCommand( _
"EXECUTE ws_ReturnThumbs " + strArgs + _
",@ReturnImage=0", conImage)
Else
adpImage.SelectCommand = New SqlCommand( _
"EXECUTE ws_ReturnThumbs " + strArgs + _
",@ReturnImage=1", conImage)
End If
' Fill the DataSet
dsThumbs = New DataSet("Thumbs")
adpImage.Fill(dsThumbs, "Thumbs")
ProcessAllThumbSizes(dsThumbs.Tables("Thumbs"), _
intThumbHeight, intThumbWidth)
' Accept the changes (To not return a complicated diffgram)
dsThumbs.AcceptChanges()
Catch ex As Exception
conImage = Nothing
ReturnThumbs = ExceptionDataset(ex)
Exit Function
Finally
If Not conImage Is Nothing Then conImage.Close()
conImage = Nothing
End Try
' Return
ReturnThumbs = dsThumbs
End Function
End Class
```

That wraps up all of the functions that we'll need in the next chapter. Now, we need to compile the code and create a DLL that we can use for the XML Web services. To compile the DLL, right-click the project and select Build, then select Build Solution from the Build menu (or press Ctrl-Shift-B) to build the solution.

Summary

You've now nearly built the data access component. The remaining functionality can be downloaded from the support Web site.

In this chapter you've learned how to use the drag-and-drop functionality and how to build data access code from scratch. Now all you need to do is build the XML Web services for the Hutchings Photography business. That's coming up in Chapter 6.

CHAPTER

6

Creating Web Services

The public part of the Hutchings Photography's case study is its Web services. The entire business model of allowing third parties to resell images depends on convenient access to those photos.

In Chapter 5, we built a relatively sophisticated class and associated DLL to create DataSet objects through several different methods. In this chapter, we use that component to provide data to our various Web services. Although this component was well designed, Hutchings Photography is a fairly large shop, and the designer of the component wasn't able to predict exactly what the needs of the Web service designers would be.

The WebData class was written entirely in Visual Basic .NET. We will be constructing the suite of Web services in C#, a very different language. This will demonstrate an important feature of .NET's cross-language compatibility.

In this chapter, we create a new project, build the Web services, show how we can improve the look of the .asmx page, and test the project.

Creating the ASP.NET Web Service Project

Our first step is to create a new project specifically geared toward XML Web services. So, fire up Visual Studio .NET. We're going to create a new project. Select File, New, Project. In the New Project form, select Visual C# Projects from the list on the left side and ASP.NET Web service from the project type selections on the right side. Create the project in http://localhost/HutchingsImages_CS. See Figure 6.1.

Once the project has been created, we want to ensure that we can use the WebData component we created in Chapter 5. There are a couple of ways to do that. We could simply add a reference to the DLL file we created, or we could add the entire project from Chapter 5 to our solution. If we do this, we still need to add a reference, but now we add the reference to the project. This is a good approach, but not technically necessary. It does, however, allow us to step through the WebData code while debugging our XML Web services. To add the project to our current solution, select File, Add Project, Existing Project, and select the project from Chapter 5.

Once the project is added, you must add a reference to either the DLL or the project as a whole. We'll add a reference to the entire project so that we can step through the WebData code if we decide we need to do so. To add a reference to the project, either right-click the HutchingsImages_CS project and select Add Reference, or right-click the References folder of the project and select Add Reference. You can now select the Projects tab to add

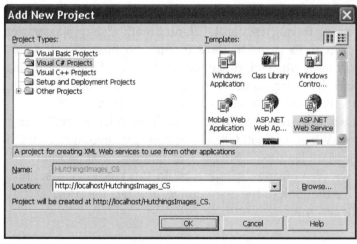

Figure 6.1   Create the Web service project in C#.

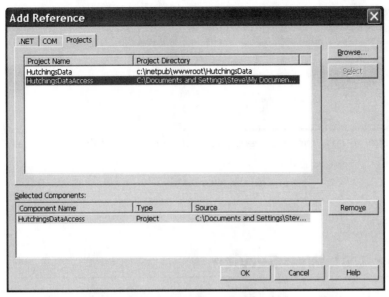

Figure 6.2   Add a reference to the HutchingsDataAccess project.

a reference to a project that is currently in the Solutions folder. Figure 6.2 shows how the screen should look just prior to pressing the OK button.

> **NOTE** One of the coolest things about .NET is the ability to debug through several languages. This shows just how deeply cross-language compatibility is embedded into the .NET Framework. In fact, the .NET Framework includes the support for cross-language compatibility at the Common Language Runtime level, the lowest level of the Framework.

Now select Service1.asmx from the Solution Explorer pane, and rename it as HutchingsImages.asmx. This renames only the filename that will contain the class that will provide the XML Web service. We want to rename the XML Web service itself, however. To do so, open the HutchingsImages.asmx file by right-clicking it and selecting View Code. This opens up the code page. You'll notice that the primary class is still named Service1. To fix this, select Edit, Find and Replace, Replace. Replace all the occurrences of Service1 with HutchingsImages. (See Figure 6.3.) The reason to use the search-and-replace tool is that occurrences of Service1 are embedded within the code that was automatically generated by Visual Studio .NET.

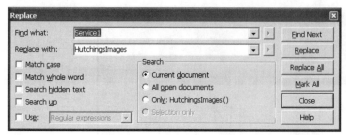

Figure 6.3 Be sure to do a complete search-and-replace through all the automatically generated code.

Coding the XML Web Service

Now, let's get into the actual code. First thing we're going to need is a variable to contain the WebData control. There are many different ways to approach this problem. One common way is to create the data access control in each of the Web method calls that Hutchings Photography supports. This is often a good approach because it reduces the amount of memory consumed by the Web service over a period of time because the WebData component is taking up memory only when a Web method using the control is being executed. In our case, though, the WebData component is used for every Web method Hutchings Photography is exposing. In addition, we hope that there will be quite a few people accessing the Web service. If that's the case, the WebData component will be constantly created and destroyed, which can cause a performance hit on the machine.

There's another method we could use: using the Cache object provided by HttpContext that the XML Web services are using. This gives us the benefits of both worlds. The component would not be continually created and destroyed, and if the component wasn't being used, it would be released from memory.

NOTE The Cache object is an excellent method for performance optimizations. It's more commonly used in ASP.NET applications, where it can increase the performance of a data-driven Web site by more than 300 percent. It is just as effective, though, for use in XML Web services.

We won't be using the Cache object at this point of development. We'll develop and test the application first, then we'll optimize our Web services using the Cache object and other optimization techniques. There are a few reasons for this. The main difficulty with using caching at the outset is that debugging can be made greatly complicated by having your Web service in cache. You might make some changes to the underlying database and expect changes in the resulting output. But you won't because the return values may have been cached, and so you get the previous results rather than the ones you were expecting.

WARNING Using the Cache object during development can make debugging your application difficult. If your XML Web service is cached, you may not see the changes reflected in the changes you may have made. That can be the source of some hard-to-find bugs.

To use the WebData component in the project, create the component as a private-class variable in our newly named HutchingsImages class. To do so, add the following line of code as a class variable. Thereafter, your project should look like the project view in Figure 6.4.

```
private HutchingsDataAccess.WebData webData = new
HutchingsDataAccess.WebData();
```

Now that we have access to the WebData component, we can begin to code the actual Web methods. On our first iteration, we'll see just how easy it is to create the code necessary to build an XML Web service with Visual

```
namespace HutchingsImages_CS
{
    /// <summary>
    /// Summary description for Service1.
    /// </summary>
    public class HutchingsImages : System.Web.Services.WebService
    {
        private HutchingsDataAccess.WebData webData = new HutchingsDataAccess.WebData();

        public HutchingsImages()
        {
            //CODEGEN: This call is required by the ASP.NET Web Services Designer
            InitializeComponent();
        }

        Component Designer generated code
```

Figure 6.4 We create the WebData control as a private-class variable because we'll be using it often.

Studio .NET. To create the ReturnThumbs() method as a Web method, simply create a normal method and prefix it with the [WebMethod] attribute (<WebMethod> in Visual Basic .NET). The code looks like this:

```
[WebMethod]
public DataSet ReturnThumbs(string Category,
    string SubCategory, string LicenseCode,
    string Keywords, string ThumbHeight,
    string ThumbWidth)
{
    return webData.ReturnThumbs(Category, SubCategory,
        LicenseCode, Keywords, ThumbHeight, ThumbWidth);
}
```

The longest part of that code is just dealing with the parameters that are being passed. It helps that we've spent time creating a good WebData control, but it shows how easy it is to create a Web method that can be used in an XML Web service.

First Test of Our Web Service

To test our code, right-click the HutchingsImages.asmx file and select Build and Browse. That tells Visual Studio .NET to build the XML Web service itself, generate all the associated .disco and .wsdl files, and create a test page. It then brings up the test page in the internal browser. The test page should look like something close to Figure 6.5.

Now, click the ReturnThumbs() method. This brings us to another page, where we can enter parameters to use to test the page. Enter *People* in the category page, and press Enter. You should be returned an XML document that contains several different images along with a fairly complex-looking XML document. Of course, you won't be able to see the images because they'll be encoded as text (using Base64 encoding). Your returned XML document should look similar to Figure 6.6.

We've tested our XML Web service successfully. (If your result doesn't look like Figure 6.6 but instead returns a DataSet that contains an error, look again at the WebData component and your database connection.)

Let's go back to Figure 6.5 and take a look at our test page, HutchingsImages.asmx. Everything is working fine and we're able to return a collection of thumbnails from Hutchings Photography. The page, though, doesn't say much about the XML Web service itself or the Web methods that it supports. In addition, there is a warning about the namespace that we are using. To ensure that our XML Web services are distinguishable from those of other companies, we should give it a unique namespace.

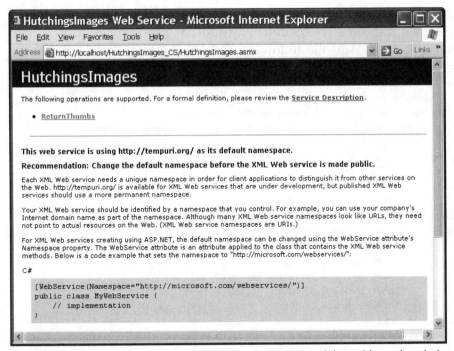

Figure 6.5   The ReturnThumbs XML Web service is exposed, but with no description and with the default namespace.

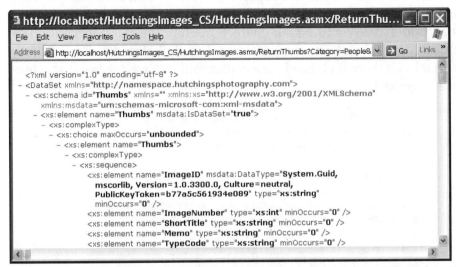

Figure 6.6   The returned XML document shows a successful call to our XML Web service.

Let's start with adding a description to the overall XML Web service. To do that, we'll use the [WebService] attribute tag to mark up our HutchingsImages class. Add the following code to the line directly above the class declaration:

```
[WebService(
    Name="Hutchings Photography Web Service",
    Namespace="http://namespace.hutchingsphotography.com",
    Description="Here are the various Web Methods that " +
"support the Hutchings Photography stock image " + "database.<br>" +
        "You should call the methods in the " +
"following order: <br><br> " +
        "  1. ReturnThumbByID(), " +
"ReturnThumbByNumber(), ReturnThumbByTitle() " +
"or ReturnThumbs()<br>" +
        "  2. ReturnImage()<br>" +
        "  3. ReturnContract()<br>" +
        "  4. NegotiateContract()<br>" +
        "  5. NegotiateContractStatus()<br>" +
        "  6. AcceptContract()<br><hr>"
)]
public class HutchingsImages : System.Web.Services.WebService
```

If you're developing code in Visual Basic .NET, your identical code will look like the following code, which is included here for comparison. (There is much more Visual Basic .NET code available for download from the support Web site.) The differences to notice that are especially important between the two languages is that the WebService attribute is wrapped in < and > brackets instead of [and] brackets. In addition, each of the named parameters and its values are separated with := instead of simply an = operator. Finally, the entire <WebService> attribute in Visual Basic .NET has an underscore continuation character before the class declaration. In both languages the attribute must come directly before the class declaration, but in C# there is no need for a continuation character, because whitespace is ignored.

```
<WebService(Name:="Hutchings Photography Web Service", _
    Description:="Here are the various Web Methods that " & _
    "support the Hutchings Photography stock image " & _
    "database.<br>" & _
    "You should call the methods in the following " & _
    "order: <br><br> " & _
    "  1. ReturnThumbByID(), ReturnThumbByNumber(), " & _
    "ReturnThumbByTitle() or ReturnThumbs()<br>" & _
    "  2. ReturnImage()<br>" & _
    "  3. ReturnContract()<br>" & _
    "  4. NegotiateContract()<br>" & _
    "  5. NegotiateContractStatus()<br>" & _
```

```
    "  6. AcceptContract()<br><hr>", _
    Namespace:="http://namespace.hutchingsphotography.com")> _
Public Class Image
    Inherits System.Web.Services.WebService
```

The WebService attribute has only three public properties to expose. We've used all three in the preceding code. Here are definitions of all three public properties:

Description.   This is a description of the XML Web service. In our code, we've explained to the user the proper methods to call our XML Web service.

Name.   This gets or sets the name of the XML Web service. We've named ours Hutchings Photography Web Service.

Namespace.   This gets or sets the name of the namespace to be used for the XML Web service. We've chosen http://namespace .hutchingsphotography.com as the namespace for our Web service.

NOTE The namespaces for an XML Web service are not the same as the namespaces used in the .NET Framework.

Now that we've spruced up the XML Web service, we'll do the same for the Web method that we've created. We will again use an attribute to provide information to Visual Studio .NET to use when creating our test Web page. Because we've already created the attribute, all we'll do in this case is add to the proper parameters to the attribute declaration. The code that follows demonstrates how to do this in C#.

```
[WebMethod
    (Description="Request Image Thumbnail(s) by combination " +
      "of one or more criteria<br><br>" +
      "  Category - (String) for the Category; " +
      "refer to Reference Tables (example: People)<br>" +
      "  SubCategory - (String) for the " +
      "SubCategory; refer to " +
      "Reference Tables (not used in Hutchings " +
      "Photography)<br>" +
      "  LicenseCode - (String) for the " +
      "type of license; refer to Reference Tables " +
      (example: Flat)<br>" +
      "  Keywords - (String) of " +
      "comma-separated values (example: Boy, School, " +
      "Friends)<br>" +
      "  ThumbHeight - (optional Int32) " +
      "Integer for the height of the thumbnail<br>" +
      "  ThumbWidth - (optional Int32) " +
```

```
            "Integer for the width of the thumbnail<br><br>" +
            "  (for best results specify height or " +
            "width or neither, but not both)")
    ]
public DataSet ReturnThumbs(string Category,
    string SubCategory, string LicenseCode,
    string Keywords, string ThumbHeight,
    string ThumbWidth)
{
    //code here
}
```

Several properties are available to the programmer of the Web method. Many of them have to do with whether state will be preserved between calls or whether the Web service will be cached. Here's the complete list:

BufferResponse.   This parameter gets or sets whether the response for this request is buffered before being returned to the client.

CacheDuration.   This parameter gets or sets the amount of time that the response should be cached. The time is in seconds.

Description.   This is a string describing the XML Web service method.

EnableSession.   This parameter indicates whether session state is enabled for this Web method.

MessageName.   This parameter gets or sets the name used by the Web method.

TransactionOption.   This parameter indicates whether transactional support of the Web method is enabled.

As you can see, these parameters are significantly more expressive than those of the WebService attribute. This makes sense, given that the Web methods are the actual methods that are called.

Now that we've built a description of the Web method and added a namespace, name, and description to the XML Web service, we can look at the HutchingsImages.asmx file again. See Figure 6.7.

We have now exposed the ReturnThumbs() Web method to the world. We can congratulate ourselves on a job well done. There's still much more to do, though, and that is to create all the additional Web methods. To view them, see the book's downloadable code.

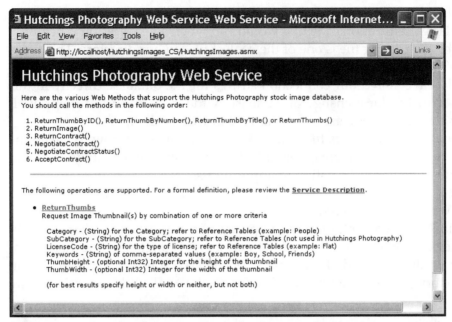

Figure 6.7 ReturnThumbs XML Web service is exposed with proper namespace and descriptions.

Understanding the Files Created by Visual Studio .NET

Before closing this chapter, let's take a quick look at the various files created in our ASP.NET Web service and their purposes.

The most important of these files is the HutchingsImages.asmx page. This is the page that actually serves up the XML Web service. There is also a HutchingsImages.asmx.cs file. This code-behind file contains the code that we've written that will be compiled into the DLL that will support our site.

There is the family of global.asax files. These files (global.asax, global.asax.cs, and global.asax.resx) contain code that is to be run when an application itself fires events. (We could have added initialization code that could have been run when the application was first run.) We could also put in place initialization code that would run when a new session is begun.

The Web.config file is one of the coolest files in our directory. This file is an XML document that contains all of the settings for our application. We could have stored our connection strings for the database directly in this file, allowing for a change of database without the need to recompile. It also contains several security settings that we can change.

The AssemblyInfo.cs file contains information about how to create the assembly. You can safely ignore this file for the most part until you start to create some fairly sophisticated applications.

HutchingsImages_CS.disco is a discovery file, which points visitors to the WSDL for this Web site.

Finally, the contents of the all-important \bin directory is where the rubber meets the road. This is the MS Intermediate Language code that encapsulates all of the code functionality of the Web site. The DLLs in the bin directory provide the functionality for all the XML Web services that are called.

Summary

In this chapter, we created our first XML Web service and a single Web method, ReturnThumbs(), that can be used to return a DataSet containing a group of thumbnails based on query criteria. You've learned about the different parameters of the WebService and WebMethod attributes, and you've seen how some of them can be applied to assist in the consumption of our XML Web service.

What's left is to advertise the site and maybe help some partners build a Web site that can consume the Hutchings Photography XML Web services. The upcoming chapters address these issues.

Deploying Web Services (UDDI)

The Universal Description Discovery and Integration, known as UDDI, is an ongoing initiative to create an independent, yet interoperable, framework of standalone Web service repositories hosted by independent companies around the world. The UDDI provides a convenient manner in which to discover, describe, and execute Web services based on business needs.

As of this writing, only 4 of the 300 companies involved in the version 2 UDDI effort host central UDDI SOAP-based Web service registries: Microsoft, IBM, Hewlett-Packard, and SAP.

Rather than memorizing the locations of the UDDI on each independent provider's Web site, you can use the following Web site as a central UDDI directory to locate the individual UDDI directories on each of the four sites: www.uddi.org/register.html (see Figure 7.1).

Although you cannot navigate to this site and simultaneously add your business to all four of the UDDI host provider registries, the site provides a great starting spot in which to locate a particular UDDI for which you might want to add your company's Web services. The site's drop-down list boxes display different providers and support the hosting of the UDDI specifications for versions 1 and 2.

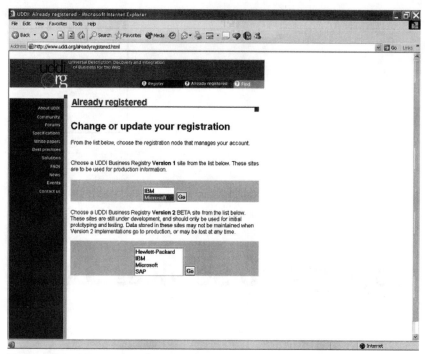

Figure 7.1   UDDI Registry home page.

The site also lets you change UDDI host providers. If you are not satisfied with the service of one provider, you can switch to another provider using tools available on the site. The UDDI is structured so that if one provider perishes, another could theoretically assume its responsibilities.

You might compare the UDDI structure to the structure of a book. The UDDI Web site is similar to the table of contents of each independent UDDI Web site, known as a UDDI host provider.

Additionally, the table of contents of a book provides a directory to the individual chapters in the book. You can't expect to read the table of contents and really know anything about the book other than the title of the chapters and to what chapters the table of contents points. The same can be said about the UDDI.org Web site.

Although it is possible to navigate to each company's Web site manually and access the UDDI, it might be extremely difficult to find . . . and more painstaking than necessary. To simplify your discovery of Web services, access the location either through a built-in tool in the IDE of an application such as .NET or through the navigational assistance of the UDDI.org Web site.

In addition to being able to access UDDI registries from this Web site, you can also register your business as a UDDI participant. Being a participant means that you still host your own Web services; however, you do not have to host your own UDDI registry.

Only Microsoft and IBM support version 1 of the UDDI, while Microsoft, IBM, Hewlett-Packard, and SAP all support the version 2–compatible UDDI. For more information on the specifications for the UDDI, version 2, visit the Web site www.uddi.org and look in the Technical Highlights section.

A nifty thing about the UDDI.org Web site is that you can switch between hosts as you please, which means that you can really use any version of the UDDI that you want. (Note: Version 2 of the UDDI specification is only in beta testing at this writing.)

Because hosts that are listed as providers in the UDDI share the same development specification, they should theoretically be able to rely on the SOAP framework of the Web services in each other's registries to communicate in an efficient and well-known manner. In other words, you should be able to call any of the UDDI-registered Web services from any of the independent UDDI host provider Web sites from your Web service consumer applications, communicating with all of them in exactly the same manner regardless of the language in which they were written and compiled.

We will pursue this issue later in the chapter by creating a data consumer and attempting to communicate with UDDI SOAP-based Web services from each of the different UDDI host registrants using the same source code syntax.

Registering as a UDDI Participant and Registering Its Web Services

Let's register as a UDDI business participant. Start by navigating to the Web site at www.uddi.org/register.html. This Web site, shown in Figure 7.1, is one of two ways to register our business in a UDDI registry. Another way would be to access the online UDDI registry form from a host UDDI Web site. Following are the four different UDDI hosts and their corresponding UDDI Web sites, which allow you to register directly with the one you choose.

As mentioned, it might be easier to let the IDE discover the Web services for you. If you are requesting information from multiple UDDI partners on multiple UDDI host registries, you can start with the following:

Microsoft.   https://uddi.rte.microsoft.com/register.aspx

IBM.   https://www-3.ibm.com/services/uddi/testregistry/protect/find

Hewlett-Packard.   https://uddi.hp.com/uddi/index.jsp

SAP.   https://www003.sap-ag.de/~form/uddi_discover

For purposes of this chapter, we used the UDDI.org Web site to register. Next, we chose the version of the UDDI specification we wanted to use. Because of the timing of our writing, we chose version 1. We would use the latest version of whatever UDDI specification is released as a recommendation at the time of registering.

Next, choose a UDDI host provider. We had to choose between Microsoft and IBM because they are the only two companies that support the version 1 specification of the UDDI. We chose Microsoft.

We were taken to the registration page at http://uddi.microsoft.com/register.aspx. On this page we were given an option to either specify an email address or use my Microsoft Passport Profile. Besides a name and a primary phone number, nothing else is required. In fact, if you use the Passport .NET option, filling in the required information is done for you. After clicking the Save button, we were taken to http://uddi.microsoft.com/registrationcomplete.aspx. (See Figure 7.2.)

An interesting thing about registering through the UDDI is that we began with a page on the UDDI.org domain and ended on a page in the Microsoft domain. This happened when we chose to use Microsoft UDDI Business Registry to register our information. As soon as we clicked Go on the initial UDDI.org page, we were redirected to Microsoft UDDI registration Web site. The same should happen for the other UDDI providers. If you choose a different UDDI provider, the browser should navigate to its corresponding UDDI registration Web page. To finish, click Continue. You should end up on the Administer page (shown in Figure 7.3). You are done registering yourself as a UDDI participant.

Now you need to fill out the information that allows you to universally describe your Web services through creation and registration, and to discover and integrate existing Web services from the UDDI registry in your own applications.

To expose your Web service through the UDDI, click the Add a New Business hyperlink on the Administer Page, as shown in Figure 7.3. That takes you to the page shown in Figure 7.4. You will find the following properties on this page:

Business Detail.   Such information as the name and description of your business.

Contacts.   Detail information of business contact and reason for contacting.

Service Detail.   The name of the UDDI Web service and its HTTP location.

Add Identifier.   Such as Dun and Bradstreet, Thomson ID, or Real-Names Keyword. These are Name/Value pairs, where the Value is a number. The purpose is to verify you as a business through either a unique identifier or branding.

Business Classification.   Creates an identifier based on your choices.

Discovery URLs.   Allows you to provide a location for a discovery file that describes the Web service.

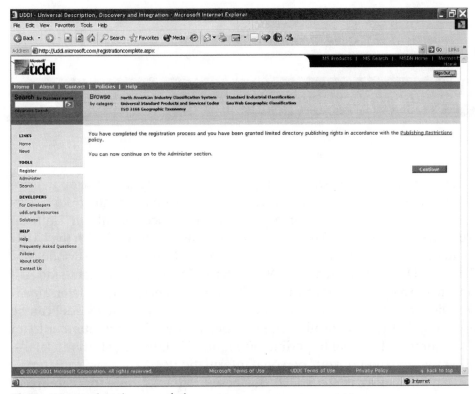

Figure 7.2   Registration completion page.

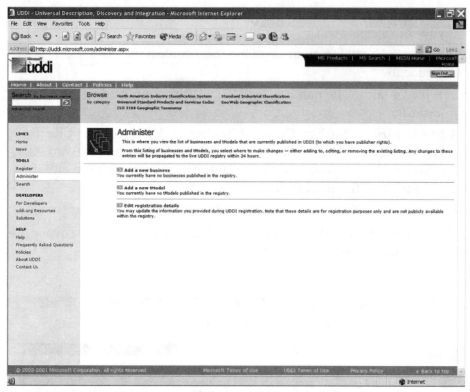

Figure 7.3   The Administer page.

If you go back to the Administer page (shown in Figure 7.3), you will see a link to add a new tModel. A tModel is a specification for categories or services. Essentially, it is a namespace that is structured like a Uniform Resource Name (URN). The tModel (business) is associated with the UUID (a unique hexadecimal-based business identifier), known as the tModelKey. This UUID, also known as the Web Service Key, is what a client-side API uses to derive detailed information about the business and to determine if the client and Web service can properly communicate. The tModel can be anything that is numerically unique, from a Social Security number to an SKU number. The final hyperlink on Figure 7.3, Edit Registration Details, allows you to modify your personal information.

By participating in the UDDI Business Program, you add visibility to your company. You might also increase your network contacts by finding companies with similar interests or complementing ideas that can increase the usefulness of your existing Web services.

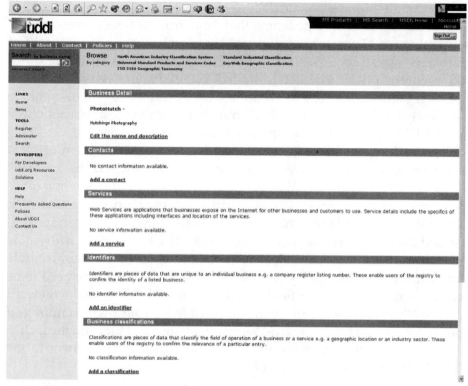

Figure 7.4   Browsing the required UDDI participant information.

Be certain to allot time to become an active participant of the host UDDI registries. The process can sometimes take days to add you as a member.

For more information on registering yourself or your company in Microsoft's UDDI Business Registry, go to http://uddi.microsoft.com/register.aspx and http://msdn.microsoft.com/library/default.asp?url=/library/en-us/dn_voices_webservice/html/service10172001.asp.

Adding Your Business to the UDDI

One major concern of the UDDI is garbage data, which is the publishing of a phony or trivial Web service to a valid UDDI directory. Garbage data provides no value to a developer who is interested in referencing a valid Web service. A bogus company, though, could create misleading or even fraudulent Web service.

For example, suppose you are a mid-sized stockbroker firm basing your clients' transactions on algorithms that your firm has been meticulously developing for 20 years. Next, suppose that you base the puts and calls of customers' stocks on a Web service that at one time was returning quick and accurate prices for stocks traded on exchanges such as NYSE, NASDAQ, and AMEX. The application works great for several months, so you slowly begin to transition all of your client data to the application that calls a UDDI Web service tracking real-time prices of stocks.

The next thing you know, your business is getting phone calls from upset customers who claim to have lost all their money. How did this happen? Maybe the providers of the Web service decided to introduce slightly modified prices of a few select stocks to drive up their prices fraudulently. Maybe they wanted to test their new random-number generator application and decided to replace their earlier stock price Web service with a new Web service. Your business may pay the consequences of the inappropriate efforts of the new third-party Web service. The point is that we need to be careful what we write and where we write it on the UDDI host. If you want to write Web services to test, then test them from your own computer. If you are testing production-grade Web services, then test them on the UDDI. When you feel they are ready for production, then migrate them to the UDDI Web service production registry.

For reasons like these, further qualification of business information is necessary before you are granted access to add information to your Web service to the UDDI provider's registry. Items such as DUNS or RealNames criteria are required when publishing a Web service to a UDDI account. Also, UDDI accounts are limited to the number of Web services they can publish based on their Tier Type (UDDI business classification).

A number of UDDI standards documents encompass the UDDI version 2.0. The specifications include the Programmers API Specification at http://uddi.org/pubs/ProgrammersAPI-V2.00-Open-20010608.pdf, the Data Structure Specification at http://uddi.org/pubs/DataStructure-V2.00-Open-20010608.pdf, the Replication Specification at Version 2.0 Replication Specification (229 KB), and the Operator's Specification at http://uddi.org/pubs/Operators-V2.00-Open-20010608.pdf.

The UDDI initiative is well marketed in the new Microsoft .NET IDE. When developers attempt to create a Web reference for applications or applet ASPX pages, they are taken to a page within a browser that allows them to either enter the URL location of the ASMX Web service that is sought or to click a UDDI link that takes them to the Microsoft UDDI Web site, where the developers can explore the availability of Web services listed on the UDDI Web site. This greatly increases the visibility of

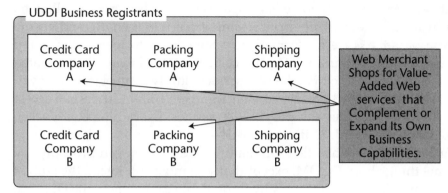

Figure 7.5   UDDI business registrants.

Microsoft UDDI participants, eliminating the burden of creating a Web service that might already be available by a UDDI participant. The companies adding Web services provide their own descriptive information when they register. Consider Figure 7.5.

Figure 7.5 illustrates the services of six companies selling three classifications of Web services. Two of the companies provide online credit card authorization services, two of the companies pack merchandise, and two of the companies ship goods.

The Web merchant might be interested in Credit Card Company A because of its popular brand name and reputation. The Web merchant might also choose Packing Company B because it offers a better price for its services. And Shipping Company A might have been chosen over Shipping Company B even though Shipping Company A might be more expensive, because of its unmatched reliability. The UDDI offers a location to find vendors that compete against your business as well as a location to find business services that complement your existing business services.

The Advantages of Web Services

In .NET, adding a Web Reference is easier than referencing a DLL in earlier versions of Visual Basic. With Web services, there is no need to register DLLs, so you can do away with the following code:

```
REGSVR32 "C:\RegisterMyDLL.dll"
REGSVR32 -u "C:\RegisterMyDLL.dll"
```

Web services are qualified by namespace and the URL used to call them. If you want to access a Web service, simply point to the URL and ensure that you pass the correct information in the correct format. Better yet, if you're using Visual Studio .NET, the correct format is already generated for you, allowing you to treat the Web service simply as an object. So, if you can use port 80, or 8080 if you are behind a firewall, and if users can access the IP address, then they can use the Web service. Everything else is taken care of using the UDDI, XML, and SOAP.

Marshalling is also handled internally by SOAP. You can probably say the same thing about DCOM, except that you must still install the stub of the DLL on a client machine, usually through the exporting of the DLL into a self-installing executable (an .exe for MTS and an .msi for COM+).

Most of the time, the self-installing executables are packaged in setup applications, so the user is oblivious until modifications are made to the COM+ DLL, which breaks the compatibility of the old interface. Thus, a new DLL must be generated containing a new CLSID, forcing the client application to create a reference to the new DLL.

Unlike DCOM, where the object's host and security properties were configured through Dcomcnfg.exe, as well as needing to be registered when an interface is broken and have a port opened on the machine and firewall when communicating across an Internet, a simple XML string can be passed to a Web service, thereby never breaking binary compatibility.

Theoretically, the structure of the XML can change as many times as needed to adapt to the data you need to send and receive. Modifications to the server-side Web service component can be made without changing the interface. Furthermore, with the support of XML for Microsoft SQL Server 2000, it is possible to add bidirectional capabilities for your XML processing. Whether your Web service is reading or writing to the SQL Server database, the string is the only datatype you really need to concern yourself with.

Having said that, there is a danger here! If you change the structure, you will likely break any of the XSLT or other processing functions that the client is doing with your XML. Thus, it can be a very bad idea—so bad, in fact, that we recommend that, once an XML Web service is published, the formats of the data never change.

NOTE Never change the interface of an XML Web service once it has been published. Although it won't break binary compatibility with any client applications, it will likely break their logic. If you have an upgrade, publish a new XML Web service rather than simply changing an old one.

As you saw in the previous chapter, Microsoft Web services are easy to create. No publishing is required if they are private, and absolutely no registering is required regardless of whether the Web services are public or private. Finally, Web services are easy to reference from the consumer standpoint.

Public and Private UDDI

The Web service specifications we have been talking about to this point have been from a public standpoint, where any user with the proper UDDI access can discover and use a Web service. Of course, there is built-in security available for the Web service through the assistance of the .NET Web.Config file, which can force a user to authenticate before using a Web service. Note that a viewer can still "see" your Web service on the UDDI.

Prior to version 2 of the UDDI, the only other solution was to simply not publish your Web service with the UDDI at all. With the release of the version 2 UDDI specifications from UDDI.org, the ability to secure private Web services in a public UDDI host Registry becomes possible. Also, version 2 of the UDDI allows you to describe your Web services, so your partners know what they are getting.

One last notable item is the new version's Web Service Inspection Language (WSIL), which is a Web specification language announced jointly by Microsoft and IBM. The WSIL complements the UDDI by making it much more developer-friendly to discover and integrate Web services on Web sites without discovery information hosted on a UDDI provider. In other words, if you are familiar with the URL of the Web service host that owns the Web service that you need, then there is no reason to rummage around the UDDI looking for the Web service. This can be an invaluable specification; as a UDDI begins to grow with participant Web services, it may become much more difficult to find specific Web services.

Specifically, the WSIL provides endpoints, which are simply pointers to the Web services, allowing you to query Web services to retrieve a list of Web services—or even methods of Web services. Keep in mind, though, that at the time of this writing the specifications for the WSIL have not yet been submitted to a standards body for approval. For a look at the WSIL standards, navigate to www-106.ibm.com/developerworks/webservices/library/ws-wsilspec.html.

Summary

The UDDI provides a convenient way to locate Web services that can complement or enhance your business. It is also an ideal way to register your own Web services for public use. In this chapter we discussed the background of UDDI, including the four hosts that allow you to publish your Web services in a common registry for public use.

We discussed the advantages of the UDDI.org Web site versus committing your business to a single UDDI Registry. We also explored the necessary step of registering your company and your Web service with a UDDI host provider. We also explained how a UDDI creates a directory service that allows businesses to form alliances or partnerships with other businesses that complement their own as well as provide links to the UDDI.org Web site's specification documents.

You saw an example of how you can choose a UDDI host and register your business as a UDDI participant. We showed you how to add your business and Web service details to the UDDI, and we demonstrated the discovery capabilities of the Web Service Locator, the advantages of Web services, and public and private UDDI capabilities. Additionally, we briefly discussed the WSIL, a new way to search for Web services via the UDDI.

CHAPTER

8

The Web Services Client Business Model

This chapter expands our case study to the next level. We introduce two clients of the Hutchings Photography Web service. The first client is Hutchings Photography itself. Yes, it invested in building the back-end Web service platform to support its partners, but it still licenses images directly to clients. The second client is Penguin Photos, a fairly new partner with no history of doing business with Hutchings. Put another way, it's a perfect test for the new security and commerce model.

Chapters 9 and 10 walk you through the design and creation of these two client Web sites. We will look at the architecture, designs, and code they use to connect to and consume the Hutchings Web services.

Who's Our Market Again?

With the legacy Web version of our application, we had to ask some questions: "Who will use our Web site?", "What existing clients are online?", "What potential customers are online?", and "Will we lose existing clients if we go online?" Fortunately, these questions were previously answered in our development effort. Now we need to ask some new, even tougher questions.

Checking on the existing system, and determining how and why we built it the way we did, can be done by asking how our online commerce has been of late. The answer is, flat! Sure, new partners find us, make contact, and then possibly come onboard, but only at a linear rate at best. Hutchings Photography had hoped for a few explosions here and there, thanks to the effects of viral marketing, but they never even sparked.

One drawback we observed was that the larger stock photography Web sites were not interested in partnering with Hutchings Photography because it didn't play by *their* standards. While our business models were similar, they were not aligned enough to interact successfully. For example, the way that Hutchings Photography licenses its images is a bit different from that of other image providers. What Hutchings calls "royalty free" is not what a partner might consider royalty free. There was no mechanism to shuttle the verbiage of Hutchings' licensing to the client via the partner's site. It all had to be done manually, which was often a deal breaker.

Another problem, aesthetic as it may seem, was in the size of the thumbnails. It seems that each partner wanted a different size: 72 x 108, 108 x 72, 74 x 110, 110 x 74, and so forth. Hutchings used 92 x 120 (portrait) and 120 x 92 (landscape), which estranged a few potential partners or simply added another bullet to the programming staff's to-do list.

We're Tired of Pushing; Let Them Pull for a While

Hutchings Photography turned upside down in its balance of effort versus reward. The online stock photography industry was changing and morphing at a fantastic rate, like almost every online sector. The short list of the major players in the business changed constantly. New names were added on a weekly basis. Hutchings would get contacted by, or passed a lead to, a new company. It would then have to decide if that firm was worth pursuing as a partner.

More importantly, Hutchings would have to decide if the potential partner was worth the effort of the analysis and programming required for integration. Remember, in the online world, it's easy to assemble a thin façade over a basically virtual and nonexistent company. Remember those commercials on TV where the board members of a large Japanese firm are deep in tough negotiations with a parts supply firm in the United States, which turns out to be a one-man shop run out of the guy's house?

It's a Matter of Effort

Well, as an online company working to make a buck, Hutchings Photography fell prey to a few shady partners. Based on a lead, the look and feel of its Web site, and some other investigative techniques attempting to judge the credibility of the firm, Hutchings might launch a programming effort to push a portion of its image database to the partner. In addition, Hutchings' developers would advise, code, or even architect the partner's system. This led to great internal debates, such as "Why spend time getting up to speed on technologies like Cold Fusion or PHP scripting, just for a single customer?"

In its haste to propagate its product to the world, Hutchings made a few bad judgment calls. What fallout would occur when the partner's site eventually folded? Due to lack of business, poor management, or a merger with another firm, its partners sometimes disappeared in the night—along with its code and the time it invested. Whatever the cause, this equated to wasted work by Hutchings.

What needed to be done was to centralize all development effort on the Hutchings Web site. We needed to put our programmers to work building code for us, not our customers. "Write once, use often" is the Holy Grail of any API. XML Web services allow us to pull this off. By simply exposing 10 Web methods (seen in Figure 8.1), Hutchings allows another Web site to fully interact with its database of images and its commerce model—the way *it* wants the interaction to occur.

Hutchings Photography's goal was to write all the code once, document it thoroughly using HTML and WSDL, and then just point potential partners at the site. Whether they are "Microphiles" (enthusiasts of Microsoft

```
┌─────────────────────────────────────┐
│ Hutchings Photography Web Service    │
├─────────────────────────────────────┤
│ +ReturnThumbByID()                   │
│ +ReturnThumbByNumber()               │
│ +ReturnThumbsByTitle()               │
│ +ReturnThumbs()                      │
│ +ReturnImage()                       │
│ +RequestContract()                   │
│ +NegotiateContract()                 │
│ +CheckNegotiateStatus()              │
│ +AcceptContract()                    │
│ +ReturnReferenceTables()             │
└─────────────────────────────────────┘
```

Figure 8.1   Hutchings Photography Web methods.

products) or "Microphobes" (detesters of Microsoft products), they'll be able to read, understand, and use these Web services because the Web services are based on published standards. Sure, Hutchings will continue to advise on the best ways to connect to and consume the Web services and, if a decision is made to use Visual Studio .NET, it will even show its partners how easy it is to drag and drop the Web references and bind to those Web methods.

It's a Matter of Trust

Remember that in the previous Web version of the system, the data (thumbnails, watermarked images, and even the pure images themselves) had to physically live on a partner's site. This became a question of trust. Hutchings would elect to push out only *some* of its portfolio, maybe the less popular or less costly images, to a new or suspicious partner. Then, assuming a transgression occurred, the amount of exposure would be less. As the partner transacted more business with Hutchings Photography, this level of trust would grow and more images would get deployed on the partner's servers.

Even though we're centralizing the code on the Hutchings Photography site, we're still not completely removing the trust factor. What we gain, however, is the ability to audit the *who* and the *when* for each thumbnail, watermarked, and, pristine image requested and transported. If we mate this with the server variables automatically supplied by ASP.NET, we are able to attach the Remote IP address, browser specifications, and other helpful metrics about the client and partner accepting our product.

As previously mentioned, we've already decided in our business model to allow anyone (end user or partner) to request a thumbnail or thumbnails as well as the watermarked image for verification. In our minds, these Web methods are safe and could be called by anonymous individuals. In fact, they serve to propagate the Hutchings Photography marketing machine. Our thinking was that, after all, what could the public do with a small thumbnail or a watermarked image? Maybe after a few days in front of PhotoShop our offender could clean up the image to the point where it would be usable. It would be cheaper, in terms of hours, for these people to just license the image. Down the road, we may decide to tighten the screws on these Web methods, allowing only registered partners to execute them, but for now they're wide open.

The security concerns are high when dealing with the pure, unwatermarked images themselves. For a partner to receive such an image, the

Web method must receive the following data to the appropriate Web method call:

PartnerID.   A Uniqueidentifier (GUID) that must match a registered, active partner in the database.

ContractID.   A Uniqueidentifier (GUID) that identifies the contract previously agreed upon by the partner.

TokenID.   A Uniqueidentifier (GUID) that relates to the current session; although not actually used in authentication, the TokenID will support the authentication process and keep a commerce session from becoming stale. We use TokenID whenever we quote a price or provide licensing verbiage so that we can control how long those offers are valid.

Figure 8.2 shows when the TokenID and ContractID are issued.

With the Partner ID, Contract ID, Image ID, date and time stamp, and Remote IP address information, Hutchings Photography will be able to audit the who, what, when, and where of the transaction. The firm will probably care about auditing only the transactions that include the pure, unwatermarked images, but the database's default behavior is to audit all requests, even those for thumbnails and watermarked images. Contract IDs will expire after so many minutes, and the uniqueidentifiers are large and random enough that hackers will not be able to guess at them. For the initial run, these GUIDs will serve as the authentication mechanism.

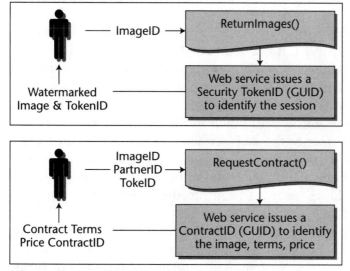

Figure 8.2   Using tokens to maintain context.

We will explore other ways to improve security, such as using SSL communication and restricting access to a specific list of IP addresses, in Chapter 11.

It's a Matter of Standards

The standards behind Web services are just that—standards. Partners who in the past hesitated or resisted interacting with us and our servers may have done so because of our tight integration with proprietary Microsoft standards. By basing their new software strategy on universal standards, like those approved by the W3C and ECMA (European Computer Manufacturers Association), partners won't have any political or, we hope, personal reasons to resist anymore. All of the popular development environments available today are able to construct and consume XML Web services because the primary technologies, XML, HTTP and SOAP, are W3C recommendations.

> **NOTE** The W3C doesn't actually issue standards. The highest level of endorsement that it gives a technology is known as the recommendation. The *recommendation* is a technical report that constitutes the end product of a long consensus-building process. This process goes through many phases: the working draft, the last-call working draft, candidate recommendation, proposal recommendation, and finally the recommendation itself. Once it is realized as a recommendation, the W3C considers that the idea, technology, or process in question is appropriate for widespread deployment. For more information on the W3C, the technologies in question, or the process itself, visit www.w3c.org.

It won't matter to the world that our Web service was constructed by Microsoft Visual Studio .NET. It also won't matter that it is running under the Microsoft .NET Framework and is hosted on a Microsoft Internet Information Server. The interface to the system is gained by using well-known, nonproprietary protocols, such as HTTP, XML, SOAP, and HTML. These universally accepted protocols are shown in Figure 8.3. Even the WSDL that describes the interface of the Web service and the UDDI that locates and advertises the Web service use nonproprietary grammar written in XML format. If it happens that a partner doesn't like the format of the XML documents that Hutchings returns, it can run the documents through its own XSL transformation.

The only drawback that we can see is the latency for a partner to get up to speed on using these standards. As we've already said, all of the popular Web tools and languages now support XML and SOAP, but to some firms, XML is still an alien life form and SOAP is an acronym to make a joke about.

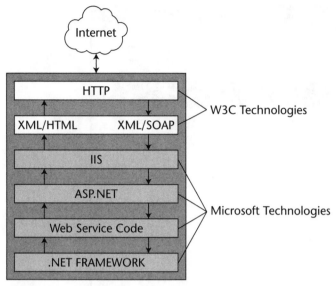

Figure 8.3 XML Web services support W3C recommendations.

Hutchings Photography plans to assist this classification of partners by assuming an advisory role. It will point the partners and potential partners toward sources for good sample code, training, and books so that they may get up to speed and successfully consume these Web services.

Partner: HutchingsPhotography.com

Because Visual Studio .NET was used to construct the XML Web services themselves, half of the effort of setting up a client Web site is already done: The developers know the tool, the languages, and the technologies. This doesn't even take into consideration the extremely RAD (Rapid Application Development) way that Visual Studio .NET can reference the Web services and write code.

Although we're talking about clients here, another benefit of building the Web services with Visual Studio .NET is that VS will write all of the WSDL code and even build and deploy a testing mechanism automatically. A software tester, or potential client Web developer, only has to call the .ASMX file directly to see an HTML-based page where the Web methods supported by the service are listed (see Figure 8.4). This test page also lists any description information for the Web service as a whole or any individual Web method.

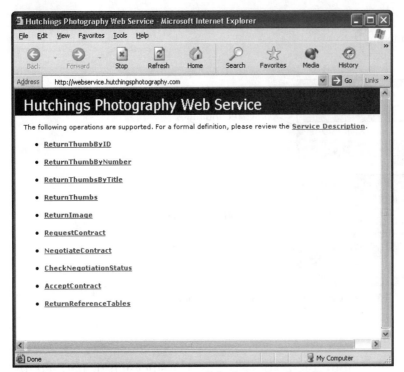

Figure 8.4 XML Web service test page built by Visual Studio .NET.

When constructing the Web service, the coder can specify a description property on the Web service or Web Method attribute. Attributes are rampant in .NET. They allow the programmer to add notes and comments to the code, most of which can guide the compiler or be fetched at runtime, using reflection. With Web services, these descriptions can be augmented to include HTML tags for formatting. One might also host some basic instructions on how to call the method, what arguments to pass, and what the return will look like:

```
Imports System.Web.Services
<WebService(Name:="Hutchings Photography", _
    Description:="Here are the various Web Methods that " & _
        "support the Hutchings Photography stock " & _
        "image database.<br>" & _
        "You should call the methods in the " & _
```

```
        "following order:<br><br>" & _
      "  1. ReturnThumbByID()<br>" & _
      "  2. ReturnImage()<br>" & _
      "  3. RequestContract()<br>" & _
      "  4. NegotiateContract()<br>" & _
      "  5. CheckNegotiateStatus()<br>" & _
      "  6. AcceptContract()<br><hr>", _
   Namespace:="http://namespace.hutchingsphoto.com")> _
Public Class HPImage
   Inherits System.Web.Services.WebService
#Region " Web services Designer Generated Code "
   <WebMethod(Description:="Request Image Thumbnail by Image ID " & _
      "(GUID) - Here is a GUID to try: " & _
      "58F1C24C-E0A6-4FF7-8AC4-8805A05F433E")> _
Public Function ReturnThumbByID(ByVal ImageID As String) As DataSet
   ' Implementation goes here
End Function
```

These descriptions are not meant to give complete technical details about the interface. That is the job of the WSDL code and, we hope, some solid, human-readable documentation. An astute programmer could study the WSDL code, fully analyzing the Web service, and learn how many parameters and of what data type to pass over, and what to expect back in return. Not only is the WSDL automatically generated by Visual Studio .NET, but if the client application is being built by Visual Studio .NET, it will be able to read the WSDL, bind to the Web service reference at design time, generate a proxy class, and give the programmer Intellisense on the Web service and its methods, parameters, and return values.

NOTE Intellisense is a feature in Visual Studio .NET that relieves the programmer from having to look up syntax and exact spellings of code. Intellisense uses the current project references, namespaces, and context to offer suggestions and automatically complete words while the coder types. Pop-up hints and drop-down lists ensure that the code follows syntax rules and uses the correct enumeration values. Most programmers find Intellisense a useful and time-saving feature, but it can be partially or completely disabled.

WSDL, however, is not that friendly to read and is reminiscent of IDL from the COM world. Figure 8.5 shows a sample of the WSDL generated by Visual Studio .NET. All the Hutchings Photography WSDL that you want to read can be found at http://code.hutchingsphoto.com.

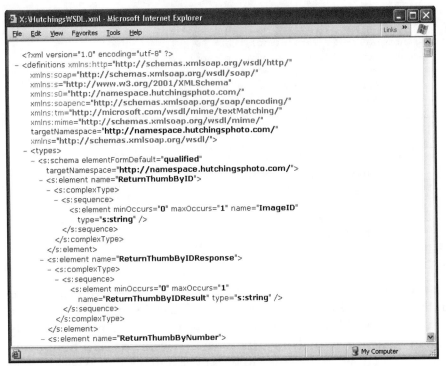

Figure 8.5 Sample WSDL from the Web service.

Finally, and probably most importantly, the visitor can use the simple HTML forms that Visual Studio .NET and the .NET Framework give you to test the different methods of a Web service. Figure 8.6 shows a page to test the ReturnThumbs Web method of the Hutchings Photography Web service. The user can enter any of the applicable parameters and then click the Invoke button to execute the method. The return information, if any, will be returned to the browser, emitted as XML. Any errors, whether caused by bad input or server-side complications, will be returned instead, also emitted as XML.

Using the automatically generated forms to test the Web service is one thing, but our goal is to build a full-scale Web application. The software requirements for this application are the same as with the previous (non-Web service) version of www.hutchingsphotography.com. These requirements are as follows:

- To search for photos by number, title, category, or keyword

- To drill down on a thumbnail to view a larger, more detailed image protected by watermark

Figure 8.6   Testing the ReturnThumbs() Web method.

- To view all of the metadata about the thumbnail or watermarked photo, such as the image number, title, description, photographer, and license types available for the image
- To select a licensing mode and be allowed to read the full verbiage
- To accept the license agreement, purchase the license, and then select the image format for download
- To download the full, unprotected image

Chapter 9 showcases the actual design and construction of the Hutchings Photography client Web site.

Partner: Penguin Photos

Penguin Photos is a fairly new online company. It would best fit into the category of image broker. Unlike other online stock houses that tend to use Hutchings Photography to augment their own image collection, Penguin Photos is essentially an intermediary that has no images of its own. Penguin saw a market opportunity, did some research on what image databases were out there, and then came into existence almost overnight.

Penguin's platform is as non-Microsoft as is possible. It runs Red Hat Linux version 7.2 and develops using Borland Kylix. Penguin Photos has a very technical IT staff and has already successfully integrated with several other image-providing vendors. Two developers from Penguin's staff, Jim and Ken, are both seasoned Web developers and will be working on the integration with Hutchings Photography's Web service. They really appreciate the XML Web service model that Hutchings chose because they already have a knowledge base in communicating using SOAP and consuming XML.

> **NOTE** Kylix is best described as "Delphi for Linux." It is the first high-performance, fully object-oriented RAD environment for Linux. Kylix version 3.0 supports C, C++, and the Delphi language and offers full support for Web programming and XML. Borland's Delphi for Windows was the first product to market that could build XML Web services (May 2001). Borland Kylix version 2.0 does the same, but on the Linux platform.

Jim and Ken both had a hand in the design of the Penguin Photos Web site, so they have intimate knowledge of the forms, controls, and code that make it run. To support the brokerage aspect of the site, Ken architected the business objects to execute a number of queries at the same time. This asynchronous approach allows the Web application to execute a separate query against each image provider on a separate thread of execution.

What this means is that very little effort is needed to drop in additional code that fires off another thread to handle the query to Hutchings Photography. They built their Web application framework like this so that it is easy to snap in new providers as they are discovered. You can witness this type of searching mechanism with a number of shopping Web sites, where shopping agents or bots (explained further in the accompanying note) become your proxies.

> **NOTE** An agent, or "bot" as it is sometimes called, is software that can execute multiple, simultaneous searches for information. Shopping agents have become popular as they will branch out and search the popular shopping Web sites for the best prices of books, computer hardware, or music. The agent returns with a compiled, sorted list of results. Visit www.botspot.com for more information as well as a comprehensive list of shopping bots available on the Internet.

Remember that Web method calls are synchronous, so the thread must wait for the results from the call; however, the overall process of searching will feel asynchronous from the user's point of view. Figure 8.7 explains how this effect is accomplished.

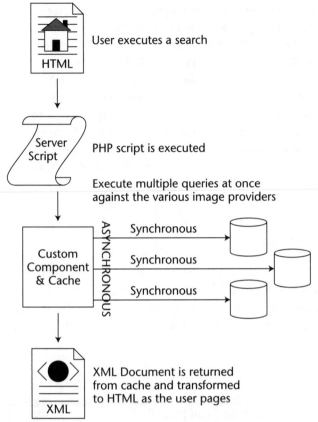

User executes a search

PHP script is executed

Execute multiple queries at once
against the various image providers

Synchronous

Synchronous

Synchronous

XML Document is returned
from cache and transformed
to HTML as the user pages

Figure 8.7   Penguin Photos' query agent architecture.

The results of some searches will return more quickly than others. This effect will be influenced by bandwidth, server locations, traffic and, most important, software design. After all, not all image vendors may be running a platform as efficient as .NET. In order to compensate for the differences in query times as well as the fact that a query may not execute, may fail, or may never finish, Jim and Ken built a buffering mechanism that returns images to the client after a threshold number of images are returned from the providers. This value can be changed by the user, but it defaults to 20 images at a time. In the back end, additional images are cached as they are returned from the various providers. The cache is then offered to the user in a next-page, previous-page interface.

NOTE Traditional patents are a grant of property right to the inventor, issued by the U.S. Patent and Trademark office. The patent goes on to protect the inventor by providing him or her with the right to exclude others from making, using, offering for sale, or selling the invention in the United States. Software patents, however, are more controversial because traditional patents don't apply to the realm of computer software very well. Decision makers at the Patent and Trademark office tend not to be very technical, so they are slow to identify software and processes that probably should not be patented—those that should remain in the public domain. More information on software patents, from the point of view of the League for Programming Freedom, can be found at http://lpf.ai.mit.edu.

User Interface Integration

Calling the Web methods is the easy part. Because thumbnails, contracts, and images are all familiar concepts to Penguin Photos and other players in the online image business, the only substantial effort will be in integrating Hutchings Photography's codes and terms with Penguin's user interface.

The Search Page

Penguin uses a search page similar to Hutchings'. There is a textbox to search for an image by name as well as by keyword. There are also two pull-down controls where the user can search for a category and licensing type. The work will be in getting Hutching Photography's master list of categories over to Penguin, where the list will be scrubbed and merged with a master list of categories conglomerated from other image vendors.

Penguin must take a passive approach here, as it is in no position to try to set a standard for potentially dozens of companies that are much larger, have been in business longer, and have more clout. This means that the programmers must shoulder the burden. The work will be a bit painful because the programmers and analysts have to look at the list of categories and make subjective decisions as to which categories from provider #1 might match with those of provider #2 so that Penguin's end user can see a single, simple pull-down list of options. If an image provider updates its list of categories, the developers will have to revisit the code.

Verification Page

Again, the verification page is similar to those of other online stock Web sites. After an image thumbnail is clicked on the search page, a larger, watermarked image is requested from the appropriate image provider and displayed in the center of the browser. Additional metadata, such as the title, description, and photographer, are displayed here as well. Penguin also lists icons at the bottom, representing the ways in which the image may be licensed. We see two areas of programming concern here.

The first problem is in standardizing the display of the metadata. It is imperative that the user sees the same types of information for each image clicked. Penguin insists on this consistency to maintain its veil and hide the fact that it is only a broker of these images. The problem is that some image providers send back the metadata in HTML format that Penguin has to screen scrape (see accompanying note), while other providers (such as Hutchings Photography) have chosen XML format. Even with XML, there is no consistency to the grammar within the document. One provider may have an element named Title while another provider uses Name and yet another uses Description.

NOTE Screen scraping is a procedure in which one application is able to interact, albeit very crudely, with another application. Lately, screen scraping is associated with HTML pages, but originally it became popular when GUI programs wanted to interact with a text mode or terminal connection, such as a mainframe application. This entails a programmer writing code to evaluate the information being displayed or returned. For a terminal session this is straightforward, as the mainframe software will always post information to the same locations on the screen. The programmer can simply count the bytes in the stream and capture the interesting items. For an HTML document, metatags and element tags must be searched and used to delimit the interesting text. With the introduction of Web services comes the craving to wrap up existing sites with a Web service. In fact, if you visit www.xmethods.com, you'll find a few examples of this. For example, a clever coder could easily build a Web service that takes two street addresses as input, silently visits www.expedia .com or www.maquest.com for driving directions, and then returns the series of driving steps as an XML document. Always be cautious when screen scraping. Not only can the format change unexpectedly, but it is usually illegal to scrape a Web page and then turn around and provide it as original content.

Penguin tackled the inconsistency problem by insisting that all metadata be maintained on its system in XML. If an image provider sends over its metadata in XML, so much the better. If, however, a screen-scraping technique or ASCII text source was used, an XML document is built and populated manually. Once all metadata is in XML, Penguin can simply maintain a separate XSL file for each provider and then transform the raw XML into HTML to be placed directly under the image on the page.

The second problem facing Penguin is in standardizing the licensing icons displayed on the page. This is mostly a business problem in determining what icons to use and how to label them to match the license required by the image provider. Fortunately, enough analysis went into the licensing aspects of the industry by both the image providers and the clients that this can be minimized to conditional processing. So, although the ideas behind the different license types might be coordinated (license for one-time use, license for multiuser, license for free use), each provider might use different terminology.

Penguin designed an algorithm to determine which image provider it is currently displaying, which licensing modes are available for the image, and how those modes map to Penguin's standard icons. Also, there are times when there needs to be a Custom license icon so the user can send a note to Penguin (who passes it along to the provider) requesting a custom quote. Not wanting to overload the verification page, Penguin uses a separate, standardized contract page where the full verbiage from Hutchings Photography, or whichever image provider, gets displayed.

Contract and Billing Page

The contract page is where the e-commerce details start to take shape. By the time this page is displayed, the user has selected an image and a licensing mode. This page simply displays the verbiage of the contract, the price and payment method, and delivery options. The content on this page is supplied by the image provider and then addended by Penguin itself.

As far as Hutchings Photography is concerned, the contract is simply an XML document that spells out all of the rules for licensing the image, the penalties for breaking these rules, and then a price element for the license itself. This price has already been adjusted by Hutchings Photography to reflect any discounts to the partner. If the contract is accepted and the image delivered, the partner is expected to pay that amount to Hutchings. It sounds simple, but you know that Hutchings' Web service enforces solid record keeping and watches every image shipped.

It is Penguin's job to display the full contract text and the price (marked up to include the partner's fees). Penguin then determines the method of payment and prompts the user for the type of image to be downloaded. The list of possible image types is provided by the image provider. Hutchings Photography, for example, can deliver the final image in JPEG, GIF, or TIFF format.

Once the transaction is complete, the pristine image is requested and sent from Hutchings Photography, and offered to the user for download in the format selected. Penguin Photos then destroys its copy of the image.

The Benefits to Penguin Photos

A company like Penguin wants to ramp up fast. By partnering with Hutchings Photography, Penguin was able to immediately boast an additional 100,000 photos in its database. The fact that these photos don't live in Penguin's physical repository is irrelevant to the end user.

Penguin appreciates XML Web services because their developers are well versed in the underlying standards. As momentum behind Web services grows, more image providers will start using them and Penguin can simply snap them into its infrastructure. In a way, Penguin is enjoying the "write once, use often" aspect of XML Web services.

More Partners Are Lining Up at Port 80

The more partners that get connected to Hutchings Photography equates to more partners doing business. The more partners doing business equates to more images being licensed. The more images being licensed equates to more people seeing the product. Remember that each licensed image must be adorned with the copyright text, *Copyright © HutchingsPhotography.com.* This notice must be on the image, or at least near it in any usage. All voyeurs of the images, including potential clients and partners, will know where to go to license their own images. Let's look at a couple of scenarios.

When Hutchings Photography gets contacted by a potential client, Hutchings will direct them toward the end-user Web site at www .hutchingsphotography.com or possibly one of their preferred partners. The hutchingsphotography.com Web site could be considered the outlet store for the Hutchings Photography Web service.

When Hutchings Photography gets contacted by a potential partner, Hutchings will direct them toward the partner Web site at http:// partner.hutchingsphoto.com for explanation of the procedure, terms, documentation, sample code, and FAQs about connecting to and consuming the Web services. The responsibilities of both parties in the partnership are also clearly spelled out. Once the partner has signed up and is ready to connect to the Web service, the partner can visit the end point at http://webservice.hutchingsphoto.com.

Anonymous partners can instantly and without authentication call the Web methods to return thumbnail and watermarked images. There are no restrictions to these two families of calls. If they wish to go further and call the contractual Web methods, a registration process must take place. If the potential partner qualifies, it is issued a PartnerID and allowed to begin commerce with Hutchings Photography. The ability for anonymous partners to play around with the first two levels of the Web service is also a clever sales and marketing technique.

The partner registration process will still be performed manually. The principals at Hutchings Photography want decision-making power over who gets registered and who doesn't. The partner registration database can be improved in other ways as well: annual fees, renewal dates, enforcement tracking, and incentive programs are just a few ideas.

Partners Who Want to Stay with Classic ASP

Those partners wanting to stay with a Microsoft platform but not necessarily migrate to .NET can make use of the SOAP toolkit. The SOAP toolkit was made available by Microsoft in June 2000 to Web service-enable Visual Basic 6.0 or any COM-based application. It is compliant with the SOAP 1.1 specification. The main thrust of the SOAP toolkit is to allow Windows DNA developers to develop and host Web services in ASP pages. SOAP listeners can then be built to run as an ISAPI DLL. The same toolkit, however, can be used to build applications that can consume SOAP-compliant Web services, which Hutchings Photography is.

The SOAP toolkit includes features that enable developers to turn existing applications into Web services without having to rewrite them or master XML. The SOAP toolkit includes wizards to turn existing Microsoft COM-based applications into Web services as well as an add-in to the Visual Studio 6.0 development system that enables developers to build applications that consume XML Web services. For example, a developer could take an existing application and use the SOAP toolkit to expose its capabilities as a Web service. Then, the developer could use the Visual Studio add-in to use that Web service from within another application, such as a database.

One object of the SOAP toolkit is ROPE (Remote Object Proxy Engine). ROPE is a COM component that allows a programmer to treat a Web service as though it were a COM component. After you instantiate the ROPE object, you can point it at a piece of SDL code, where it will parse it, identifying the methods and then providing programmatic access to those methods as though they were COM methods.

```
' Sample code on using the ROPE proxy from Visual Basic 6.0
Dim myROPE as Rope.Proxy
Dim myTemp as String
Dim myURI as String
' Initialize
myURI = "http://webservice.hutchingsphoto.com/wsdl.xml"
' Instantiate
Set myROPE = New Rope.Proxy
' Retrieve the SDL
If myROPE.LoadServicesDescription(icURI,myURI) <> 0 then
' Call the various Web methods as normal methods
    strTemp = myROPE.ReturnReferenceTables()
    strTemp = myROPE.ReturnThumbsByNumber("100001")
End If
' Cleanup
Set myROPE = Nothing
```

To download the SOAP toolkit, samples, or redistributable files, visit www.microsoft.com/downloads and perform a keyword search on SOAP. You might also want to go through the www.microsoft.com/xml Web site to find sample code as well as a really helpful FAQ.

Summary

The cliché "If you build it, they will come" is especially applicable for Hutchings Photography. By standardizing on XML Web services, Hutchings is able to attract new clients and put the effort back on them to perform the integration. The next two chapters focus on building partner Web sites. These Web sites will become the consumers of our Web services.

Chapter 9 considers our first partner site. It is not really a partner at all, but actually Hutchings Photography itself. Just because it has built a robust Web service back end doesn't mean it's out of the business of licensing images. Hutchings Photography has invested in .NET to carry its Web service, so naturally it will leverage that same skill set and tool set to design its own ASP.NET client application.

Chapter 10 showcases Penguin Photos, a partner that is taking an approach to consuming Web services in a 180-degree opposite fashion. While it has bought into the Web services way of doing business, it is a non-Microsoft shop through and through. None of the tools, servers, or Web browsers Penguin uses is created by Microsoft. Penguin is, however, a firm believer in the solid recommendations of the W3C and will demonstrate how to connect to and consume data as efficiently as the Hutchings client Web site, but without using .NET.

Hutchings Photography

In this chapter, we create a consumer of the XML Web services using Visual Studio .NET. Hutchings Photography is a consumer of its own Web service; although its business model is primarily about providing images to other stock photography Web sites. It still maintains a Web site of its own for existing clients and as a separate revenue source. Prior to the .NET RTM release on the MSDN download Web site on January 16, 2002, the Microsoft SOAP Toolkit 2.0 was Microsoft's de facto standard for creating SOAP-based Web services. The Toolkit provided a wizard-like manner of guiding developers through the creation of WSDL and WSML files that is the catalyst for Internet and intranet SOAP-based calls. The SOAP Toolkit 2.0 experienced some shortcomings, including limited data type support. Also, if an external Web client wished to access a remote Web service, the client would be forced to download a component to provide SOAP support.

Since the release of the RTM version of the .NET Framework Developer SDK, the world of Web services hasn't been the same. The wizard-like approach to creating Web services has evaporated. The creation of Web services is as simple as creating a DLL, and consuming a Web service has never been easier. The Microsoft Development IDE includes a UDDI locater, so finding UDDI registered Web services has been greatly simplified.

Essentially, Web services are referenced in nearly the same way as DLLs. The calls are the same, qualifying the reference to the object by its namespace and class name. Microsoft Intellisense is available once a Web service has been discovered, making the development of Web services incredibly easier than using its predecessor, the SOAP Toolkit.

The full Microsoft .NET Framework Software Development Kit (SDK) is 131 MB and is available for download from http://msdn.microsoft.com/downloads/default.asp?url=/downloads/sample.asp?url=/msdn-files/027/000/976/msdncompositedoc.xml. It includes everything you need to create a .NET application, including the .NET Framework, tools to build applications, and tools to test and deploy the .NET applications.

Furthermore, if all you need is the .NET Framework class library and ASP.NET, then the 21 MB Redistributable Framework is available for downloading at: http://msdn.microsoft.com/downloads/default.asp?url=/downloads/sample.asp?url=/msdn-files/027/000/976/msdncompositedoc.xml. You won't be able to create things like Web services with this framework as you can with the .NET Framework SDK, but you can support them if they are developed elsewhere and deployed to the machine containing the framework.

This chapter discusses the benefits of consuming Web services while focusing on the Hutchings Photography .NET Web site. You will learn how to reference a Web service, consume its methods, and display the data. We will dissect the incoming and outgoing SOAP information to give you a better understanding of what's going on behind the scenes.

This chapter also discusses the validating capabilities of the XML Schema Definition (XSD) document and how you can validate the Extended Markup Language (XML) with an XSD. The chapter also provides an example of how to create a schema using .NET and deploy it in code.

Creating a Basic .NET Web Service Consumer

A .NET consumer is responsible for referencing a Web service and initiating communication with a Web service with the goal of using functionality or returning data from the Web service. The returned data doesn't necessarily need to be meaningful because at times you might decide to simply test your Web service connection capabilities by exploiting a Web service, such as a test Web service on a UDDI host's test registry. But this still qualifies you as a Web service consumer.

Using the .NET IDE, you can access a Web service using any language supported by the Microsoft Common Language Runtime (CLR). As an

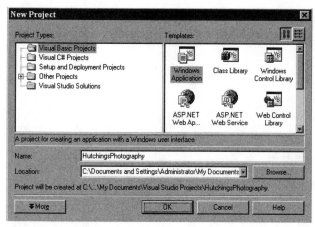

Figure 9.1 Creating a new project.

example, open your .NET IDE and choose Visual Basic .NET as your development language. Use HutchingsPhotography as the name of your project, as shown in Figure 9.1.

Now, click the OK button, and Form1 will appear in your new project. Now, to add a Web Reference, you can do one of three things. You can click the Project menu to drop down a list of menu choices that includes the item Add Web Reference, as shown in Figure 9.2.

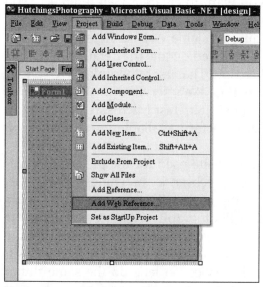

Figure 9.2 Add a Web reference through the menu bar.

Figure 9.3 Add a Web reference through the Solutions Explorer pane.

You also can right-click References in the Solution Explorer Pane to display a pop-up menu of choices that includes Add Web Reference, as shown in Figure 9.3. (Further, you can use the hotkeys, ALT–P and then ALT–R.)

Using the Web Service Locator

Once you have chosen the way you want to create a Web reference, you will be taken to the UDDI Locator as shown in Figure 9.4. The purpose of this browser is to assist you in finding available Web services.

The Web Service Directories that are listed denote the default UDDI host registries that are supported by Microsoft. The first hyperlink, UDDI Directory, transports you to the production Web services available on the Microsoft UDDI host registry. The next link, Test Microsoft UDDI Directory, brings you to the Test UDDI Directory available on the Microsoft UDDI host registry.

To get to the Hutchings Photography site used for the purposes of this chapter, type the following URL, http://webservice.hutchingsphotography .com, in the URL address bar at the top of the UDDI Locator. You should now find yourself at the Hutchings Photography Web service shown in Figure 9.5. Notice that the Add Reference button toward the right-bottom corner of the screen is enabled. If you remember from Chapter 7, this is what we used to reference the Web service, so let's do the same things again. Click the Add Reference button.

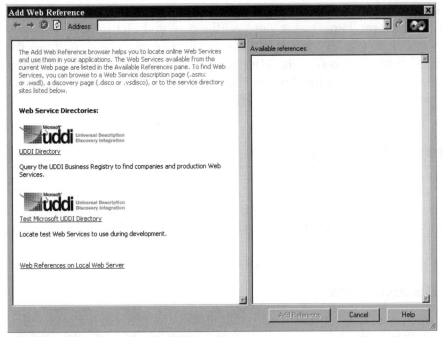

Figure 9.4   The built-in UDDI Locator.

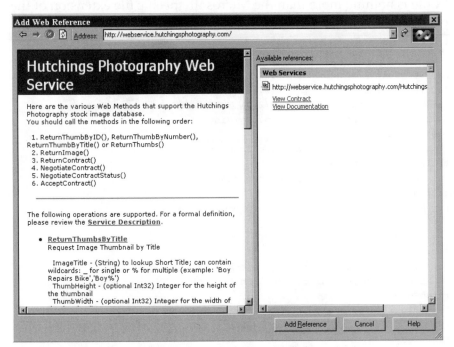

Figure 9.5   Referencing the Hutchings Photography Web services.

You are taken back to the .NET IDE. Notice that the Reference Node in the Solution Explorer Pane has a new addition, com.hutchingsphotography .webservice1. If you expand this node in the tree view, you will see the HutchingsImage.disco file, the HutchingsImage.wsdl file, and the Reference.map. Double-clicking any of these nodes in the Solution Explorer pane provides a description of each file.

The Web Reference Files

The Web reference files describe to the .NET Framework and to the developer much of the information required to use the Web service. There are three files to be aware of: the Discovery File (DISCO), the WSDL file, and the Reference Map.

The Discovery File

The Discovery (DISCO) File's responsibility is to provide links to other libraries that further illustrate the Web service, such as the WSDL and ASMX files. The WSDL file is discussed in the next section, while the ASMX file is nothing more than the Microsoft-specific file extension of the compiled Web service or multiple Web services. Shown here is an example of a DISCO file:

```
<?xml version="1.0" encoding="utf-8"?>
<discovery xmlns:xsi="http://www.w3.org/2001/XMLSchema-instance"
    xmlns:xsd="http://www.w3.org/2001/XMLSchema"
    xmlns="http://schemas.xmlsoap.org/disco/">
    <contractRef
        ref="http://webservice.hutchingsphotography.com/
HutchingsImage.asmx?wsdl"
        docRef="http://webservice.hutchingsphotography.com/
HutchingsImage.asmx"
        xmlns="http://schemas.xmlsoap.org/disco/scl/"
    />
    <soap address="http://webservice.hutchingsphotography.com/
HutchingsImage.asmx"
        xmlns:q1="http://namespace.hutchingsphotography.com"
        binding="q1:Hutchings_x0020_Photography_x0020_Web_x0020_
ServiceSoap"
        xmlns="http://schemas.xmlsoap.org/disco/soap/"
    />
</discovery>
```

The WSDL File

The WSDL file contains information such as the schema, the message names and type, the SOAP ports, the operation names, the binding names, the binding transport, and the service name. Following is a description of related terminology:

Schema.   The expected input. Specifies structure and valid input.

Message.   The named parameters and their corresponding function and data types (such as In and Out).

Types.   The parameterized order of data types that will be transmitted from the client to the Web service as well as the return value data type that will be sent back to the client.

Port.   The qualified name of the Web services operations.

Operation.   The name of the exposed Web method.

Binding.   The name of bind and what protocol language you will use as a transport (such as SOAP over HTTP).

Binding Transport.   SOAP, HTTP, POST, GET, or some other valid method.

Service.   The name of the service to which you will bind.

The Reference Map

The Reference Map is a list of files that consist of the URLs you are referencing in your consumer application. It is what allows you to close an application after referencing a Web service and still maintain a reference. It is a late-bound reference because the application will not be able to determine if the interface of the Web service changes after the initial reference until the consumer is executed, the Web service is called, and the client fails. The following code illustrates an internal Reference.map:

```
<?xml version="1.0" encoding="utf-8"?>
<DiscoveryClientResultsFile
xmlns:xsi="http://www.w3.org/2001/XMLSchema-instance"
xmlns:xsd="http://www.w3.org/2001/XMLSchema">
<Results>
   <DiscoveryClientResult
      referenceType="System.Web.Services.Discovery.ContractReference"
      url="http://webservice.hutchingsphotography.com/
HutchingsImage.asmx?wsdl"
```

```
        filename="HutchingsImage.wsdl"/>
    <DiscoveryClientResult

referenceType="System.Web.Services.Discovery.DiscoveryDocumentReference"
        url="http://webservice.hutchingsphotography.com/
HutchingsImage.asmx?disco"
        filename="HutchingsImage.disco" />
    </DiscoveryClientResultsFile>
</Results>
```

Objects, Properties, and Code

There are numerous objects in our Web consumer that we need to add and modify to build a working application. We've only just started our application, but now is the time to actually build it. We'll begin with Form1, changing the name and adding several pieces of functionality. Then we'll continue with the rest of the Hutchings Photography Web application.

Form1: frmImages.vb

Change the name of the default Form1 to frmImages and change the text to Hutchings Photography. Now, add the following objects to frmImages and make the corresponding modifications to the properties of each object as demonstrated in the text that follows.

Form1 (already present as the default form).   Name: frmImages

PictureBox.   Name: picMyPhoto Image: Supply an image of your choice.

Label1.   Name: lblCategories Text: Categories Font: Microsoft Sans Serif, 8.25pt, style=Bold

ComboBox1.   Name: cboCategories Font: Microsoft Sans Serif, 8.25pt, style=Bold TabIndex: 1

Button1.   Name: cmdSendCategory TabIndex: 2

Label2.   Name: lblLicenseType Text: License Type   Font: Microsoft Sans Serif, 8.25pt, style=Bold

Combo Box2.   Name: cboLicense Font: Microsoft Sans Serif, 8.25pt, style=Bold TabIndex: 3

Button2. Name: cmdSendLicense TabIndex: 4

Group Box. Name: grpPhotos Text: Please Enter Only One Search Criteria

Label3. Name: lblTitle Text: Title Font: Microsoft Sans Serif, 8.25pt, style=Bold

Textbox1. Name: txtTitle Font: Microsoft Sans Serif, 8.25pt, style=Bold TabIndex: 5

Label4. Name: lblKeyword Text: Keyword Font: Microsoft Sans Serif, 8.25pt, style=Bold

Textbox2. Name: txtKeyword Font: Microsoft Sans Serif, 8.25pt, style=Bold TabIndex: 6

Button3. Name: &cmdSend Font: Microsoft Sans Serif, 8.25pt, style=Bold TabIndex: 7

Button4. Name: cmdExit Font: Microsoft Sans Serif, 8.25pt, style=Bold TabIndex: 8

This completes the objects necessary for frmImages.vb. Your form should look similar to Figure 9.6.

Next, add the following lines of code to the frmImages_Load Event of frmImages.vb:

```
Private Sub frmImages_Load(ByVal sender As System.Object, ByVal e
As System.EventArgs) Handles MyBase.Load
'Early bind using the cached web service files in Reference.map.
```

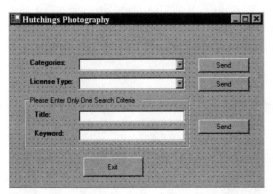

Figure 9.6 The frmImages data consumer.

```
Dim objConsumer As
com.hutchingsphotography.webservice4.Hutchings_x0020_Photography_x0020_
Web_x0020_Service
    objConsumer = New
    com.hutchingsphotography.webservice4.Hutchings_x0020_
Photography_x0020_Web_x0020_Service()
    'This is our local error handling for the sub procedure.
    '(i.e. Try, Catch, Finally, End Try)
    Try
        'Try to return a dataset using the initial web service method.
        dsRetVal = objConsumer.ReturnReferenceTables("1688FA5C-5FA0-444C-
B969-67896C89FAE7")
    Catch
        'Try failed. Remove the reference to the web service object.
        objConsumer = Nothing
        'Status the user on the error.
        MsgBox("An error has occurred. Application failed because the
service failed.")
        'Exit the sub procedure.
        Exit Sub
    Finally
        'Try succeeded. Set data source values of the objects equal to the
        'values returned from the tables.
        cboCategories.DataSource = dsRetVal.Tables("Table1").DefaultView
        cboLicense.DataSource = dsRetVal.Tables("Table7").DefaultView
        cboLicense.DisplayMember = "LicenseCode"
        cboCategories.DisplayMember = "CategoryCode"
        objConsumer = Nothing
    End Try
End Sub
```

Now, test to make sure that your Web reference is working by executing the application. After the application executes, the cboCategories object should be populated. If it is, then you have successfully created a Web service data consumer as illustrated by Figure 9.7.

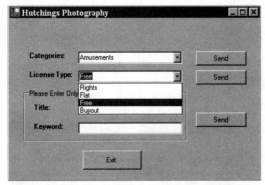

Figure 9.7 Make sure the application and Web service are communicating.

Based on our earlier test, we know that our application is able to communicate with the remote Web service via SOAP. We should now be able to query the remote ReturnThumbs() Web service to retrieve any image files based on our entry. The ReturnThumbs() Web service uses the following information to query for associated files:

Category.   Obtains a single JPEG and multiple ImageIDs that allow us to query another Web service that will supply the information to find additional photos that fall under the same category.

SubCategory.   Allows us to query for subcategories.

LicenseCode.   Allows us to query for various types of images based upon their licensing type.

Keywords.   Allows us to search text, including comma-separated values.

The ReturnThumb() Web service also allows two additional parameters to specify the height and width properties of the returned thumbnail. They are as follows:

ThumbHeight.   An integer data type specifying the desired height of the thumbs, in pixels.

ThumbWidth.   An integer data type specifying the desired width of the thumbs, in pixels.

Now, using our main form, double-click the cmdSendCategory object. You will be taken to this object's click event. Enter the following lines of code:

```
Private Sub cboCategories_SelectedIndexChanged(ByVal sender As
System.Object, ByVal e As System.EventArgs)
    If blnStartNow = True Then
        Select Case cboCategories.Text
            Case Is = ""
                Exit Sub
            Case Else
                MsgBox(cboCategories.Text)
        End Select
    End If
End Sub
```

Our Global Module

Let's add a module to the solution. Right-click the HutchingsPhotography Project and then click Add in the pop-up menu. On the sub-pop-up menu, click Add New Item. Click Module in the Add New Item dialog box, and name the new module GeneralModule.vb, as shown in Figure 9.8.

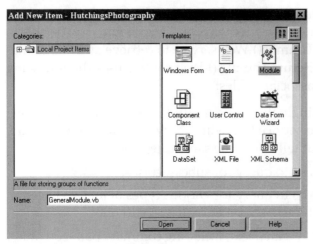

Figure 9.8 New Item dialog box.

Now add the following lines of code to GeneralModule.vb:

```
Module Module1
'Enumerate the Search Types.
Friend Enum SearchType
    SEARCH_CATEGORY = 1
    SEARCH_TITLE = 2
    SEARCH_KEYWORD = 3
    SEARCH_LICENSE_TYPE = 4
End Enum
Friend intSearchType As Integer
'Create a friend variable to store the
'integer associated with the chosen
'search type.
Friend Search_Type As Integer
Friend dsRetVal As DataSet
Friend dsData(0)
Friend intArrPos As Integer
Friend intColumnCount As Integer
Public Function ByteArrToImage(ByVal bytImage As Byte()) As Image
Dim msMemStream As System.IO.MemoryStream
    Try
        msMemStream = New System.IO.MemoryStream(bytImage)
        ByteArrToImage = ByteArrToImage.FromStream(msMemStream)
    Catch ex As Exception
        ByteArrToImage = Nothing
    End Try
MsMemStream = Nothing
End Function
```

As we have described in the earlier comments section of the code, we are creating an enumeration of valid search types. This way we don't have to concentrate on remembering the search type as we navigate from form to form. Also, the types of searches and returned information can be different depending on the search type we use, so we'll use this enumeration as criteria for the different requirements for each query. In the long run, it will help us make better reuse of the code.

As you might recall, one of the biggest battles using XML prior to the existence of the dataset was the presentation of the XML. Key criteria such as sorting the presentation data meant implementing rigorous code using the DOM and a scripting language to handle client-side XML Data Islands or, from a server perspective, implementing an XSL sort on the server.

Some people might confuse a dataset as being strictly for XML, which is incorrect. The dataset doubles as an in-memory database. It is so diverse that it can handle a relational data structure in the same manner that it can handle a hierarchical structure. It can also amalgamate each data access approach by simply manipulating its various methods and properties while maintaining the relational structure with which it was created.

We will use the ByteArrToImage function to extract and decode the large streams of embedded ASCII that contains the JPEG image files we will illustrate throughout the application. This is a unique approach to passing binary graphical streams across the Internet, as opposed to the traditional method of creating a hyperlink that references the location of the image file.

Form2: frmArtistInfo.vb

Now that we have the objects placed on our main form and enough code behind the objects to demonstrate the application, let's focus on the next form. Add another form to the project by right-clicking the Project in the Solution Pane and clicking Add in the pop-up menu followed by clicking Add Windows Form. Name this form frmArtistInfo, and add the following controls and the corresponding properties to the form.

Form2 (already present as the default form).   Name: frmArtistInfo.

Next, add the following labels to the form. Name the labels anything you like, but use the following as a guide for the Text:

Image ID

Image Number

Short Title

Memo

Type Code

Category Code

Subcategory Code

Resolution Code

Material Code

Orientation Code

Color Code

Date

Artist ID

Artist Company

Artist Last Name

Artist First Name

Artist Email

Artist Website

Artist Summary

Copyright

Image ID

Click to Enlarge

Now add corresponding textboxes for the labels you just created. Use the following as a guide and set their Locked properties to True:

txtImageID

txtImageNumber

txtShortTitle

txtMemo

txtTypeCode

txtCategoryCode

txtSubCategoryCode

txtResolutionCode

txtMaterialCode

txtOrientationCode

txtColorCode

txtDate

txtArtistID

txtArtistCompany

txtArtistLastName

txtArtistFirstName

txtArtistEmail

txtArtistWebsite

txtArtistSummary

txtCopyright

txtImageID

Now add three command buttons like these:

Button1.   CmdPrevious.

Button2.   CmdReturn.

Button3.   CmdNext.

Finally, add a Picturebox, and call it picThumbnail. The results should be similar to Figure 9.9.

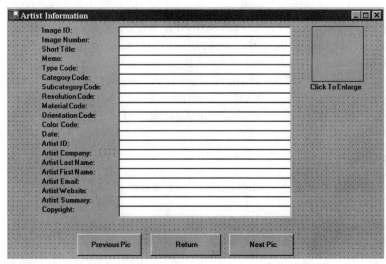

Figure 9.9   frmArtistInfo.vb.

Implementing the Load Event Code for frmArtistInfo.vb

Copy the following lines of code into the load event of the frmAritistInfo.vb file:

```
Private Sub frmArtistInfo_Load(ByVal sender As System.Object,
ByVal e As System.EventArgs) Handles MyBase.Load
   'Select the proper search using the public
   'enumeration of available search types. You can
   'simply take the cases out and just have this
   'event call the Display_QueryType. However, you
   'might want to keep if for statistical purposes.
   Select Case intSearchType
      Case Is = SearchType.SEARCH_LICENSE_TYPE
         Call Display_QueryType()
      Case Is = SearchType.SEARCH_CATEGORY
         Call Display_QueryType()
      Case Is = SearchType.SEARCH_TITLE
         Call Display_QueryType()
      Case Is = SearchType.SEARCH_KEYWORD
         Call Display_QueryType()
   End Select
End Sub
```

In this code we are searching through the search type enumeration to determine what action should be taken corresponding to the search the user commenced on frmImages. In this case, SearchType.SEARCH_LICENSE_TYPE calls the FillDS Method to populate the results of the Web service response in an array, which is presented in the code that follows.

The importance of this is that the image information that we return may contain additional photos and information. The code also sets the cmdNext.Visible property to True if more than one node of graphic information is returned in our SOAP XML Response. This allows the user to click the cmdNext button to browse the other graphical nodes.

Filling the DataSet

Here's the code for the method to allow users to browse those other graphical nodes:

```
Public Sub FillDS()
'Declare the local variables.
Dim intOutterCounter As Integer
'Clear the array.
System.Array.Clear(dsData, 0, UBound(dsData))
'For each row of data that is queried by us and passed back from the web
'server, loop.
   For intOutterCounter = 0 To dsRetVal.Tables("Thumbs").Rows.Count - 1
```

```
      'If the number of records exceeds the default
      'array bound value of the array, then redim preserve the contents in
      'the array.
         If intOutterCounter > 0 Then
            ReDim Preserve dsData(intOutterCounter)
               cmdNext.Visible = True
         End If
         Try
            'For each column in the web service, loop.
            For intColumnCount = 0 To
dsRetVal.Tables("Thumbs").Columns.Count - 1
               'Try to populate the dsShort Object.
               Try
                  'Qualify a short name for the properties of the dataset.
                  dsData(intOutterCounter) = dsRetVal.Tables("Thumbs")
.Rows(intOutterCounter).Item(dsRetVal.Tables("Thumbs")
.Columns(intColumnCount).ColumnName)
               Catch ex As Exception
                  'Throw an error if there are no graphics.
                  MsgBox("No graphics available per your selection, please
try again.")
                  Throw ex
               End Try
            Next
         Catch
            'Deallocate the datasets and form.
            dsRetVal = Nothing
            dsData = Nothing
            MyBase.Finalize()
         End Try
      Next
   Call Set_Pic(intArrPos)
   Exit Sub
End Sub
```

In this code, notice that at the end we call Set_pic(intArrPos). This positions our focus on each node that contains graphical information. The method uses the dataset array that we have created and uses the intArrPos index to extract the information from the dataset array to populate the frmArtistInfo.vb objects.

Using a DataSet Array to Display the Information

Here's the method to accomplish the method discussed in the preceding section:

```
Public Sub Set_Pic(ByVal intOutterCounter As Integer)
'Declare local variable.
Dim guidTemp As System.Guid
```

```
Dim intColumn
    If intOutterCounter <= UBound(dsData) Then
        If intOutterCounter = UBound(dsData) Then
            cmdNext.Enabled = False
        ElseIf intOutterCounter = LBound(dsData) Then
            cmdPrevious.Visible = False
        End If
        'Hide Previous if position entered is zero.
        If intOutterCounter = 0 Then
            cmdPrevious.Visible = False
        End If
        'For each column in the web service, loop.
        For intColumnCount = 0 To dsRetVal.Tables("Thumbs").Columns
.Count - 1
            'Try to populate the dsShort Object.
            Try
                'Qualify a short name for the properties of the dataset.
                dsData(intOutterCounter)=
dsRetVal.Tables("Thumbs").Rows(intOutterCounter).Item(dsRetVal.Tables
("Thumbs").Columns(intColumnCount).ColumnName)
            Catch ex As Exception
                'Throw an error if there are no graphics.
                MsgBox("No graphics available per your selection, please try
again.")
                Throw ex
            Finally
                'If the value of the column value is not null, then get the
                'column value.
                If Not dsData(intOutterCounter) Is System.DBNull.Value Then
                    'Populate the form-level GUI objects.
                    Select Case
dsRetVal.Tables("Thumbs").Columns(intColumnCount).ColumnName
                        Case Is = "ImageID"
                            guidTemp = dsData(intOutterCounter)
                            txtImageID.Text = guidTemp.ToString
                        Case Is = "ImageNumber"
                            txtImageNumber.Text = dsData(intOutterCounter)
                        Case Is = "ShortTitle"
                            txtShortTitle.Text = dsData(intOutterCounter)
                        Case Is = "TypeCode"
                            txtTypeCode.Text = dsData(intOutterCounter)
                        Case Is = "CategoryCode"
                            txtCategoryCode.Text = dsData(intOutterCounter)
                        Case Is = "SubCategoryCode"
                            txtSubcategoryCode.Text = dsData(intOutterCounter)
                        Case Is = "ResolutionCode"
                            txtResolutionCode.Text = dsData(intOutterCounter)
                        Case Is = "MaterialCode"
                            txtMaterialCode.Text = dsData(intOutterCounter)
```

```
                        Case Is = "OrientationCode"
                           txtOrientationCode.Text = dsData(intOutterCounter)
                        Case Is = "ColorCode"
                           txtColorCode.Text = dsData(intOutterCounter)
                        Case Is = "Date"
                           txtDate.Text = dsData(intOutterCounter)
                        Case Is = "ArtistID"
                           guidTemp = dsData(intOutterCounter)
                           txtArtistID.Text = guidTemp.ToString
                        Case Is = "ArtistCompany"
                           txtArtistCompany.Text = dsData(intOutterCounter)
                        Case Is = "ArtistLastName"
                           txtArtistLastName.Text = dsData(intOutterCounter)
                        Case Is = "ArtistFirstName"
                           txtArtistFirstName.Text = dsData(intOutterCounter)
                        Case Is = "ArtistEmail"
                           txtArtistEmail.Text = dsData(intOutterCounter)
                        Case Is = "ArtistWebsite"
                           txtArtistWebsite.Text = dsData(intOutterCounter)
                        Case Is = "Copyright"
                           txtCopyright.Text = dsData(intOutterCounter)
                        Case Is = "ImageThumbnail"
                           'Perform the byte array to image decoding.
                           picThumbnail.Image =
     ByteArrToImage(dsData(intOutterCounter))
                           picThumbnail.Name = txtImageID.Text
                     End Select
                  End If
               End Try
            Next
         Else
            MsgBox("Sorry, out of data")
         End If
      End Sub
```

The Truth about Embedded Base64 Binary Images

Delightfully, the code we have created to this point is completely reusable, regardless of the query requested by the Web service and the information that is returned. Later in this chapter you will witness this when we make additional calls using additional query methods on frmImages.vb.

In the earlier code example, you will notice that we used ByteArrToImage to use the System.IO.MemoryStream to "automagically" set the picThumbnail .Image equal to the information returned by the Web service. It's as easy as that.

You might assume that the Base64Binary data type that is associated with the Thumbnail needs to be converted using the System.Security,

Cryptography.FromBase64Transform class, but this is not so. The image was simply streamed up to the Web service by using the inverse of the code used in the ByteArrToImage method. The Web service handles this by assigning it a data type that conforms to the information sent. So, when you think about it that way, it makes sense that you should only have to stream the contents of the Thumbnail Image Node into an image object.

From a practical standpoint, you might also write the binary contents of our data to a file in a folder that has been enabled to cache thumbnails with a .jpg extension. This way you could avoid reacquiring the encoded jpeg each time you made a call to obtain information about the graphic. But, in our case, the binary is included in the response each time we query for information, regardless of whether we have consumed this information in the past, so we might as well take advantage of it. After all, reading and writing to disk is "expensive," so we should use it from the dataset each time.

One impractical method of operation included in our example is the same item that will make our coding life easier, the dataset array. We grab the information from each node before doing anything else.

This is bad if the user wanted to display information about only the first JPEG and nothing else. We would have wasted precious memory for nothing. If the user wants to review the bulk of the images that are included in our example, though, the dataset array is our key to speed.

Displaying the Data

Based on the code examples to this point, your Visual Basic application should return the results in Figure 9.10 when you query the Web service by using the Category option.

You will notice that the cmdNext button (Next Pic on the user's monitor) is now visible, symbolizing that we have more than one image available to browse through. However, before you begin to use it, add the following lines of code to its Click Event.

```
Private Sub cmdNext_Click(ByVal sender As System.Object, ByVal e As
System.EventArgs) Handles cmdNext.Click
    intArrPos = intArrPos + 1
    cmdPrevious.Visible = True
    Call Set_Pic(intArrPos)
End Sub
```

In the preceding code you will notice that we make the cmdPrevious button visible, thereby allowing us to decrement our picture count as well as increment it. So, add the following lines of code to the cmdPrevious button's Click Event.

```
Private Sub cmdPrevious_Click(ByVal sender As System.Object, ByVal e As
System.EventArgs) Handles cmdPrevious.Click
    intArrPos = intArrPos - 1
    Call Set_Pic(intArrPos)
End Sub
```

You will now be able to browse back and forth through the text and graphic images made available by the Web service. Don't forget about the cmdReturn button. Enter the following lines of code to activate it. You will need it to get back and forth between forms.

```
Private Sub cmdReturn_Click(ByVal sender As System.Object, ByVal e As
System.EventArgs) Handles cmdReturn.Click
    'Deallocate and dispose of the form.
    frmArtistInfo.ActiveForm.Dispose()
End Sub
```

Before we begin to write code for our other Web service queries, let's finish one final commitment, the ability to retrieve the thumbnail into a full-fledged image. To get started, add the following lines of code to the Click Event of the picThumbnail PictureBox object. This will query the Web service using the name applied to the picThumbnail when it was populated by the memorystream.

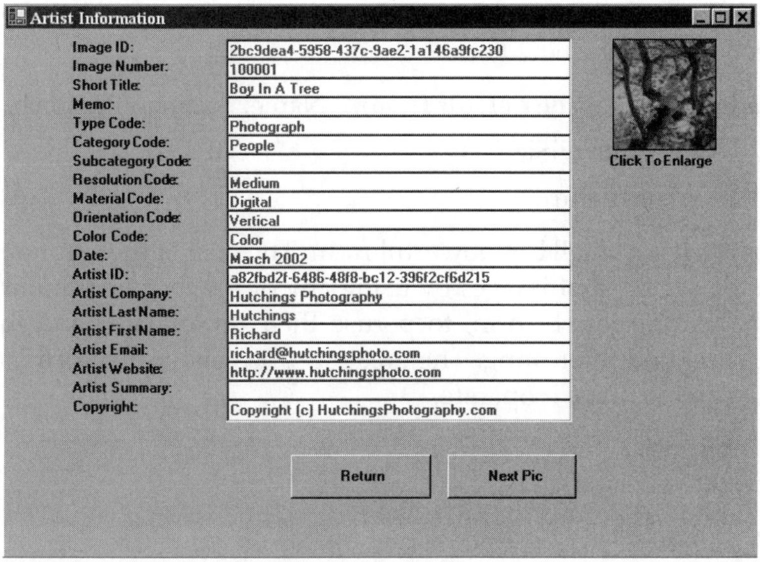

Figure 9.10 The results of frmArtist Info.

```
Private Sub picThumbnail_Click(ByVal sender As System.Object,
ByVal e As System.EventArgs) Handles picThumbnail.Click
'Declare local variables.
Dim objConsumer As com.hutchingsphotography.webservice4.Hutchings_x0020_
Photography_x0020_Web_x0020_Service
Dim frmSP As New frmShowPhoto()
    'Change the mousepointer to wait.
    Windows.Forms.Cursors.WaitCursor.Show()
    'Reference the web services.
    objConsumer = New
com.hutchingsphotography.webservice4.Hutchings_x0020_
Photography_x0020_Web_x0020_Service()
    'Set the dataset to the query used by the consumer
    'object. Pulls down the streamed binary of the graphic.
    dsRetVal = objConsumer.ReturnImage(Trim(picThumbnail.Name), 300, 300)
    'Show the referenced form.
    frmSP.Show()
    objConsumer = Nothing
    'Change the cursor back to normal.
    Windows.Forms.Cursors.Default.Show()
End Sub
```

Form3: frmShowPhoto.vb

As you can see, the method presented in the previous section calls another form, the final form used to create the total number of objects in our solution. You will add it to the new form in the same way you added the frmArtistInfo.vb form. After you have added the form, insert the following objects and properties to the new Form.

Form3 (already present as the default form).   Name: frmShowPhoto.vb.

PictureBox.   Name: picFullSize.

Button1.   Name: cmdReturn.

frmShowPhoto.vb is a small but powerful form. The goal of the solution is to be able to derive a list of images by using any of the four operations listed in on the frmImages.vb form, to peruse their thumbnails, and to enlarge images you find interesting. The great surprise about this form is the few lines needed to make it operate.

```
Private Sub frmShowPhoto_Load(ByVal sender As System.Object,
ByVal e As System.EventArgs) Handles MyBase.Load
    'Display the enlarged image using the dataset table structure
    'and jpeg conversion.
    picFullSize.Image =
```

```
ByteArrToImage(dsRetVal.Tables("Images").Rows(0).Item(dsRetVal
.Tables("Images").Columns("Image").ColumnName))
End Sub
Private Sub cmdReturn_Click(ByVal sender As System.Object,
ByVal e As System.EventArgs) Handles cmdReturn.Click
    frmShowPhoto.ActiveForm.Dispose()
End Sub
End Class
```

Only two lines of code make this form operate. The Load Event performs a single ByteArrToImage on the streamed-in XML graphic image and sets it equal to the PictureBox Object picFullSize.Image on the form, and the Button Object, cmdReturn, disposes of the form when it is clicked.

Let's view our progress before adding additional search methods to our solution. Query the Web service using a category on the drop-down listbox on frmImages.vb. When the form frmArtistInfo.vb appears, click the image in the right-hand corner of the picThumbnail form. You will see the results in Figure 9.11.

Adding the Code for the Other Searches

Let's add some more functionality to our search page, frmImages.vb. We can start by adding some query functionality to the License Type. In the cmdSendLicense Click Event, add the following lines of code:

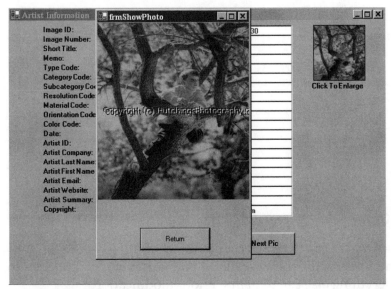

Figure 9.11   The full image.

```
Private Sub cmdSendLicense_Click(ByVal sender As
System.Object, ByVal e As System.EventArgs) Handles cmdSendLicense.Click
'Declare local variables.
Dim objConsumer As
com.hutchingsphotography.webservice4.Hutchings_x0020_Photography_x0020_
Web x0020_Service
Dim frmAI As New frmArtistInfo()
    'Change the mousepointer to wait.
    Windows.Forms.Cursors.WaitCursor.Show()
    'Set the search type.
    intSearchType = SearchType.SEARCH_LICENSE_TYPE
    'Reference the web services.
    objConsumer = New
com.hutchingsphotography.webservice4.Hutchings_x0020_Photography_x0020_
Web_x0020_Service()
    'Set the dataset the query used by the consumer
    'object. It searches using the selected category.
    dsRetVal = objConsumer.ReturnThumbs("", "", CStr(cboLicense.Text),
"", 100, 100)
    'Show the referenced form.
    frmAI.Show()
    objConsumer = Nothing
    'Change the cursor back to normal.
    Windows.Forms.Cursors.Default.Show()
End Sub
    'Now, in the frmArtistInfo.vb Load Event, add the following entry:
    Private Sub frmArtistInfo_Load(ByVal sender As System.Object,
ByVal e As System.EventArgs) Handles MyBase.Load
    'Select the proper search using the public
    'enumeration of available search types.
    Select Case intSearchType
        Case Is = SearchType.SEARCH_LICENSE_TYPE
            Call Display_QueryType()
        Case Is = SearchType.SEARCH_CATEGORY
            Call Display_QueryType()
        Case Is = SearchType.SEARCH_TITLE
            'TODO Later
        Case Is = SearchType.SEARCH_KEYWORD
            'TODO Later
    End Select
    End Sub
```

Testing the Other Searches

As you will see by running the application, everything is now complete.
Aside from the code for the initial search, we have developed our code to
ensure that everything else can remain without modification.

Let's next add some functionality to the Title Search. Add the following code to the cmdSendTitleKey commands button's Click Event.

```
Private Sub cmdSendTitleKey_Click(ByVal sender As
System.Object, ByVal e As System.EventArgs) Handles
cmdSendTitleKey.Click
'Declare local variables.
Dim objConsumer As
com.hutchingsphotography.webservice4.Hutchings_x0020_
Photography_x0020_Web_x0020_Service
Dim frmAI As New frmArtistInfo()
    If Len(txtTitle.Text) > 0 And Len(txtKeyword.Text) > 0 Then
        MsgBox("Only one text entry can contain text for this search.
Please remove one.")
        Exit Sub
    Else
        'Change the mousepointer to wait.
        Windows.Forms.Cursors.WaitCursor.Show()
        'Set the search type.
      intSearchType = SearchType.SEARCH_LICENSE_TYPE
        'Reference the web services.
        objConsumer = New
com.hutchingsphotography.webservice4.Hutchings_x0020_
Photography_x0020_Web_x0020_Service()
        'Set the dataset the query used by the consumer
        'object. It searches using the selected category.
        If Len(txtTitle.Text) > Len(txtKeyword.Text) Then
            dsRetVal = objConsumer.ReturnThumbsByTitle(txtTitle.Text, 100,
100)
        Else
            dsRetVal = objConsumer.ReturnThumbs("", "", "",
txtKeyword.Text, 100, 100)
        End If
        'Show the referenced form.
        frmAI.Show()
        objConsumer = Nothing
        'Change the cursor back to normal.
        Windows.Forms.Cursors.Default.Show()
    End If
End Sub
```

Use Boy% as the txtTitle.txt entry, or Boy, Tree as the entry for the txtKeyword.txt while running the application. You will see the results just as you did for the Categories and Licensing Types. This is what a little upfront planning will do for the reusability of the code in your application. The code segments that are encapsulated in each method or function are atomized for reuse, and the Web service is standardized to return the results to the client each time in a reliable manner and format.

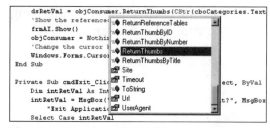

Figure 9.12 Microsoft IntelliSense makes it easy to learn about Web services.

Two Features that Make Building Web Services Easy

One feature that makes understanding Web services easy is the Web Service Locator, which allows us to look for a Web service using the UDDI links that are provided as defaults on the page, as well as the URL Locator that can permit us to look for Web service files on the Internet and on our own hard drive. Without this tool, creating client applications that interact with Web services would be much more difficult, as it was with Visual Studio 6.0, where you manually included the location of the Web service.

Another feature that really makes life with Web services easy is Microsoft's Intellisense, with which you can find almost everything you need to know about a Web service. Figure 9.12 demonstrates how easy it is to learn about a Web service using this handy, built-in feature.

As well as being able to display the list of parameters (see Figure 9.13) for the exposed method you have selected, you can use Intellisense to find more information about a Web service.

```
dsRetVal = objConsumer.ReturnThumbs(CStr(cboCategories.Text), "", "", "", 100, 100)
'Show the refere  ReturnThumbs (Category As String, SubCategory As String, LicenseCode As String, Keywords As String,
frmAI.Show()                     ThumbHeight As String, ThumbWidth As String) As System.Data.DataSet
objConsumer = No
'Change the cursor back to normal.
Windows.Forms.Cursors.Default.Show()
```

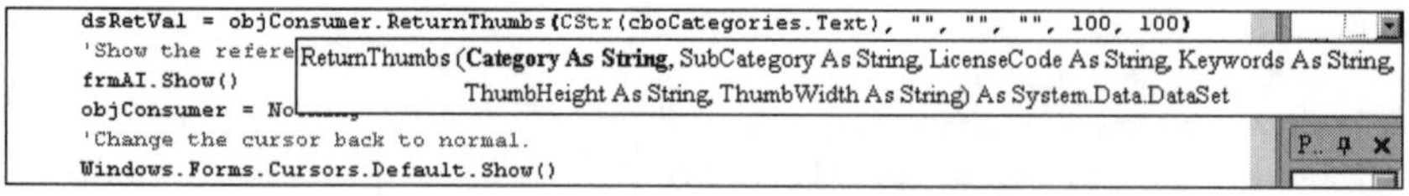

Figure 9.13 Microsoft Intellisense offers additional information about a Web service.

Web Services and Lesser-Known XML Schema Validations

After you connect to a Web service using the Web Service Locator discussed in Chapter 7, you can freely browse the WebMethod-enabled functions, the

```
<?xml version="1.0" encoding="utf-8" ?>
- <DataSet xmlns="http://namespace.hutchingsphotography.com">
  - <xs:schema id="Thumbs" xmlns=""
      xmlns:xs="http://www.w3.org/2001/XMLSchema"
      xmlns:msdata="urn:schemas-microsoft-com:xml-msdata">
    - <xs:element name="Thumbs" msdata:IsDataSet="true">
      - <xs:complexType>
        - <xs:choice maxOccurs="unbounded">
          - <xs:element name="Thumbs">
            - <xs:complexType>
              - <xs:sequence>
                  <xs:element name="ImageID"
                    msdata:DataType="System.Guid,
                    mscorlib, Version=1.0.3300.0,
                    Culture=neutral,
                    PublicKeyToken=b77a5c561934
                    e089" type="xs:string"
                    minOccurs="0" />
                  <xs:element name="ImageNumber"
                    type="xs:int" minOccurs="0" />
                  <xs:element name="ShortTitle"
                    type="xs:string" minOccurs="0"
                    />
                  <xs:element name="Memo"
```

Figure 9.14 Schema information included in Web services.

parameter list that the Web method expects to receive (Input Parameters), and the return data type (RetVal) that contains the data that will be sent back to the caller. It makes working with Web services pretty simple.

In Chapter 7 we talked about the UDDI being a great tool to discover and display important information about Web services. UDDI participants provide information about their UDDI-enabled Web services so a potential client can easily locate and understand the descriptive information about the exposed Web service methods without much complexity.

Some lesser-known discovery items of the Web service involve schema validation routines, such as the XSD (see Figure 9.14). Some people consider the schema validations an optional item, but it is difficult to justify not using them.

The schema contains metadata, describing the input to or output of a Web service. It categorizes things about the element's structure such as the element name, the corresponding data type, the number of occurrences, and whether the data consists of a complex or simple structure. It can also be atomic enough to restrict the type of data it receives, such as a specific character string, even getting as selective as examining the case of the letters it receives before processing anything.

The Inline Schema

The type of schema displayed in Figure 9.14 is called an inline schema because it is an embedded part of the returned XML document. In this document you will view some of the items discussed in the last section, such as the complex type, data type, and the number of occurrences of the data. Figure 9.14 is the XML schema that is returned with the XML data from the Hutchings Web service when you perform a query by Category.

Why would clients want schema information returned to them? Earlier we spoke of Microsoft's Intellisense being able to provide the methods, input parameters, and return values that are either offered or required to execute the Web service, artificially simulating an early bind with a remote object and making you aware of the information that is required to make it run.

So, what if you are able to run a Web service that you know little about and it returns the data that you know absolutely nothing about? What good would the data be if you don't know what it is comprised of, its limitations, or how to use it? Without an inline schema, you have absolutely no proof that the data or structure of the data embedded in the XML document is correct.

Using a provided inline schema, we are able to provide evidence that the data coming in should be there in a specific format if required. The XSD will also provide a roadmap that we can use to decode the data, returned data, the data's attributes, and even the order in which they should appear in the XML document. It provides hardcore evidence that the Web service we engaged is capable of handling the job that we want it to do.

In the example we used for the Hutchings Photography Web service, the dataset drove the functionality behind the forms. We could have just as easily used a simple DOM (Document Object Model), which the dataset already leverages as a W3C-compliant component, as the primary driver had the return type from the Web service been a simple string. It can be as simple or complex as you want it to be. As you can see in Figure 9.14, our Web services contain an inline schema to help you understand how to use the information that is returned to your data consumer.

Microsoft's .NET Framework offers a wide array of schema validation types, including DTD, Schema, XDR, and Auto. For flexibility, an application should preferably determine how it should validate the consumed inline schema.

Building the Code

The following code example demonstrates how we can implement schema validations in our application. Note the highlighted text, because this is where we will modify most of the code:

```
Private Sub frmImages_Load(ByVal sender As System.Object, ByVal e As
System.EventArgs) Handles MyBase.Load
```

```
'Early bind using the cached web service files in Reference.map.
Dim objConsumer As
com.hutchingsphotography.webservice4.Hutchings_x0020_Photography_x0020_
Web_x0020_Service
objConsumer = New
com.hutchingsphotography.webservice4.Hutchings_x0020_
Photography_x0020_Web_x0020_Service()
    'This is our local error handling for the sub procedure.
    '(i.e. Try, Catch, Finally, End Try)
    Try
        'Try to return a dataset using the initial web service method.
        dsRetVal = objConsumer.ReturnReferenceTables("1688FA5C-5FA0-
444C-B969-67896C89FAE7")
    Catch
        'Try failed. Remove the reference to the web service object.
        objConsumer = Nothing
        'Status the user on the error.
        MsgBox("An error has occurred. Application failed to load because
the Web service failed.")
        'Exit the sub procedure.
        Exit Sub
    Finally
        'Dim the variables to do store our XML and Schema validator.
        'Because the dataset stores the schema and the xml
        'in different properties, you'll need to append them to one
        'another and wrap
        'root tags around them.
        Dim strXMLReader As New IO.StringReader ("<Image>" &
dsRetVal.GetXmlSchema & dsRetVal.GetXml & "</Image>")
        Dim trXMLInput As New System.Xml.XmlTextReader(strXMLReader)
        Dim vrSchemaReader As New
System.Xml.XmlValidatingReader(trXMLInput)
        'Designate the appropriate validation type of the
        'Schema Reader. In our case it is a schema, but
        'other validation types are available as well.
        vrSchemaReader.ValidationType = System.Xml.ValidationType.Auto
        'Set the Address of the schema readers even handler
        '(error handler).
        AddHandler vrSchemaReader.ValidationEventHandler,AddressOf
XMLValidator
        'Read the entire XML string that was input, and
        'compare its contents and values to those specified
        'in the XSD.
        While vrSchemaReader.Read()
            'Will loop on its own here.
        End While
        'If trXML contains contains info then
        'deallocate all the references. Otherwise
        'status the user that the text reader failed
        'to initialize (accept our XML and XSD).
        If IsNothing(trXMLInput) = False Then
```

```
                    'If the Text Reader is instanced, then
                    'close the document and dereference
                    'all of the referenced objects.
                    trXMLInput.Close()
                    strXMLReader = Nothing
                    trXMLInput = Nothing
                    vrSchemaReader = Nothing
                Else
                    'If the Text Reader is not instanced, then
                    'dereference everything anyway and return
                    'the following string.
                    strXMLReader = Nothing
                    trXMLInput = Nothing
                    vrSchemaReader = Nothing
                    MsgBox("Text Reader Failed To
                    Initialize!!!")
                End If
                'If the lenght of the XML error collector is
                'greater than zero, then return the errors to the
                'caller. Otherwise, return a zero to the user
                'to specify there are no errors to report back.
                If Len(m_resulting_errors) = 0 Then equal to the values returned
from the tables.
                    cboCategories.DataSource =
                    dsRetVal.Tables("Table1").DefaultView
                    cboLicense.DataSource = dsRetVal.Tables("Table7").DefaultView
                    cboLicense.DisplayMember = "LicenseCode"
                    cboCategories.DisplayMember = "CategoryCode"
                    objConsumer = Nothing
                Else
                    MsgBox(m_resulting_errors)
                    End
                End If
            End Try
    End Sub
```

We need to add a sub to contain our ValidationEventHandler to capture and store errors for us. It needs to reside in the GeneralModule.vb, or add it as a sub in frmImages.vb. Here is the code for that:

```
Protected Friend Sub XMLValidator(ByVal sender As Object,
ByVal args As system.Xml.Schema.ValidationEventArgs)
    'The validator will accept the information provided by
    'the sender, including arguments.
    'Receive the errors provided in the args parameter,
    'and append them to the errors that might already exist.
    m_resulting_errors = m_resulting_errors & " " & args.Message
End Sub
```

Test-Driving the XSD

Notice that Sub XMLValidator makes a reference to m_resulting_errors, a variable that currently does not exist in our application. You can add m_resulting_errors to the GeneralModule.vb or just below the line of code that defines our frmImages.vb, just like this:

```
Public Class frmImagesInherits System.Windows.Forms.Form
Dim m_resulting_errors
```

The correct result will display frmArtistInfo.vb as if nothing has changed since we last touched the application. The schema in this case ensures that the content the XSD expects is contained in the XML body.

When everything is working, you don't even notice that it is there. So, how do you know that it is actually working? Here is an easy test that you can perform. Change this line of code:

```
vrSchemaReader.ValidationType = System.Xml.ValidationType.Auto
```

to this:

```
vrSchemaReader.ValidationType = System.Xml.ValidationType.XDR
```

When you now run the application, you will encounter the error displayed in Figure 9.15.

You have now learned how to validate an inline XSD. This is code you can use in either the client or server process that allows you the flexibility to handle erroneous XML.

Occasionally, it doesn't make any sense to include the XSD in your document. For instance, if your application parameters change often, then you

Figure 9.15 This error validates the XML.

might want to store the XSD external to your application. The XSD can reside on a local server on your domain, or even on one that can be accessed across the Internet via HTTP.

In the next section we will discuss how to build an external XSD using the Microsoft .NET IDE. We will build a basic XML sample and use it to build the structure of the XSD document.

Building an Out-of-Process XSD

XSD is an acronym for XML Schema Definition. The XSD serves as an important validation tool when applied against its companion XML string. The XSD can consist of a number of rules that the incoming XML string must adhere to, including but not limited to structure, patterns, values, sequence, total digits or characters, and type.

Without the XSD or a comparable validation document, the XML rules would have to take place in the source code. Of course this would work, but it isn't a very malleable solution because acceptable data constraints and patterns can change. Every time an acceptable constraint or pattern changed, the code that contains your XML validations might have to be modified as well to conform to these changes, forcing a recompilation and republishing of the .dll, .vdisco, or .wsdl files. In turn, this could result in a cascading nightmare, as other internal applications that rely on this .dll or Web service begin to fail, or even worse, as you watch hopelessly as your clients' applications, those that contain references your Web service, begin to fail, one after the other.

Therefore, it is probably more realistic to store this information externally and in a format that can be easily modified if needed, as well as be republished after being modified without disrupting or harming the current processing application or its constituents. XSD may be your answer. Let's next demonstrate how to construct an XSD document from within the .NET IDE and put it to use in a VB.NET Web service.

Constructing an XSD Document

If you look at a lengthy XSD document from anywhere but a XSD development tool, it might appear a bit intimidating. You will probably see things like simpleType or complexType, restriction base, nillable, whiteSpace, min and maxLength, pattern value, and more. Luckily for us, there are XSD development tools that simplify the building of XSD documents. Microsoft has one completely built into .NET, and the XML Spy IDE offers a feature-rich XML development environment. Using either of these integrated development environments or others, you can put together an XSD document in no time.

Because we will be using the Microsoft .NET IDE to create our solution, we will also use it to create the XSD document. To do this, open the .NET IDE and create a new Web service. You can use WebService1, the default, for the name of your new Web service project.

After the project has been rendered in the .NET IDE, then right-click your project in the Solution Explorer pane of the IDE and then select Add, and then Add New Item. The Add New Item dialog box will appear. Select XML Schema from the Templates list box and provide a name. Let's call it XMLMix because it will be a combination of element-based and attribute-based XML items. You will find yourself in the XMLMix.xsd file.

Now, let's construct our XSD to match the example of the mixed attributed-based and element-based XML demonstrated earlier in this chapter. We can initiate this process by dropping an element from the XML Schema Toolbox on the .xsd form as shown in Figure 9.16.

Next, rename element1 to match the name of our root node, root_tag. Then, drop an attribute control on top of the root_tag element and change the name of the attribute from attribute1 to Customer_ID.

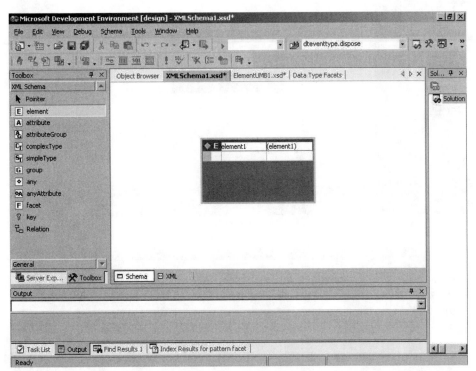

Figure 9.16 Using objects in the XML Schema Toolbox to build an XML validating XSD.

> **NOTE** XML and the XSD are case sensitive. Be sure that their corresponding element and attribute names match.

Now, repeat the previous procedure by adding another attribute, but this time try doing it without dropping the attribute control on the element. Use Add New (*) by clicking the first column of the next line. A drop-down list box will appear on the grid. Select Attribute, tab to the next sequential column, and change the name of the attribute from attribute1 to Date_Time_Arrival. Your example should look like Figure 9.17.

Notice that both of the attributes, Customer_ID and Date_Time_Arrival, are strings. Change the data type of each attribute to Unnamed Simple Type by clicking the data type column and choosing it from the drop-down list box.

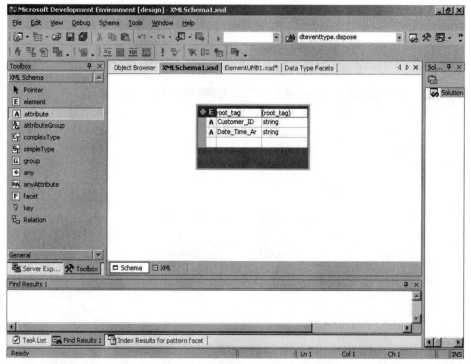

Figure 9.17   Using objects in the XML Schema Toolbox to build an XML validating XSD in another way.

Next, click the first column of the second row on either of the ST (Simple Type) controls, located directly beneath where the ST are displayed. A drop-down list box appears. Choose Facet. Facets allow you add constraints to your XSD document.

Click the column adjacent to the grayed out Customer_ID and change the data type from a string to a long using the drop-down list box. Next, click the first column of the bottom row, directly below where the word *facet* appears. Another drop-down listbox appears, displaying the various constraints you can place on your attribute.

You don't need to use all of them, just those that you feel satisfy your criteria. In our case, let's choose the whiteSpace property and, on the adjoining column, enter the word *collapse*. Thus, if there are any spaces in the value, they will be trimmed. Next, add another facet on the next row. Choose pattern from the types in the next column and set its value to \d\d-\d\d\d. Add another facet, whiteSpace and type *collapse* in the adjoining column.

What you have done at this point is specify that the XML format consist of a digit, a dash, and three more digits, and that any spaces will be trimmed. If the format of the XML attribute does not match this format, then the validation routine will throw an error.

Next, perform the same routine on the Date_Time_Arrival attribute, only keep its data type as a string. Also, use the following pattern, \d\d\d\d-\d\d-\d\dT\d\d:\d\d:\d\dZ-\d\d, set its length property to 23, and collapse the whiteSpace as you did with the Customer_ID attribute. You have now specified that the pattern corresponds to a specific W3C-compliant DateTime pattern, that its length is a total of 23 characters (the default would be characters because it's a string, but our pattern property overrides this property), and that it's trimmed of all spaces.

Now that the validations of the attributes have been satisfied, let's work on the validations for the child XML elements. Start by creating or dropping an element property on the root_tag element. This process is similar to the way you created the attributes. Change element1 to Menu (remember that it is case sensitive).

You will now see that the IDE created a new box for the Menu element. Now, in the Menu element either drop or create another element. Name this element Food. Set the data type of Food as String. When you get done, your XSD Project should look like the one in Figure 9.18. Make sure you save your work.

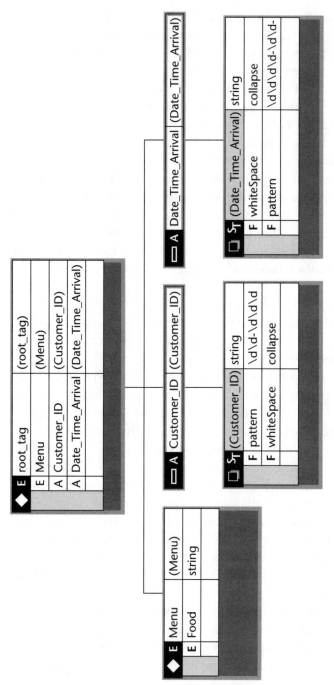

Figure 9.18   Our XSD document after completion.

Writing the Code to Use the XSD for Validating XML

Next, we will write a .NET Web service to handle server-side XML requests from the client as well as a .NET .aspx page to initiate client-side XML requests to the server. Our project began as a Web service, so simply double-click the .asmx file in the Solution Explorer window and enter the following lines of code.

```
Imports System.Web.Services
Imports System.Xml.Schema
Imports System.Xml
<WebService(Namespace:="http://tempuri.org/")> _
Public Class OurXMLExample
Inherits System.Web.Services.WebService

'Global variable declarations.
Friend m_resulting_errors
Friend Const ROOT_BEGIN As String = "<ERROR>"
Friend Const ROOT_END As String = "</ERROR>"
Friend Const NODE_ERR_BEGIN As String = "<DESCRIPTION>"
Friend Const NODE_ERR_END As String = "</DESCRIPTION>"
#Region " Web Services Designer Generated Code "
Public Sub New()
MyBase.New()
'This call is required by the Web Services Designer.
InitializeComponent()
'Add your own initialization code after the InitializeComponent() call
End Sub
'Required by the Web Services Designer.
Private components As System.ComponentModel.IContainer
'NOTE: The following procedure is required by the Web Services Designer.
'It can be modified using the Web Services Designer.
'Do not modify it using the code editor.
<System.Diagnostics.DebuggerStepThrough()> Private Sub
InitializeComponent()
components = New System.ComponentModel.Container()
End Sub
Protected Overloads Overrides Sub Dispose(ByVal disposing As
Boolean)
'CODEGEN: This procedure is required by the Web Services Designer.
'Do not modify it using the code editor.
    If disposing Then
        If Not (components Is Nothing) Then components.Dispose()
        End If
    End If
    MyBase.Dispose(disposing)
```

```
        End Sub
#End Region
'Web service that will simply validate our incoming XML.
<WebMethod()> Public Function ValidateXML(ByVal strInput As String) As
String
'Local variable declarations.
Dim strXMLReader As New IO.StringReader(strInput)
Dim trXMLInput As New XmlTextReader(strXMLReader)
Dim vrSchemaReader As New XmlValidatingReader(trXMLInput)
    'Designate the appropriate validation type of the
    'Schema Reader. In our case it is a schema, but
    'other validation types are available.
    vrSchemaReader.ValidationType = ValidationType.Schema
    'Add the appropriate XML Schema to the schema reader.
    vrSchemaReader.Schemas.Add(Nothing,
""http://localhost/WebService1/XMLMix.xsd")
    'Specify the address of the function or sub that
    'handles the events of the Schema Reader.
    AddHandler vrSchemaReader.ValidationEventHandler,AddressOf
XMLValidator
    'Read the entire XML string that was input, and
    'compare its contents and values to those specified in the XSD.
    While vrSchemaReader.Read()
        'Will loop on its own here.
    End While
    'Determine if the Text Reader is instanced.
    If IsNothing(trXMLInput) = False Then
        'If the Text Reader is instanced, then
        'close the document and dereference
        'all of the referenced objects.
        trXMLInput.Close()
        strXMLReader = Nothing
        trXMLInput = Nothing
        vrSchemaReader = Nothing
    Else
        'If the Text Reader is not instanced, then
        'dereference everything anyway and return
        'the following string.
        strXMLReader = Nothing
        trXMLInput = Nothing
        vrSchemaReader = Nothing
        Return ROOT_BEGIN & NODE_ERR_BEGIN & _
        "Text Reader Failed To Initialize!!!" & _
        NODE_ERR_END & ROOT_END
    End If
    'If the length of the XML error collector is
    'greater than zero, then return the errors to the
    'caller. Otherwise, return a zero to the user
    'to specify there are no errors to report back.
    If Len(m_resulting_errors) > 0 Then
```

```
        Return m_resulting_errors
    Else
        Return ROOT_BEGIN & NODE_ERR_BEGIN & "0" & NODE_ERR_END & ROOT_END
    End If
End Function
'The validator will accept the information provided by
'the sender, including arguments.
Protected Friend Sub XMLValidator(ByVal sender As Object, ByVal args As
ValidationEventArgs)
    'Receive the errors provided in the args parameter,
    'and append them to the errors that might already exist.
    m_resulting_errors = m_resulting_errors & NODE_ERR_BEGIN &
args.Message & NODE_ERR_END
    End Sub
End Class
```

Adding the Web Reference and Testing the Solution

Next, add a Web reference to our project by right-clicking its project name in the Solution Explorer window. Click Add Web Reference; the Add Web Reference dialog box will appear. Type the URL to your .asmx file in the Address textbox. Using the same solution, project, and object names as we have in this chapter, it will look something like this:

```
http://localhost/WebService2/Service1.asmx
```

Now, add an .aspx file to your solution by repeating the steps you did to add the .xsd file to your solution, except choose Web Form in the Add New Item dialog box. On the .asmx form, drag and drop a button, then double-click the button to get to the codebehind page, the .aspx.vb*. Then, copy the following lines of code into the click event of the object.

```
Dim objMyXMLValidator As localhost1.XMLMix
Dim strRetVal As String
objMyXMLValidator = New localhost1.XMLMix()
    strRetVal = objMyXMLValidator.ValidateXML("<root_tag
Customer_ID='12345' " & "Date_Time_Arrival='2002-12-12T17:30:00PMZ-04'>"
& "<Menu><Food>T-Bone Steak</Food></Menu></root_tag>")
    Response.Write(strRetVal)
```

In the Solution Explorer, right-click the .aspx file and choose Set As Start Page from the drop-down list, then run the page by pressing F5 or pressing the Start icon on the menu bar. Press the Command button; a list of items will be returned to you that violate the constraints of your XSD file.

The error message returned is self-explanatory. The XSD file rejected the XML because it clearly violated our constraints. In your ASPX page, copy the following code over the bad Web service method call.

```
strRetVal = objMyXMLValidator.ValidateXML("<root_tag
Customer_ID='12-345'" & "Date_Time_Arrival='2002-12-12T17:30:00Z-04'>" &
    "<Menu><Food>T-Bone Steak</Food></Menu></root_tag>")
```

Summary

Web services are an important feature of the .NET Framework. Web services allow us to communicate across the Internet without the painstaking process of DCOM configuration or custom WinSock programming—and the 21MB .NET Framework is free and downloadable from the Microsoft MSDN.

.NET Web services are capable of communicating with various Web clients via the SOAP protocol, which is supported by the W3C. The client is responsible for initiating the communication and sustaining this communication bilaterally and in a well-known way.

The Web Resource Locator allows you to easily find published Web services using the Microsoft UDDI. It also aids you in finding unpublished Web services or internal services for remoting. Using the URL provided earlier in this chapter, you will be able to test Web services using the Hutchings Photography Web site.

You can use the Web Resource Locator by either right-clicking the project in the Solution pane and then clicking Add Web Reference in the pop-up menu or adding one by clicking Project in the IDE menu bar. When the submenu appears, click Add Web Reference.

After you add a Web service, you can look at the internal files that further define a Web service, such as the Discovery File, the WSDL file, and the Reference.map file. They are located in the Solution Pane after adding a Web reference.

An interesting thing about Web services is that they can be consumed by Microsoft Visual Basic .NET applications and aren't constrained to the Web genre. Adding a Web reference to a Visual Basic .NET Windows application is identical to the way you would do it to an ASPX file.

Building applications in Visual Basic .NET is simple and much more powerful than it used to be. The namespaces that are available to Visual Basic .NET are the same namespaces that are made available to C# or C++.NET. Developing with Visual Basic has never been so powerful! It's quick and easy to learn if you are a seasoned Visual Basic software developer, and the more than 1,500 classes will keep you coming back to learn more.

Speaking of namespaces, it was through the use of the System.DataSet and the System.IO.Stream that we were able to extract the embedded binary image from the XML document to stream the contents into the PictureBox. We used an array to store the groups of datasets that were returned by the various Web services available on the Hutchings Photography Web site.

Microsoft IntelliSense is a built-in and configurable tool that allows us to view the various namespaces, classes, and methods that are available to us once we reference a Web service. IntelliSense makes objects look early bound, when in fact they are not. It does this by leveraging the locally cached DISCO, WSDL, and Reference.map files. These files are exposed to a client application by navigating and referencing the Web service using the Web Service Locator.

Additionally, an inline or out-of-process schema can be used to further identify the types of data that will be sent or returned to a Web service. The Web service should also have its own schema or code to validate the incoming XML using an inline schema from a client. It is important to do this for data integrity.

By using a schema, you will know whether you received all the data that was sent to you. It might be more advantageous to reference an external schema from the location of the Web service and use it to validate the incoming information. It is possible to link to a remote schema using a ValidatingReader Object.

Penguin Photos

This chapter looks at another partner Web site of Hutchings Photography. Penguin Photos is a relatively new business in the world of online stock photography. Its role is also somewhat unique in that it is a broker of images rather than an owner and direct licenser. Penguin Photos saw a niche in the marketplace and filled it. It owns zero photographs or artwork and is, instead, simply an agent between the online shopper and the image purveyor. Image providers such as Hutchings Photography have created XML Web services to support their partners. We will take a technical look at how the development team at Penguin Photos connected to and consumed the XML Web services served up by Hutchings Photography and .NET.

Penguin's platform is as non-Microsoft as possible. It runs Red Hat Linux version 7.2 and develops using Borland Kylix. Penguin Photos has already successfully integrated with several other image-providing vendors. Two developers from Penguin's staff, Jim and Ken, are seasoned Web developers and will be working on the integration with Hutchings Photography's Web service. They really appreciate the XML Web service model that Hutchings chose because they already have a knowledge base in communicating using SOAP and consuming XML.

This chapter is written from the perspective of the developers at Penguin Photos.

About Penguin Photos

Penguin Photos finds Web sites on the Internet that sell stock images. These images are sold for presentations, advertisements, or anything else the buyer desires. What Penguin does is present several images as the result of a user's search criteria. For example, if you need an image of several kids in a playground for your next presentation, then you've come to the right place. The images can be in several different formats so the buyer can get what is needed. What made working with Hutchings Photography interesting is that Hutchings had created an XML Web service that provides a way to query the stock images that it carries. Compared to the old way of getting images by screen scraping the returning HTML documents for the data needed, XML Web services sounded very exciting. With the promise from Hutchings Photography that this would give Penguin the control we needed, letting us send queries to its database and then getting a live result set, an agreement was made.

Hutchings Photography sent us the required information necessary to invoke its Web service. We began by checking out the functions that were exposed to us. We noted that this Web service was one of the first business-oriented Web services published using Microsoft's .NET platform. This concerned us a bit at first because our Web site is not hosted on a Microsoft platform, but rather on Red Hat Linux version 7.2. We prefer to use the Linux operating system for several reasons:

- No fees to install on a new server
- Increased security
- Not plagued by as many viruses and bugs
- Performance significantly better than that of Windows on the same hardware

Because Linux and Windows applications do not normally communicate without some level of difficulty, the XML Web service model is a great benefit to our shop. Integration with non-Linux platforms is part of our everyday existence. With the hopes of making Linux and Windows applications play together nicely, we were excited to start consuming the Hutchings Web service.

Conventions Used in This Chapter

In this chapter all the code blocks are formatted similarly to the syntax highlighting used as default in Kylix. Syntax highlighting makes reading source code significantly easier. Many developers devise their own syntax-highlighting scheme along with their own code style, but for simplicity we use the default.

- Reserved words (**bold**). These are words that cannot be redefined or used as identifiers. A few examples include **begin**, **end**, **if**, **then,** and **else**. A complete list of Kylix reserved words can be found in the Kylix help file.

- Comments (*italic*). The italic includes the comment delimiters, which in Object Pascal are the pairs { } and (* *), or // for a single line.

The most noticeable difference between the syntax highlighting used here and the syntax highlighting used in the Kylix IDE is that in Kylix the comments are also in color, which we can't reproduce in black-and-white text such as is used for this book. For the HTML we used similar syntax highlighting. The tags and properties are in **bold,** with the property values and all other text and symbols in Roman ("regular") text.

Borland Kylix

We had several tool choices in trying to consume the .NET Web service from the Linux platform. After evaluating a few of them, we chose Kylix, Borland's Rapid Application Development environment for the Linux platform. Currently, Kylix uses the Object Pascal language, which was made popular by Borland's Delphi product on the Microsoft Windows platform. The next version of Kylix (version 3) will also support C++ as well the .NET Framework's Common Language Runtime (CLR). Figure 10.1 shows the Kylix IDE running on the Linux KDE desktop.

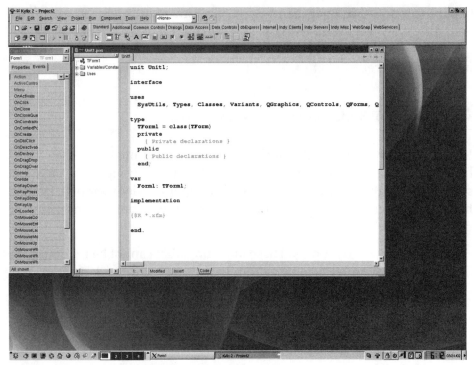

Figure 10.1 Kylix IDE running on KDE (Red Hat 7.2).

Because Kylix is based on Delphi, many people refer to Kylix as Delphi for Linux. All of the source code we developed is cross-platform compatible with Delphi 6 and will run on Microsoft Windows. The only necessary changes regard which path delimiter to use (forward slash versus back slash) and some fixed paths. This is easily handled using conditional defines or some of the built-in path-handling functions. As a result, the properly written source code files can be opened in either Kylix 2 or Delphi 6 on either Linux or Windows (respectively), where they can be compiled into native binaries for the respective platforms and run without any modification.

Here are the major features of Kylix 2:

- 100 percent native Linux ELF object format executables

- Built-in support for Web Services, SOAP, WSDL, XML, and other related technologies

- Integrated data-access solutions to Oracle, Informix, DB2, Interbase, PostgresSQL, and MySQL

- Cross-platform code compatibility with Borland Delphi 6
- Apache Web server and application development

Anders Hejlsberg was the leading engineer for Turbo Pascal, Delphi's predecessor, as well as for Delphi. Anders left Borland to work for Microsoft and was the chief architect in charge of designing the C# language and other elements of the .NET Framework. Because of this common heritage, many elements and conventions in Delphi are also found in the new C# language. Being familiar with C# and the .NET Framework makes the transition to Kylix all the easier.

Kylix 2 was chosen to create the client for Hutchings Photography because of the incredibly short time to market required for our product. We wanted to start making money fast. We are a business, and taking time to finish an application means a loss of dollars. Kylix is a one-stop development environment, providing all the support we needed to create the Linux Web service client and our entire Web server application in little time.

For more information on Kylix 2, visit Borland's Web page at www .borland.com/kylix, where you can download the open edition of Kylix 2 for free.

NOTE The source code for this chapter is available at http://code .hutchingsphoto.com. The Enterprise Edition of Kylix 2 or Delphi 6 is required to compile the Web services code from this chapter.

Consuming XML Web Services with Kylix 2

Borland's Delphi 6 was the industry's first RAD Web services development solution when it was released in May 2001. Due to the changing nature of the SOAP standard, there have been two updates in the time since to be more in line with newer implementations. Kylix has been supporting the Linux platform since March 2001, but it wasn't until November 2001 and the release of Kylix 2 that an integrated Web services solution became available.

The built-in support for Web services for Kylix 2 provides a wealth of tools for creating both Web service clients and servers. For most needs, you can use the Web Services Importer to import the WSDL information into Kylix when creating a client by providing the URL or local file path to the WSDL or XML document. Kylix then creates the units containing the

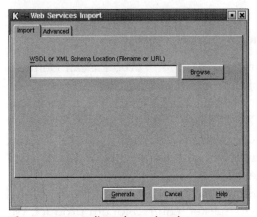

Figure 10.2 Kylix Web services importer.

source code for an interface to the Web service. By including the created units in your project, your program can invoke the Web service.

The Web Services Importer (Figure 10.2) allows you to specify either a filename or URL for the WSDL or XML Schema describing the desired Web service. Kylix connects to the Web, if necessary, to obtain and parse the Web service information. Once completed, the Importer generates the Kylix source code providing the interface to the Web service.

The communication with the Web services imported through this means is accomplished via the THTTPRIO component in Kylix. This component handles the sending of HTTP messages to remote SOAP objects. The importer automatically creates the code to dynamically create the THTTPRIO components. Figure 10.3 shows the THTTPRIO component icon as it will be shown on the Kylix design surface.

The THTTPRIO component also provides functionality outside the Web Services Importer. THTTPRIO is a mouthful, and stands for Type of Hyper-Text Transfer Protocol Remote Interface Object. Properties are provided

Figure 10.3 The THTTPRIO component icon.

that allow the developer to specify the WSDL location (local or on the Web), the selected Web service, and the selected port. Additional properties are provided to allow fine-tuning of the component, including proxy information and security credentials (usernames and passwords).

This simplified interface to Web services by the THTTPRIO component frees the developer to work on the goal of the program instead of worrying about interfacing with the Web service. While the THTTPRIO simplifies working with Web services, it does not limit the developer in the kind of access he or she has to the Web service. In most cases the THTTPRIO component provides all the access necessary to create a Web services application.

Web Applications with Kylix

Kylix provides a *TPageProducer* component to facilitate the creating of Web pages from a template. This template allows the creation of the bulk of the Web page (layout, graphics, HTML, CSS, and so on) by a Web designer, while a developer spends his or her time producing the functionality of the page using Kylix. This separation allows everyone to concentrate on his or her area of expertise. Figure 10.4 shows the TPageProducer component icon as it will be shown on the Kylix design surface.

The Web designer simply builds the Web page using whatever tools and techniques he or she wants. Once the pages are completed, the specified HTML-transparent tags are added to the source of the Web pages. These tags have the following form:

```
<#TagName Param1=Value1 Param2=Value2 ...>
```

When the Web application uses these templates, it fires an event for each tag, allowing the Web server application to replace these tags with customized content, as defined by the developer. Server-side scripting, such as JavaScript or any other ActiveScript language, can also be used in these templates. Kylix provides all the power necessary for most Web server applications. Giving Web developers power on the server side helps

Figure 10.4   The TPageProducer component icon.

balance the workload and gives the designers more control of the Web presence.

There are two different ways in which you can use HTML-transparent tags. The first way is to load up your document with tags so your designers can have more of a say in how they would like the page to look. The second way is to just place a tag in the HTML document and leave the formatting to the developers. Both ways work well. We did both in the creation of our Web application, as you will see later on in this chapter.

Integrating Kylix and .NET

In our efforts to integrate with Hutchings Photography's .NET Web service, we discovered that .NET Web services use Document Literal (Doc | Lit) encoding for their SOAP requests by default. Borland, releasing its framework first, chose the more common Remote Procedure Call (RPC | Encoded) format as its default for SOAP invocation. This choice of different standards has created difficulty in interfacing the two systems. Once the Microsoft implementation was released, Borland has improved support for Doc | Lit and communication with Microsoft Web services through updates.

Attempting to use the Kylix 2 Web Services Importer on the Hutchings Photography works, but when we ran the resulting code, we discovered that the Web service returned a .NET DataSet. While this would be great if all the clients were created with .NET, this is a problem for non-.NET clients. This use of proprietary formatting and communication between diverse platforms is a problem that Microsoft acknowledges. Kylix simply does not know as of this writing what to do with a proprietary .NET DataSet.

Fortunately for us, the flexibility of Kylix 2 provides an alternative. By using the TidHTTP component (Figure 10.5), we can invoke the Web service via HTTP and then parse the .NET DataSet with the TXMLDocument component (Figure 10.6). This option no longer uses the robustness of the Borland Web services framework, but when communicating with nonstandard implementations, it is nice to have such flexibility. As we will see, implementing a Web service client through this means is still quite simple.

Figure 10.5   The TidHTTP component icon.

Figure 10.6 The TXMLDocument component icon.

The TidHTTP is part of the Internet Direct (Indy) component suite. This is an open-source Internet component suite supporting popular Internet protocols and is included as standard equipment with Kylix. Indy uses blocking sockets as opposed to the more complex (for programming) non-blocking sockets. This results in ease of use in client development because you write your transactions in a sequence. We will be using the Get method of the TidHTTP component to retrieve the .NET DataSet as an XML document, after passing in specific parameters through the URL.

The TXMLDocument component provides a hierarchical interface to an XML document through the use of an XML DOM (Document Object Model) parser. Access to the root node of the parsed XML document is provided through the DocumentElement property. From there we can traverse and access the various ChildNodes throughout the document. We will be using the XML document to extract the meaningful information from the resulting .NET DataSet we receive from the Web service.

Consuming Hutchings Photography's Web Service

According to the published interface at http://webservice.hutchingsphoto.com, several methods of the Web service are at our disposal. We will illustrate our implementations of only a couple of them:

ReturnReferenceTables. This function populates the search option boxes to let users refine their search.

ReturnThumbs. This function returns the thumbnails that meet the criteria that the user selected on the search screen.

ReturnImage. This function returns a full-size watermarked image so the user can better decide if it is the image wanted.

Because all the functions are invoked by the same client, we created a function to build the HTTP POST header to invoke the Web service. This is what we will use instead of SOAP to accomplish the same end result. For simplicity in documenting this, we have hard-coded the base URL. Because all other applications invoke the same Web service, Penguin Photos as well as other developers trust Hutchings Photography to keep up with its end of the contract by providing the Web service for our application.

The BuildHTTPPost function returns a string with all the parameters to the calling Web service function in the proper order. This makes it easier to add functionality to our application if and when the need arises. This function takes several parameters; most of them are optional, denoted by the string = '' syntax. We pass in the Web service function name as well as any parameters that are required by the calling function. Two functions that we use are worth mentioning: AnsiSameText and Format.

AnsiSameText compares two strings that are passed in and returns true if they are the same text; it does not care what case the values are. MyFunction and MYFUNCTION are the same. Format makes it easier to add values to a string. Format takes the first string parameter and replaces the format codes with the values that are passed in as the second parameter. In this case, the format code that we are using is %s, which tells the Format function that the value that needs to be replaced is a string.

Our resulting function looks something like this:

```
function BuildHTTPPost(func: string; p1: string = ''; p2: string = '';
    p3: string = ''; p4: string = ''; p5: string = ''; p6: string = ''):
string;
begin
// this is the base URL for invoking the web service
    Result :=
'http://webservice.hutchingsphotography.com/HutchingsImage.asmx/';
// if ReturnThumbs is the specified function then this will format
// the URL for invoking that method
if AnsiSameText(func, 'ReturnThumbs') then
    Result := Result + Format('ReturnThumbs?Category=%s&SubCategory=%s&'+
    'LicenseCode=%s&Keywords=%s&ThumbHeight=%s&ThumbWidth=%s',
    [p1, p2, p3, p4, p5, p6]);
// if ReturnReferenceTables is the specified function then this will
// format the URL for invoking that method
if AnsiSameText(func, 'ReturnReferenceTables') then
    Result := Result + Format('ReturnReferenceTables?PartnerID=%s', [p1]);
// if ReturnImage is the specified function then this will format
// the URL for invoking that method
if AnsiSameText(func, 'ReturnImage') then
    Result := Result +
    Format('ReturnImage?ImageID=%s&ImageHeight=%s&ImageWidth=%s',
    [p1, p2, p3]);
end;
```

This function takes the parameters passed in and places them in the post header, thus creating the correct URL for each function call. We will now take a look at the specific code for calling each of the various Web methods from Hutchings Photography.

The ReturnReferenceTables Web Method

Hutchings Photography provided this method for their partners to populate their Web site controls. In order for us to know all of their categories to offer our users as a choice for searching, we need to call the ReturnReferenceTables method of the Web service. Using the Get method of the TidHTTP component, with the resulting URL from BuildHTTPPost, it returns the .NET DataSet for us.

Our call looks something like this:

```
XMLDocument.XML.Text :=
    HTTP.Get(BuildHTTPPost('ReturnReferenceTables',
    '1688FA5C-5FA0-444C-B969-67896C89FAE7'));
XMLDocument.Active := True;
```

HTTP is an instance of the TidHTTP component, and XMLDocument is an instance of the TXMLDocument. We pass in the name of the method we are calling, in this case ReturnReferenceTables. This method requires only the Partner ID provided by Hutchings Photography. Because this PartnerID will be the same for the duration of our contract with them, we again hard-coded this value into our Web application. Setting the Active property of the TXMLDocument to True takes the resulting .NET DataSet and parses it in the TXMLDocument for easy access.

Because the returning XMLDocument has several child nodes and most of them are usable only by .NET clients that are using the .NET DataSet, we need to skim past them and get to the meat of the XML Document—the nodes that we want. Figure 10.7 shows the location of the desired child nodes within the XML document with the schema tags taken out because we will not be using them. At the first level we want the second node (which is node 1 because we are base 0). At the second level we want the first node and then we want the count of nodes at that level. Then we iterate through those nodes looking for specific nodes by name.

Now that we have the XML document, we need to obtain the types from this dataset. We can get the count of the types by examining the count property of the correct child node here:

```
XMLDocument.DocumentElement.ChildNodes[1].ChildNodes[0].ChildNodes.Count;
```

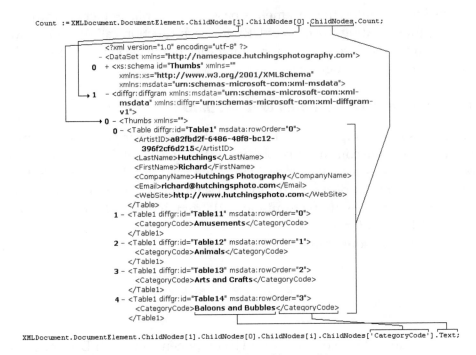

Figure 10.7 The DataSet XML document returned by Hutchings.

By simply iterating through these child nodes we can extract the type information with this code:

```
XMLDocument.DocumentElement.ChildNodes[1].ChildNodes[0].
    ChildNodes[i].ChildNodes['CategoryCode'].Text;
```

and again ...

```
XML.DocumentElement.ChildNodes[1].ChildNodes[0].ChildNodes[i].
    ChildNodes['LicenseCode'].Text;
```

In the preceding code, *i* is the local variable from our *for* loop. We are able to return the CategoryCode and LicenseCode, respectively. These values are cached locally and used for populating the pull-down lists for our Web application, as we will see a bit later.

The ReturnThumbs Web Method

Now that we have obtained these reference codes, we can perform a search by invoking the ReturnThumbs method. This code starts out similarly to how we obtained the types:

```
XMLDocument.XML.Text :=
    HTTP.Get(BuildHTTPPost('Returnthumbs', 'people', '', 'flat'));
XMLDocument.Active := True;
```

With our call to ReturnThumbs, we pass the category and the license type to the BuildHTTPPost function and then pass that result to the HTTP.Get method. Once again, we set the Active property to True to parse the returned .NET DataSet into our TXMLDocument.

We now iterate through the XML document, extracting the individual image thumbnails and related information. This is accomplished by referencing the correct node just as we did in the ReturnReferenceTables section. The Image is encoded as a long string using Base64 encoding. We have written a function called Base64toJpeg that converts this string into an actual JPEG image file.

```
procedure Base64ToJpeg(const s: string; ImageFile: string);
var
    st: TStringStream;
    ms: TMemoryStream;
begin
// Convert the String into a Stream of type TStringStream
    st := TStringStream.Create(s);
    try
// Create a TMemoryStream to store the converted image in
        ms := TMemoryStream.Create;
    try
        DecodeStream(st, ms);
        ms.Position := 0;
        ms.SaveToFile(ImageFile);
    finally
        ms.Free;
    end;
    finally
        st.Free;
    end;
end;
```

The actual conversion from Base64 is accomplished by calling the DecodeStream procedure. To that procedure we pass a TStringStream created from the image string passed in and a destination, TMemoryStream. We then take the contents of the TMemoryStream and save them to disk as an actual JPEG image file as specified in the parameter. Saving the files to disk allows us to cache the images locally so we do not needlessly bog down the system requesting the same images multiple times. If we were not interested in caching the images, we could just stream them back to the client directly. Once again, this is an advantage of the flexibility offered by Kylix.

The ReturnImage Web Method

Once users find a thumbnail that looks interesting, they can request a full-blown image, which has been watermarked to prevent, or at least dissuade, theft. To obtain the full-size image, we call the ReturnImage method with the ImageID parameter. Again, we use the same technique to get the .NET Dataset, only changing the parameters:

```
XMLDocument.XML.Text :=
    HTTP.Get(BuildHTTPPost('ReturnImage', ImageID));
XMLDocument.Active := True;
```

What we get back in the .NET Dataset is a really large Base64 JPEG string as well as additional information about the author, image type, and size. Once again, we use the Base64toJpeg procedure to convert this into a JPEG.

Creating the Web Application

Now that we can invoke the Web service and parse the relevant information that we need to give to our users, we need to create a Web server application to take our Web service client code and generate HTML to be viewed in any browser on any platform, which is our goal here at Penguin Photos.

To create a Web Server Application, select File, New menu, and then from the New tab choose Web Server Application (see Figure 10.8).

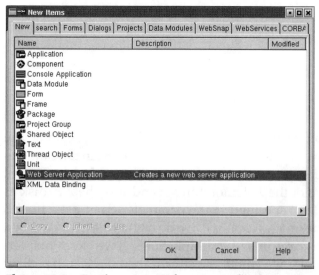

Figure 10.8 Creating a new Web server application.

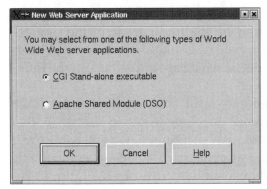

Figure 10.9   Selecting the type of Web server application.

From the New Web Server dialog, choose the type of Web service you want (see Figure 10.9). For simplicity of debugging, we chose to create a standalone CGI executable. These executables do not require the restarting of the Web server to update an application. Apache Dynamic Shared Objects (DSO) are shared modules, similar in function to IIS's ISAPI extensions.

At this point, we have an empty WebModule (see Figure 10.10). In Kylix, the TWebModule serves as a container for placing nonvisual components used in the creation of Web services. It also has a powerful property called Actions. Actions let us call our Web applications by using paths in the URL. Paths make it easier to call different functions in our application, as discussed later in this chapter.

The components necessary for creating our Web server application include the two we mentioned earlier: a TXMLDocument named

Figure 10.10   An empty WebModule container.

XMLDocument and a TidHTTP component named HTTP. The TXMLDocument component is found on the Internet tab of the Component pallet, while the TidHTTP component is found on the Indy Clients tab. We also need three TPageProducers, which are also found on the Internet tab.

TPageProducers are yet another powerful component that lets Web designers create HTML content and developers create the code that replaces the special tags that we previously mentioned. We will name these components ppResult, ppThumbs, and ppSearch. Once these components are placed, the WebModule should look similar to the one in Figure 10.11.

Next we assign the TPageProducers to the actions of the WebModule. By the time we are finished, we will need three actions, each with a different calling path, one for each page producer. Figure 10.12 shows the empty listing of actions for our module. By pressing the Insert key, a new blank action is added.

The first action is named *search*, with a path of /search. This allows us to access this method with the following URL: http://servername/cgi-bin/cginame/search. It will be the default action and will link to the TPageProducer ppSearch. The process of linking the page producer to the Action enables Kylix to know what TPageProducer goes with which action. The default action is what gets called if no path is set in the URL (the CGI is called directly).

Figure 10.11   WebModule containing our components.

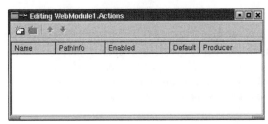

Figure 10.12   Empty collection of actions for our WebModule.

The second action is named "thumbs," with a path of /thumbs and will be linked to ppThumbs. The third action is named "result," with a path of /result and links to ppResult. Figure 10.13 shows the three actions and their respective properties now properly defined in our module.

Using the TPageProducer is just one of many ways to create a Web server application with Kylix. We chose this way because it promotes divide-and-conquer strategies to Web development. One developer creates templates in a favorite editor while another developer writes the code to populate it with dynamic content based on the user requested. As Penguin Photos wanted to ramp up quickly, this appeared to be the fastest method.

Each of these actions also needs an OnAction event defined. OnAction occurs when TWebDispatcher matches the action to an HTTP request message when it arrives. OnAction allows us to define the response, or the page, that will be returned to clients when they connect to the Web server application. It also allows us to read in the Request object. The Request and Response objects are similar to those in ASP/ASP.NET. In our event handler, we load the template file and return that as the response. The

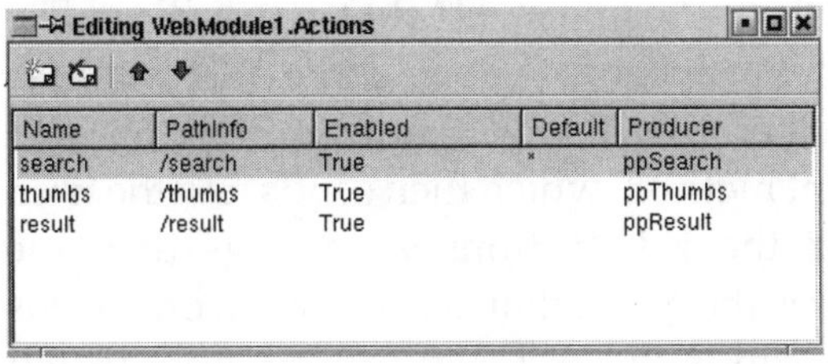

Name	PathInfo	Enabled	Default	Producer
search	/search	True	*	ppSearch
thumbs	/thumbs	True		ppThumbs
result	/result	True		ppResult

Figure 10.13   Three actions with properties defined.

TPageProducer replaces the necessary tags before the response is returned to a client.

The OnAction event for the search action looks like this:

```
procedure TWebModule1. WebModule1searchAction(Sender: TObject;
    Request: TWebRequest; Response: TWebResponse; var Handled: Boolean);
begin
// Implementation code
end;
```

We use the Request object when necessary to read in values from the user and then generate the proper Response, the final HTML, and send it back to the user. The completed code for the searchOnAction event looks like the following:

```
procedure TWebModule1.WebModule1searchAction(Sender: TObject;
    Request: TWebRequest; Response: TWebResponse; var Handled: Boolean);
begin
  // Load up the search template form
  if fileExists('search.html') then
  begin
    ppSearch.HTMLDoc.LoadFromFile('search.html');
// Return it - the tags will be replaced before the return
    Response.Content := ppSearch.Content;
end
else
    Response.Content := 'Error: Could not load search.html';
end;
```

Because the search does not require any input from the users before it can return a response, we are not even checking if there is a request from the user. The *if* statement just checks to see if the search.html template file exists; if not, it returns an error message that the template could not be loaded. If the template is found, we load it into the ppSearch's HTMLDoc LoadFromFile property (ppSearch being the TPageProducer we added earlier). This causes the template file to be loaded. We then take the content from the ppSearch and return it to the Response content method, which then sends it to the user.

If the template file has any of the HTML-transparent tags then the OnHTMLTag of the page producer is the event that is fired when one needs to be replaced. This is where we include the Web service code we created earlier in the chapter. To minimize trips to the Web service we will cache the categories and license types in local files. We check the freshness of the cache before using it. If the cache is too old or missing then we invoke the ReturnReferenceTables method in the Web service. Once we have obtained the category lists from either the cache or the Web service, we replace the HTML-transparent tags with these lists. We load the values from the Web service into TStringLists because they are easier to read and write data to disk, and to manipulate over arrays. Here is our search template with the CATEGORYS and LICENSE tags:

```html
<html>
<head>
<title>Penguin Photo Search</title>
<meta http-equiv="Content-Type" content="text/html; charset=iso-8859-1">
</head>
<body bgcolor="#FFFFFF">
<p>Welcome to penguin photos search form. This form will allow you to
search from many photos that are availible.</p>
<br><hr>
<table>
<form action="/cgi-bin/search/thumbs" method="post">
<tr><td>Category</td><td><select
name="Category"><#CATEGORYS></select></td></tr>
<tr><td>Title</td><td><input type="text" size="50"
name="Title"></td></tr>
<tr><td>Keywords</td><td><input type="text" size="50"
name="Keywords"></td></tr>
<tr><td>License Type</td><td><select
name="License"><#LICENSE></select></td></tr>
<tr><td><input type="Submit"></td><td><input type="Reset"></td></tr>
</form>
</table>
</body>
</html>
```

Here is our code that replaces the CATEGORYS and LICENSE tags found in our template:

```pascal
procedure TWebModule1.ppSearchHTMLTag(Sender: TObject; Tag: TTag;
    const TagString: String; TagParams: TStrings; var ReplaceText: String);
var
    Count, i: Integer;
    tmp: string;
    slCats, slLic: TStringList;
    cats, lic: string;
begin
// Replace all the <#...> tags in the document that we loaded up
// above on the WebModule1searchAction event
// Reference URL
// http://webservice.hutchingsphotography.com/HutchingsImage.asmx/
// ReturnReferenceTables?PartnerID=1688FA5C-5FA0-444C-B969-67896C89FAE7
// Create lists to hold the values from the return document
    slCats := TStringList.Create;
    slLic := TStringList.Create;
```

```
    try
// check for the existence and age of the locally cached lists
    if FileExists('cats') and FileExists('lic') and
      not (OldFile('cats') or OldFile('lic')) then
    begin
// We have a cached file so load it up
    slCats.LoadFromFile('cats');
    slLic.LoadFromFile('lic');
    end
    else
    begin
// retreive the .NET dataset into our XML document
    XMLDocument.XML.Text :=
    HTTP.Get(BuildHTTPPost('ReturnReferenceTables',
    '1688FA5C-5FA0-444C-B969-67896C89FAE7',
    '', '', '', '', ''));
// Parse the XML document
     XMLDocument.Active := True;
// determine the number of child nodes
// that may contain type information
    Count := XMLDocument.DocumentElement.ChildNodes[1].
    ChildNodes[0].ChildNodes.Count;
// Try to get all the seperate types from the document
    for i := 0 to pred(Count) do
    begin
// Since all the Codes for all the lookups come back in this one
// document, we will parse them all out at once.
// Look for a CategoryCode
    tmp := '';
    tmp := XMLDocument.DocumentElement.ChildNodes[1].
    ChildNodes[0].ChildNodes[i].ChildNodes['CategoryCode'].Text;
    if tmp <> '' then
      slCats.Add(tmp);
// Look for a LicenseCode
      tmp := '';
      tmp := XMLDocument.DocumentElement.ChildNodes[1].ChildNodes[0].
      ChildNodes[i].ChildNodes['LicenseCode'].Text;
      if tmp <> '' then
        slLic.Add(tmp)
      end;
// cache the newly retreived types to disk for later use
      slCats.SaveToFile('cats');
      slLic.SaveToFile('lic');
      end;
// Now that we have the codes we need to place them in the template
// Create <option> tags for each search and license elements
    cats := '<option value="" SELECTED></option>';
    lic := '<option value="" SELECTED></option>';
    for i := 0 to pred(slCats.Count) do
      cats := cats + Format('<option value="%s">%s</option>',
      [StringReplace(slCats[i],' ', '%20', [rfReplaceAll]), slCats[i]]);
// StringReplace is used to ESC encode the spaces in the code
```

```
    for i := 0 to pred(slLic.Count) do
    lic := lic + Format('<option value="%s">%s</option>',
    [StringReplace(slLic[i],' ', '%20', [rfReplaceAll]), slLic[i]]);
    finally
// Clean up after ourselves
    slCats.Free;
    slLic.Free;
    end;
// replace the appropriate tag with the appropriate list
    if TagString = 'CATEGORYS' then
        ReplaceText := cats;
    if TagString = 'LICENSE' then
        ReplaceText := lic;
end;
```

When the ppSearchHTMLTag event is called, the TagString parameter will be the transparent tag that we want to replace. Because both the CATEGORYS and LICENSE tags are going to be the option values of a select HTML element, we need to make sure we format the ReplaceText properly. Also, because there are some Categories with spaces in them, we are making sure that the spaces are converted to %20 so that they are transmitted properly. Figure 10.14 shows the culmination of these efforts and the search page generated:

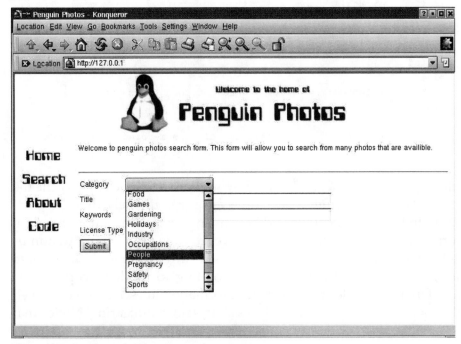

Figure 10.14   Penguin Photos search page.

When a user clicks the Submit button, the form data will be posted in the HTML header and sent to the /thumbs method of our Web application. For the OnAction event of the thumbs action we want to make sure that the user has provided some search parameters. If no search parameters are provided, then the Web service will return an empty set, so checking for parameters will once again eliminate extra, and in this case unnecessary, trips to the Web service. We can check to make sure data was selected on the form by reading in the Request.ContentFields. The content fields are a list of values that were returned from the Request in a Name=Value format. Because we know what the Names are, we just read in the Values property of the ContentFields. This code sample shows how to query those ContentField values:

```
procedure TWebModule1.WebModule1thumbsAction(Sender: TObject;
   Request: TWebRequest; Response: TWebResponse; var Handled: Boolean);
var
   cat, key, lic: string;
begin
// retreive the search parameters
   cat := Request.ContentFields.Values['Category'];
   key := Request.ContentFields.Values['Keywords'];
   lic := Request.ContentFields.Values['License'];
// Since Return thumbs may take awhile we will make sure there
// is something to search for
   if (cat <> '') or (key <> '') or (lic <> '') then
   begin
      if FileExists('thumbs.html') then
      begin
         ppThumbs.HTMLDoc.LoadFromFile('thumbs.html');
         Response.Content := ppThumbs.Content;
      end
   else
      Response.Content := 'Error: Could not load thumbs.html';
   end
   else
      Response.Content := 'You need to select something to search for';
end;
```

Although caching is a good thing, it would prove inefficient to cache the thumbnails returned from a search because it is unlikely that the exact same search would be repeated again anytime soon. After invoking ReturnThumbs, the OnHTMLTag event code for the ppThumbs PageProducer extracts the images from the XML document, saves them locally, and then creates an IMG tag pointing to the local copy of the image. Finally, the title and copyright information lines are added, as well as the company name and Web address if it is not a null string. Notice that the image tag is enclosed in an <a href> tag. This allows us to send the requested ImageID to the Result method that will be shown later.

Here is the HTML code with the THUMBS tag:

```
<html>
<head>
<title>Penguin Photo Search Results</title>
<meta http-equiv="Content-Type" content="text/html; charset=iso-8859-1">
</head>
<body bgcolor="#FFFFFF">
<p><b>Note: Clicking on a thumbnail will request a larger watermarked
image from the server.<br>This may take some time.</b><br></p>
<table width="85%" align="center">
<#THUMBS>
</table>
</body>
</html>
```

Here is the code that replaces the THUMBS tag with relevant information. Notice that the developer has to create the appropriate HTML, which gives some creation process to the developer.

```
procedure TWebModule1.ppThumbsHTMLTag(Sender: TObject; Tag: TTag;
    const TagString: String; TagParams: TStrings; var ReplaceText: String);
var
    s: string;
    Count, i: Integer;
    Image: string;
    Node: IXMLNodeList;
Begin
//'http://webservice.hutchingsphotography.com/
//    HutchingsImage.asmx/ReturnThumbs
//    ?Category=people&SubCategory=&LicenseCode=flat&Keywords=
//    &ThumbHeight=&ThumbWidth='
// invoke the Returnthumbs method of the web service
    XMLDocument.XML.Text := HTTP.Get(BuildHTTPPost('Returnthumbs',
        Request.ContentFields.Values['Category'],
        '',
        Request.ContentFields.Values['License'],
        Request.ContentFields.Values['Keywords'],
        '', ''));
// Parse the XML document
    XMLDocument.Active := True;
// Make sure we got something back
    if XMLDocument.DocumentElement.ChildNodes[1].HasChildNodes then
    begin
// Get all images that are returned from the count
// using ChildNode[1] to skip over the header information
```

```
// from the dot net web service
  Node := XMLDocument.DocumentElement.ChildNodes[1].
  ChildNodes[0].ChildNodes;
  Count := Node.Count;
  for i := 0 to pred(Count) do
  begin
      Image := Node[i].ChildNodes['ImageThumbnail'].Text;
// If there are not any more images then exit the loop
      if Image = '' then break;
      if (i mod 2) = 0 then // display the images two across
        s := s + '<tr><td align="center">'
      else
        s := s + '<td align="center">';
// Save the image to disk
      {$IfDef Win32} // use a Windows path
        Base64toJpeg(Image, '..\htdocs\img\' +
        Node[i].ChildNodes['ImageNumber'].Text + '.jpg');
      {$Else} // use a Linux path
        Base64toJpeg(Image, '../html/img/' +
        Node[i].ChildNodes['ImageNumber'].Text + '.jpg');
      {$EndIf}
// create the tag necessary to display the thumb and link
// to the results page
      s := s + Format('<a href="/cgi-bin/search/result?id=%s">'+
      '<img src="/img/%s" border="0"></a><br>',
        [Node[i].ChildNodes['ImageID'].Text,
         Node[i].ChildNodes['ImageNumber'].Text + '.jpg']);
      s := s + '<b>' + Node[i].ChildNodes['ShortTitle'].Text + '</b><br>';
      s := s + Node[i].ChildNodes['Copyright'].Text + '<br>';
// include copyright information
      if Node[i].ChildNodes['ArtistWebsite'].Text <> '' then
      begin
        s := s + Format('<a href="%s">%s</a><br>',
        [Node[i].ChildNodes['ArtistWebsite'].Text,
        Node[i].ChildNodes['ArtistCompany'].Text]);
      end;
      s := s + Format('<a href="mailto:%s">%s %s</a><br>',
        [Node[i].ChildNodes['ArtistEmail'].Text,
         Node[i].ChildNodes['ArtistFirstName'].Text,
         Node[i].ChildNodes['ArtistLastName'].Text]);
      // This has to be at the end to close the table
      if (i mod 2) = 0 then
        s := s + '</td>'
      else
        s := s + '</td></tr>';
      end;
  end
  else
      s := 'Sorry, no images came back';
```

```
    if TagString = 'THUMBS' then
        ReplaceText := s;
end;
```

Figure 10.15 shows the thumbnail result page generated in part by the preceding code.

If users select a thumbnail, they will be requesting a larger image. Because we coded our images to call the result Action of our Web application and to pass it the ImageID, we will be reading that from the Request Query Strings property. The resultAction event does what all other events have done thus far. If the template exists, it sends it to the user. If not, then it sends an error.

The OnHTMLTag event code for ppResult invokes ReturnImage to retrieve a larger, watermarked image along with more complete image

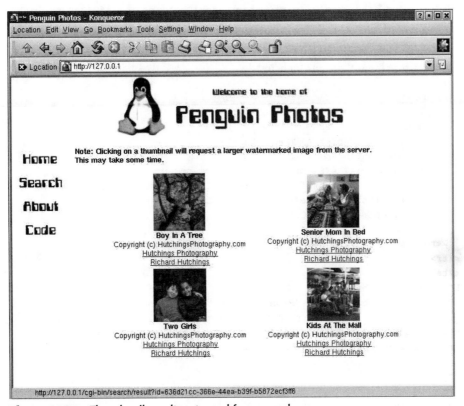

Figure 10.15 Thumbnail results returned from search.

information. Because of the size of the resulting XML document and the fact that there are multiple tags, each firing a separate event, we will cache the entire XML document locally. Then on future calls we check the freshness of the cached file. Once the image is extracted and decoded, then we replace the HTML-transparent tags with image tags and image information. This also improves performance if multiple users request the same image within a short period of time. The first request will be the only one invoking the Web service.

Here is the HTML template that supports the search results. This shows several tags placed by the designer, which puts more layout control in the designer's instead of the developer's hands:

```html
<html>
<head>
<title>Penguin Photo Search Results</title>
<meta http-equiv="Content-Type" content="text/html; charset=iso-8859-1">
<style type="text/css">
   pre { background-color: #e5e5cc; padding: 5px; font-family: Courier
   New; font-size: small; margin-top: -5px; border: 1px #f0f0e0 solid;}
</style>
</head>
<body bgcolor="#FFFFFF">
<table width="85%" align="center">
<tr>
   <td>
       Title: <b><#SHORTTITLE></b><br>
       Type: <#TYPECODE><br>
       Category: <#CATEGORYCODE><br>
       Resolution: <#RESOLUTIONCODE><br>
       Date: <#DATE><br>
       Artist: <a href="mailto:<#EMAIL>"><#NAME></a><br>
       Website: <a href="<#URL>"><#COMPANY></a><br>
       Copyright: <#COPYRIGHT><br>
   </td>
   <td><img src="/img/<#IMAGE>" border="0"></td>
</tr>
</table><p>
License photo:<br>
<input type="submit" name="Rights Protected" value="Rights
Protected"> <input type="submit" name="Flat Rate" value="Flat
Rate"> <input type="submit" name="Royalty Free" value="Royalty
Free"> <input type="submit" name="Custom" value="Custom">
<p>
<hr>
<P>
<p>The returning XML Document:<p>
<pre>
<#XML>
```

```
</pre></p>
</body>
</html>
```

Here is the code that invokes the ReturnImage method and replaces several tags. Figure 10.16 shows the final HTML page.

```
procedre TWebModule1.ppResultHTMLTag(Sender: TObject; Tag: TTag;
    const TagString: String; TagParams: TStrings; var ReplaceText: String);
var
    Node: IXMLNodeList;
    key: string;
    tmp: string;
    sFileName: string;
begin
    {This is showing that you can create a page without
    having a developer know html!
    There are more tags here, make more work for us
    but give the designer(s) more flexibility
    }
// Reference:
    // http://webservice.hutchingsphotography.com/HutchingsImage.asmx/
    //       ReturnImage?ImageID=636D21CC-366E-44EA-B39F-B5872ECF3FF6
    //       &ImageHeight=&ImageWidth=
    // Get the PhotoID from the request
    key := Request.QueryFields.Values['id'];
// we know that all the Image IDs are 36 bytes in size
    if Length(key) = 36 then
    begin
        sFileName := key+'.XML'; // XML cache file name
        // do we have a fresh cache of the result?
        if not (FileExists(sFileName) and not OldFile(sFileName)) then
        begin
// invoke the ReturnImage method of the web service
            XMLDocument.XML.Text := HTTP.Get(BuildHTTPPost('ReturnImage',
            key, '', '', '', '', ''));
            XMLDocument.XML.SaveToFile(sFileName); // cache it locally for later
        end
        else
            XMLDocument.XML.LoadFromFile(sFileName); // load from the cache
// parse the XML document
        XMLDocument.Active := True;
// Using ChildNode[1] to skip over the header information
// from the dot net web service
        Node := XMLDocument.DocumentElement.ChildNodes[1].
        ChildNodes[0].ChildNodes;
// We don't care how many images come back from the
// web service, we are only concerned with the first one [0]
        Image := Node[0].ChildNodes['Image'].Text;
```

```pascal
    if Image <> '' then
    begin
// image cache filename
      {$IFDEF Win32} // use a Windows path
      sFileName := '..\htdocs\img\' + key + '.jpg';
      {$Else} // use a Linux path
      sFileName := '../html/img/' + key + '.jpg';
      {$ENDIF}
// no need to reconvert the image if it is fresh in the cache
      if not (FileExists(sFileName) and not OldFile(sFileName)) then
      Base64toJpeg(Image, sFileName);
// replace the individual tags with the correct information
      if TagString = 'IMAGE' then
        ReplaceText := key + '.jpg';
      if TagString = 'SHORTTITLE' then
      begin
        tmp := Node[0].ChildNodes['ShortTitle'].Text;
        if Trim(tmp) = '' then
          tmp := 'N/A';
          ReplaceText := tmp;
      end;
      if TagString = 'TYPECODE' then
      begin
        tmp := Node[0].ChildNodes['TypeCode'].Text;
        if Trim(tmp) = '' then
          tmp := 'N/A';
          ReplaceText := tmp;
      end;
      if TagString = 'CATEGORYCODE' then
      begin
        tmp := Node[0].ChildNodes['CategoryCode'].Text;
        if Trim(tmp) = '' then
          tmp := 'N/A';
          ReplaceText := tmp;
      end;
      if TagString = 'RESOLUTIONCODE' then
      begin
        tmp := Node[0].ChildNodes['ResolutionCode'].Text;
        if Trim(tmp) = '' then
          tmp := 'N/A';
          ReplaceText := tmp;
      end;
      if TagString = 'DATE' then
      begin
        tmp := Node[0].ChildNodes['Date'].Text;
        if Trim(tmp) = '' then
          tmp := 'N/A';
          ReplaceText := tmp;
      end;
      if TagString = 'EMAIL' then
      begin
```

```
        tmp := Node[0].ChildNodes['ArtistEmail'].Text;
      if Trim(tmp) = '' then
        tmp := 'N/A';
      ReplaceText := tmp;
    end;
    if TagString = 'NAME' then
    begin
        tmp := Node[0].ChildNodes['ArtistFirstName'].Text + ' ' +
        Node[0].ChildNodes['ArtistLastName'].Text;
        if Trim(tmp) = '' then
            tmp := 'N/A';
            ReplaceText := tmp;
    end;
    if TagString = 'URL' then
    begin
     tmp := Node[0].ChildNodes['ArtistWebsite'].Text;
     if Trim(tmp) = '' then
        tmp := 'N/A';
        ReplaceText := tmp;
    end;
    if TagString = 'COMPANY' then
    begin
        tmp := Node[0].ChildNodes['ArtistCompany'].Text;
        if Trim(tmp) = '' then
            tmp := 'N/A';
            ReplaceText := tmp;
    end;
    if TagString = 'COPYRIGHT' then
    begin
        tmp := Node[0].ChildNodes['Copyright'].Text;
        if Trim(tmp) = '' then
            tmp := 'N/A';
            ReplaceText := tmp;
    end;
// just for fun we return the entire XML document to the user
    if TagString = 'XML' then
    begin
        tmp := Node[0].XML;
 // Format this for ALL browsers to view
        tmp := StringReplace(tmp, Image, 'Image Data', [rfReplaceAll]);
        tmp := StringReplace(tmp, '><', '&gt;@@br@@&lt;', [rfReplaceAll]);
        tmp := StringReplace(tmp, '>', '&gt;', [rfReplaceAll]);
        tmp := StringReplace(tmp, '<', '&lt;', [rfReplaceAll]);
// use @@br@@ so the above two functions
// do not replace the > and <
        tmp := StringReplace(tmp, '@@br@@', '<br>', [rfReplaceAll]);
        ReplaceText := tmp;
      end;
    end;
  end;
end;
```

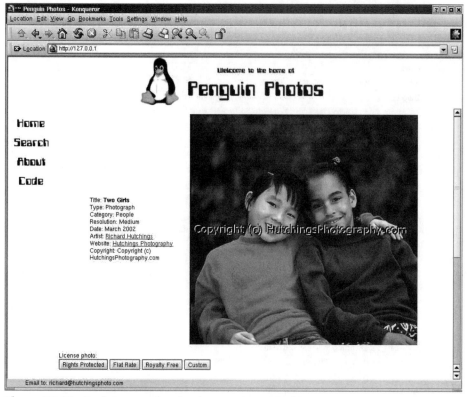

Figure 10.16   Review page showing large watermarked image.

Viewing a watermarked image, the user is able to decide whether to license the image. We follow a similar pattern as was shown previously. We create an HTML template for the page, create an Action with an OnAction Event, invoke the Web service, and replace any tags that need to get replaced, either with raw data or more HTML tags.

Apache Shared Modules

Once the CGI has been tested, we decided to create an Apache Shared Module. The shared module has additional advantages over the CGI application, including less memory consumption. These modules are much like an ISAPI extension, as shown in the following code.

First, here is the resulting project file when you select a CGI application:

```
program search;
{$APPTYPE CONSOLE}
```

```
uses
   WebBroker,
   CGIApp,
   webmod in 'webmod.pas' {WebModule1: TWebModule};
{$R *.res}
begin
   Application.Initialize;
   Application.CreateForm(TWebModule1, WebModule1);
   Application.Run;
end.
```

And here is the resulting project file when you select an Apache Shared Module:

```
library search_dso;
uses
   WebBroker,
   HTTPD,
   ApacheApp,
   webmod in 'webmod.pas' {WebModule1: TWebModule};
exports
   apache_module name 'search_module';
begin
   Application.Initialize;
   Application.CreateForm(TWebModule1, WebModule1);
   Application.Run;
end.
```

Because these two projects use the same Web module and Kylix can have both projects loaded at the same time, it is easy to switch between them.

NOTE Before you can get your Apache Shared Module to work with Apache, you need to rebuild Apache with shared module (DSO) support. This is well documented on the Apache site (http://httpd.apache.org/docs/install.html) as well as in the Kylix documentation.

Summary

Though Hutchings Photography and Penguin Photos are on two distinctly different platforms, integrating the two systems is possible. Using Kylix, the creation of our Linux Web application to consume the .NET Web Service was easy to do. At first there were a few bumps, thanks to Microsoft's proprietary formats and obscure implementations, but, thanks to using a tool as flexible as Kylix, we were able to still interact with the Web service to our business' advantage.

Because we are a small business that couldn't afford to waste money and time, Kylix turned out to be a great investment—allowing us to create our code and finished the application quickly and effectively on the Linux platform. Because of the RAD nature of Kylix, we were also able to rapidly prototype our application, which kept our managers happy. With Borland's ongoing support for SOAP, WSDL, and compatibility with the .NET platform, Kylix is a great tool for any Linux developer's toolbox.

Our implementation isn't the only way to use .NET Web services, but it meets our needs today. If for some reason we need to run on a Microsoft Windows machine in the future, the cross-platform compatibility of Kylix and Delphi allows us to easily load the same code up into Delphi 6 and compile it with zero trouble. For the purpose of this chapter, we made the changes necessary to the source so that it can be compiled in Delphi 6 or Kylix 2.

CHAPTER

11

Securing the Web Service

As of this writing, Web services have been around for about four years. As we mentioned in Chapter 1, the SOAP Toolkit was introduced to the public in 1998, allowing software developers to create Web services that shy away from special systems configurations that open up additional ports on your domain and possibly create security risks. Instead, they could use XML exchanged over port 80 to provide for a less hackable way of calling remote objects.

Security provides peace of mind, giving you the feeling that your objects and functionality don't lend themselves to revealing otherwise hidden source code or even compromising the system on which your application runs. In addition to the built-in security that separates it from its predecessors, the .NET Framework also integrates custom Web service authentication methods directly into the Web service itself. The XML-based Web.Config file is responsible for supplying security information to drive the Web service, as we'll see in this chapter.

Web.Config is stored in a virtual directory that is automatically created when the Web service solution is created. There can be only one Web.Config file per directory; however, each subfolder within the root virtual directory can have its own Web.Config file that overrides the configurations in the folder above it. The Web.Config file provides information about IIS authentication methods. It also occupies several of its own security and authentication settings. This chapter also discusses additional security features of Web services.

IIS Authentication Methods

The primary IIS authentication methods are Anonymous, Basic, and Digest. (See Figure 11.1.) Anonymous Authentication is the default.

Anonymous Authentication offers no true means of authentication. It is the least secure method that Microsoft offers to IIS Web servers, meaning anyone with the know-how can intercept your HTTP packet streams and see what you are seeing on the Internet. One way to protect the information you are sending to your users is to add SSL (Secure Sockets Layer) to encrypt the HTTP stream before it is sent to the user.

Basic Authentication is undoubtedly the most commonly used authentication method on IIS Web servers today. Web administrators choose a domain or realm to authenticate users, then users log in using their membership information.

The IIS Web Server then looks to that domain or realm to determine if the user that signed in has privileges to the folder in which the information is housed in the virtual directory that corresponds with the URL (Uniform Resource Locator) entered by the user. The downside is that the username and password supplied by the individual logging in are sent to the Web server in a plain-text format. Thus, someone with a TCP/IP packet sniffer

Figure 11.1 Available IIS authentication methods.

could potentially intercept your information and see your private credentials. For many sites where security is not really an issue but membership is, however, this is the perfect tool because it is so easy to deploy.

As with the Anonymous Authentication, you can employ SSL to create a secure environment while using this as a viable authentication method. Otherwise, your personal information can potentially be compromised by a hack.

After you choose the Basic Authentication setting in IIS, everything else is taken care of for you by the Microsoft Windows NTLM Challenge Response System. An example of the NTLM Authentication dialog box is shown in Figure 11.2.

Digest Authentication is new and requires clients to use Microsoft IIS 5.0 and the Web server to use Microsoft IIS 2000 in a Domain Server environment using Active Directory. It uses the HTTP 1.1 to offer an NTLM Challenge Response System that forces the username and passwords to be encrypted using MD-5 cryptography.

Digest Authentication exercises an arithmetic algorithm that is standard and well known to the client and the server. The product of this form of encryption is a fixed-length result, better known as a digest, that varies in size as the level of the encryption (such as 40-bit or 128-bit) is increased or decreased. If the level of encryption remains constant, then so will the size of the encryption result.

This method takes advantage of the user credentials and some other items to encrypt the information. This type of cryptography algorithm is a one-way hash, or irreversible encryption, meaning that even if others were to intercept this information in its plain-text form, they could not easily use the hash to impersonate you using normal HTTP techniques. Obviously they could not log in using the hash because the encryption method will encrypt their entered hash before sending the credentials, making them incorrect.

Figure 11.2 The Basic Authentication NTLM Challenge Response dialog box.

Individuals may have their doubts about the security of this authentication method because individuals who can sniff packets of information undoubtedly have the ability to inject an HTTP stream to a Web server in the same manner. But again, this type of encryption uses variables outside the username password credentials, making the hacker's computer-generated HTTP request incorrect.

Additional Authentication methods supplied by .NET include Forms Authentication, Integrated Windows Authentication, and Passport Authentication.

Forms Authentication. .NET Web services offer built-in Form-Level Authentication services through the use of the Web.Config file. This method of authentication allows you to supply the name of your Login.aspx file and contains redirections to other Internet applications if your login information is correct. In the past, Form-Level Authentication credentials were sent in a page, making them unsecured. Someone with the ability to spoof a Web site might be able to intercept your credentials and potentially impersonate you.

Fortunately, a passwordFormat property allows you to specify the type of cryptography that was used to store the credentials in a cookie, either SHA1 or MD-5. It also allows you to specify a clear property value if you do not wish to provide cryptographic capabilities to your login credentials.

The previous properties will not offer encryption to your application; instead, they offer you clues as to how the credentials were encrypted and what cryptographic technique is necessary to compare the value of the encrypted cookie to the credentials on the server.

Consequently, there is a protection property within the Forms Authentication Web.Config node that allows you to verify the credentials of a cookie using a 3DES cryptographic algorithm to transmit the credentials via HTTP from the client to the server, thereby offering a secure cryptographic product of the hash value of the credentials.

Another well-known method you can use to secure this form of authentication is SSL. SSL allows you to encrypt all page-level information from the client to the server. SSL supports a multitude of varying cipher suites.

Integrated Windows Authentication.   .NET Web services offer built-in Windows Authentication, whereby your name and password are verified using either Kerberos Authentication or the NTLM Challenge Response comparing the user's supplied credentials with the Windows Computer Management or Active Directory Membership Directory.

Windows Kerberos Authentication is automatically applied when a client is using a Microsoft Internet Explorer browser version 5.0 or later to authenticate against a Microsoft Windows 2000 or later Web application server using IIS as an authentication facilitator. Should the previous amalgamation not exist, then NTLM will automatically supply the login provisions for a user.

Integrated Windows Authentication uses the Kerberos protocol for encryption to pass a one-way hash, much like Digest Authentication. Integrated Windows Authentication will work with Internet Explorer from version 2 to the present and does not require Active Directory to work, unlike Digest Authentication.

Passport Authentication.   .NET Web services offer built-in Passport Authentication that allows you to use your existing Microsoft Passport Account as a PUID (Passport Unique Identifier) challenge against the credentials you supply in the Passport Login.

Passport data is protected using 3DES and SSL technology that is built into the Passport SSI (Single Sign-In) version 2.0 Service. Encrypted cookies allow you to navigate from site to site using your credentials without requiring you to log on to each new site.

Build Your Own Secure Web Service.   Let's consider an example to get a better feel for how to integrate Microsoft IIS security into a .NET Web service. Fire up your .NET IDE and choose the entries shown in Figure 11.3. Choose ASP.NET Web Service and change the name in the Location textbox from WebService1 (or whatever the next sequential default shows up in this textbox) to SecurityChapter.

You are taken to the Visual Basic .NET Design Environment. In the Solution Explorer Pane, you will see a default Web service by the name of Service1.asmx. Right-click this Web service, and click Properties in the pop-up menu. Using the File Name property, change the name of the Web service from Service1.asmx to SecurityChapter.asmx.

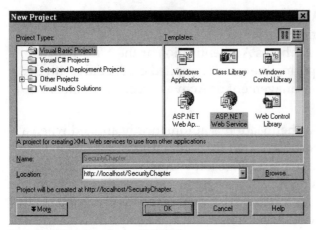

Figure 11.3   Creating a .NET Web service.

Understanding the Web.Config File

Next, in the Solution Explorer Pane, double-click the Web.Config file. This file exposes the configuration that controls many of the mechanisms about your Web service, including the following:

Dynamic Debug Compilation.   Debugging symbols are inserted into a page that is compiled through the .NET IDE. These symbols are used for debugging your application. If you are inexperienced with using symbols to debug an application that communicates with a Web service, visit www.microsoft.com/ddk/debugging/ for additional details. This site offers a download for Windows XP and Windows .NET Server Beta 3 debugging symbols, as well as being able to get them on the fly during your debugging session. Debugging Tools for Windows are also available for download. A download is also available for the Windows ME operating system.

Custom Error Messages.   Custom Error Messages allow you to use your own ASPX error-handling pages instead of the standard Microsoft error messages. You might want to manipulate this if you want to give your error messages a universal look and feel.

Authentication.   We discuss this property in this chapter. It allows you to designate different types of security, including those available in the IIS Authentication Methods dialog box as well as some of its own methods of authentication.

Authorization.   This property supplements the Authentication property. We will also use it as a security measure in the Web service that we build in this chapter. It permits you to authorize users by name, IP address, or group. Its properties resemble the properties you will find in the Security Accounts dialog box in the Microsoft Default FTP Site Properties box, where you can grant privileges to various site operators by a Member-Level or Group-Level relationship. It also offers properties similar to the Directory Security Tab of the FTP Site Property box, allowing you to permit or deny individuals based on their IP addresses, which can be handy if your Web site allows anonymous users.

Application-Level Trace Logging.   This property stores statistics for your ASPX Web page and gives you the ability to view these statistics as well as the lower-level details of each user's page hit. It uses the name of your application as part of the URL to retrieve the results of the file it stores, which is an AXSD file. To retrieve the statistics for the secure ASPX page that we will build on our SecurityChapter virtual directory, you will use the following URL: http://localhost/SecurityChapter.axsd.

Session State Settings.   Here you can define things such as whether your client is expected to support cookieless sessions, which is a SessionID that is placed within the URL as well as an identifier in the ASPX page to support cookieless sessions.

The stateConnectionString is also stored in this section. It allows you to store session state on your local server or on a remote server. The individual properties that it offers lend themselves to IP address and port settings used to connect to a remote machine or your own IP LoopBack address.

The sqlConnectionString allows you to store session state information in SQL Server by declaring it active and configuring the IP address and username and password to allow access to the database.

You can set the mode, which defines whether the state is being stored locally or remotely, here as well.

The Timeout property controls the duration that the session stays active. It is controlled in minutes via the Web.Config file, but it can also be overridden in your .NET source code where you can specify the duration in an array of different durations.

Globalization.   This refers to the encoding type that you expect to receive and remit to a caller. The default encoding type is UTF-8. You might notice that most Web services communicate via the UTF-8 protocol. You will generally want to use the UTF-8 encoding type in your Web services except under special circumstances.

Laying Down the Code

Now that we understand the individual properties associated with the Web.Config file, let's manipulate a few and build ourselves a secure Web service.

WARNING **If you are building your applications on a network domain controller, then you will want to read an article from Microsoft at the following URL before you start: http://support.microsoft.com/default.aspx?scid=kb; EN-US;q315158.**

Start by adding a Web Form to our solution. You can do this by clicking File on the Visual Basic .NET IDE and then, in the submenu that appears, clicking Add Project, New Project (see Figure 11.4).

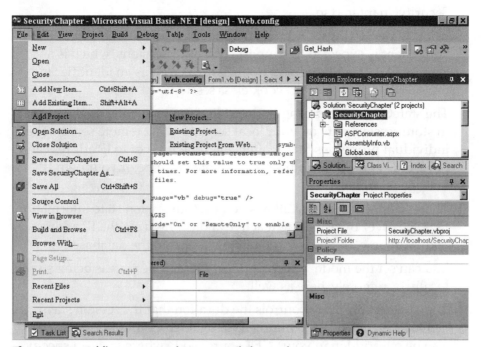

Figure 11.4　Adding a new project to an existing project.

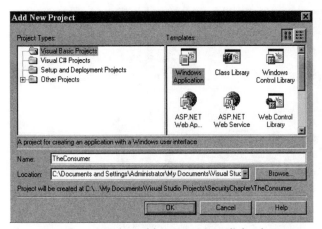

Figure 11.5   Using the Add New Project dialog box.

Next, click Windows Application and name the project TheConsumer (see Figure 11.5).

We now have a Visual Basic application that we can use to consume the returned information from our Web service. Even though the client and the Web server reside on the same machine, their content is stored in separate physical locations on the disk.

Now what we need is a Web service. We have the file; we just need the content, so double-click the SecurityChapter.asmx File in the Solution Explorer Pane, and the SecurityChapter.asmx.vb Design Window will appear (see Figure 11.6). Click the link that displays to reveal code for the file.

We are now in the Code View window. If you look closely at the commented code, you will see that Microsoft offers you a WebMethod as a template to leverage while building your .NET exposed Web methods.

All you need to do is uncomment the lines of code and change the function name, the input parameters, and the return value, then compile the code to have a Web service with an exposed Web method. So, let's copy the template and build our own .NET Web service from the template (see Figure 11.7).

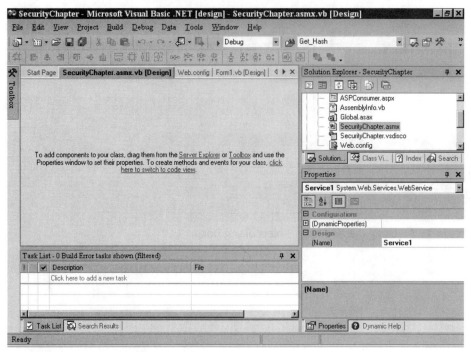

Figure 11.6 Getting to the Code View.

Listed here is the entire code used to create our Microsoft .NET Web service:

```
Imports System.Web.Services
<WebService(Namespace:="http://SecurityChapter.org/")> _
Public Class Service1
Inherits System.Web.Services.WebService
<WebMethod()> Public Function DataProvider(ByVal strGetInputAs String)
As String
```

Figure 11.7 Leveraging the WebMethod template.

```
    Select Case strGetInput
        Case Is = "Cole", "Tami", "Kyrstin", "G.A. Sullivan",
"John", "<<Your Name Here>>"
        DataProvider = "Welcome: " & strGetInput & ", thanks for " & _
"stopping by. The time is: " & CStr(Format(Now, "hh:mm AM/PM"))
    End Select
End Function
End Class
```

Testing Our Web Service

Let's test our new Web service. Either press the F5 key or click the standard Microsoft Run control on the IDE's icon bar, which is located just below the menu bar.

The first thing you see when you run the Web service is your class name and your Web method (see Figure 11.8), which together make up the Web service. You might want to change the class name from the default, Service1, to something more applicable to the Web methods that you include in your class. Note that your Web service could contain multiple classes and multiple Web methods. This is merely an example of how to build one. The code for the additional Web methods is the same as the first one.

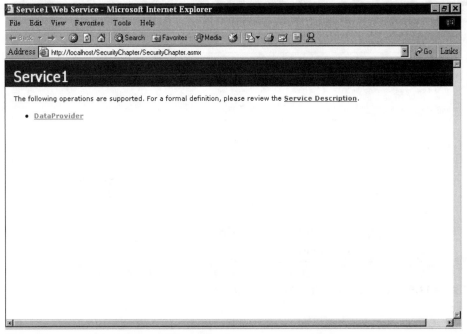

Figure 11.8   Displaying your Web method.

Now, click the DataProvider hyperlink, which takes you to a location in your virtual directory that will allow you to test the Web method you clicked (see Figure 11.9). Supply the input as one of the names you mentioned in the Select Case statement in your source code, and click the Invoke button. If we had a Web service that contained multiple parameters in our method, they would show up on top of one another in Figure 11.9. Furthermore, the lower half of the screen in Figure 11.9 demonstrates different ways you can invoke the Web service, including SOAP, GET, and POST, which are supportable types in IIS under the .NET Framework.

In Figure 11.10, the results of your Web service are displayed. This is the format that will be returned to the application that references and calls the Web method of this class.

Now that we know that the Web service works properly, it is time for us to add security to it. We can achieve this by modifying a single parameter in the Web.config file. Open that file, and scroll down to the Authorization property. Identify the location of the lines of code displaying the following:

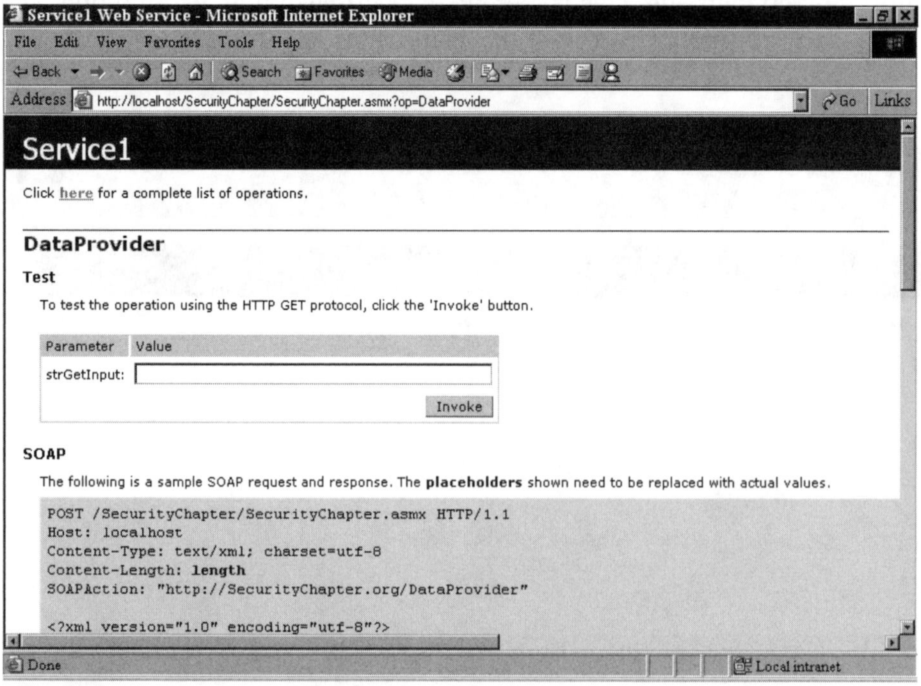

Figure 11.9 Supplying your Input parameter.

```
<authorization>

<allow users="*" /> <!-- Allow all users -->

<!-- <allow users="[comma separated list of users]"
   roles="[comma separated list of roles]"/>
   <deny users="[comma separated list of users]"
   roles="[comma separated list of roles]"/>
-->
</authorization>
```

Now, change these lines of code so that they resemble the lines of code that follow:

```
<authorization>
    <allow users="*" /> <!-- Allow all users -->
    <!-- <allow users="[comma separated list of users]"
    roles="[comma separated list of roles]"/>-->
    <deny users="?"
    roles="Users"/>
    -->
</authorization>
```

Now, run the application again, and notice the NTLM Response/Challenge. To run the Web service, you must log in using a valid Windows username and corresponding password credentials.

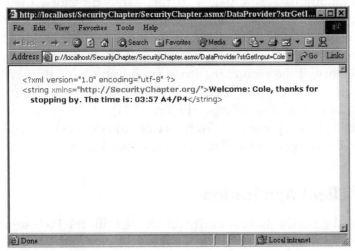

Figure 11.10 The test results.

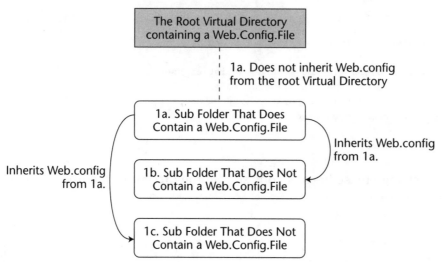

Figure 11.11   Web.Config inheritance structure.

What you have done in the preceding code is deny anonymous users under the Windows Security Account. The *?* symbolizes anonymous users, and the *** symbolizes everyone. By adding the question mark to deny users, you have affirmatively denied all anonymous users for the virtual directory that hosts the Web service.

If you added autonomous ASPX pages to this same directory, they would be subjected to the same form of authorization. So, if you wanted to supply a separate security scheme while still using the same virtual directory, then simply create a new Web.Config file in a secondary structure off the root virtual directory. If the secondary structure doesn't have its own Web.Config file, then it will become an heir to the Web.Config security information in the root virtual directory (see Figure 11.11).

Complete this section by building your Web service. You do this by clicking Build, Build The Consumer on the IDE menu bar. (See Figure 11.12.)

Build a VB.NET Client Application

Now that you know the basics about security and have built the Web service, let's hook our client application up to the Web service and test the

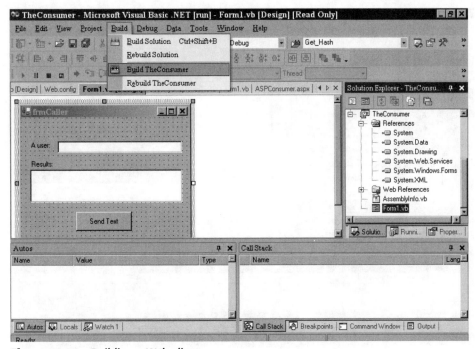

Figure 11.12 Building a Web client.

results. Open the Form1.vb file from the Solution Pane. Drag and drop the following objects on the form and change the properties to match those listed here:

Form1.   Name: frmCaller Text: frmCaller

Label1.   Name: lblUser Text: A user:

Label2.   Name: lblCallerResults Text: Results:

Textbox1.   Name: txtUser Text: [Nothing]

Textbox2.   Name: txtCallerResults Text: [Nothing]

Button1.   Name: cmdSendText Text: Send Text

Add a reference to the Web service by clicking Project, Project, Add Web Reference. See Figure 11.13. (You could have also added a reference by right-clicking the project in the Solution Pane and following the dialog.)

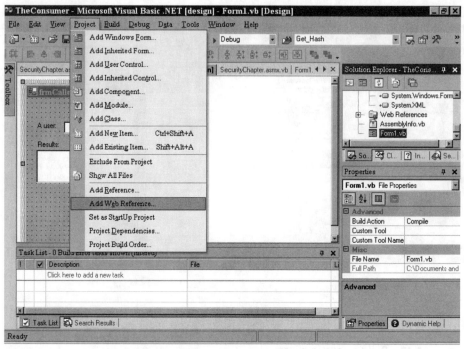

Figure 11.13 Adding a reference to a Web service.

When done, make sure that your Visual Basic form mirrors Figure 11.14. Next, finish adding the Web Reference by looking for the .asmx file that was generated by the building of our Web service in the Web Service Locator tool discussed in Chapter 7. Once you find the .asmx file, click Add Reference so that we can start writing code.

Figure 11.14 The Data Consumer form.

Double-click the cmdSendText button, which takes us to the Microsoft Visual Basic Code View. Add the following lines of code to the cmdSendText_Click Event:

```
Private Sub cmdSendText_Click(ByVal sender As _
System.Object, ByVal e As System.EventArgs) _
Handles cmdSendText.Click
Dim objWebService As localhost.Service1
objWebService = New localhost.Service1()
Dim strReturnString As String
    Try
        strReturnString = objWebService.DataProvider(Trim(txtUser.Text))
    Catch ex As Exception
       MsgBox(ex.Message.ToString)
    Finally
        txtCallerResults.Text = strReturnString
    End Try
Set objWebService = Nothing
End Sub
```

Build an ASP.NET Client Application

We will now build an ASP.NET application to test the security. Right-click the SecurityChapter Project on the Solution Explorer Pane of your IDE, and choose Add, Add New Item (see Figure 11.15).

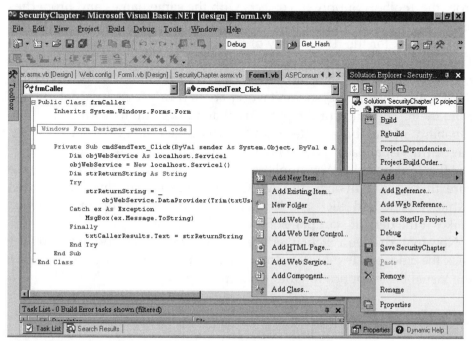

Figure 11.15 Adding an ASPX page to the SecurityChapter virtual directory.

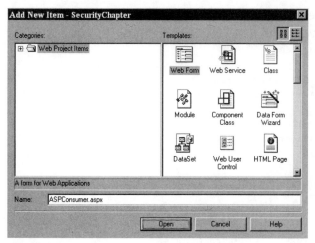

Figure 11.16   Giving a name to the ASP consumer.

In the Add New Item dialog box, choose Web Form and name the object ASPConsumer.aspx (see Figure 11.16). Click Open; the new .aspx page will be added to the SecurityChapter Virtual Directory.

Add the same objects to the .aspxConsumer.aspx page as we did on the TheConsumer.vb form by dragging and dropping the Web Forms Objects from the Toolbox. Supply the objects with the same names and properties as we did with the TheConsumer.vb Form.

Don't look for the ID Property of the ASPX page, because it isn't there. The name of the .aspx page serves as its ID. Just work with properties of the labels, textboxes, and the button. The default text of the textboxes in .NET is already nothing, so don't worry about trying to remove default text from them. The name of the property that allows you to set the multiline capability of the lblCallerResults Object is called TextMode in ASP.NET pages. (In Visual Basic .NET it is called the Multi-Line Property.)

After building the Web application, it should like Figure 11.17. Make sure that you right-click the ASPConsumer.aspx page in the Solution Explorer Pane and click Set As Start Page in the pop-up menu, which makes it the default start page of the entire Solution.

Now that we have a client interface, let's add the server-side code. Double-click the cmdSendText button, then copy and paste the code we wrote for the Visual Basic application into the .aspx application.

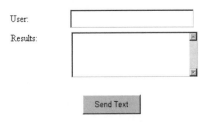

Figure 11.17 The ASPX consumer page.

After that, you make a couple of minor modifications to the variable you declare that references the Web service object. Use the code that follows as a guide. The highlighted text denotes the changes between the code in your Visual Basic application and the Visual Basic code behind the .aspx web form:

```
Private Sub cmdSendText_Click(ByVal sender As System.Object,
ByVal e As System.EventArgs)
Handles cmdSendText.Click
Dim objWebService As SecurityChapter.Service1
objWebService = New SecurityChapter.Service1()
Dim strReturnString As String
   Try
      strReturnString = _
      objWebService.DataProvider(Trim(txtUser.Text))
   Catch ex As Exception
      MsgBox(ex.Message.ToString)
   Finally
      txtCallerResults.Text = strReturnString
   End Try
Set objWebService = Nothing
End Sub
```

Testing the .aspx Web Form Client

Now let's run the ASPX application by pressing F5 to reach the Windows Challenge/Response NTLM Dialog Box. (See Figure 11.18.)

Enter your domain username and password into the dialog box, and click OK. You should see the .aspx page. Now enter *Kyrstin* as the user. You should see the information shown in Figure 11.19.

Figure 11.18   The Basic Authentication NTLM Challenge Response dialog box.

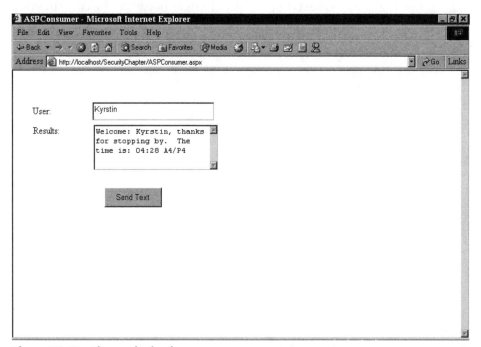

Figure 11.19   The results for the .aspx page.

Testing the Visual Basic .NET Application

Next, make sure you set the TheConsumer.vb Project as the StartUp Project. (See Figure 11.20.)

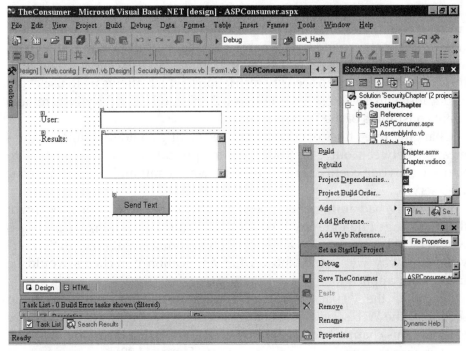

Figure 11.20 Setting the Startup Project.

Now let's test the results by executing the application. Try to enter a user and send the text to the Web service. Whoops, you are greeted with failure! (See Figure 11.21.)

The reason for this unexpected event is that the Web service has no way of knowing who or what the client application is. Trying to raise the NTLM Challenge Response dialog box from an application on a remote computer is difficult to do, especially if the application is COBOL on an SCO UNIX machine.

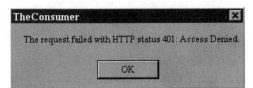

Figure 11.21 Access is denied!

The point of security consists not only of implementation, but also careful planning. If you intend to implement security on your Web site, know who your clients are and have a game plan that will allow you and them to succeed. The Hutchings Photography Web site is an excellent example of this. Currently, it has no security restrictions, which allows us to use client applications like Microsoft Visual Basic .NET and Borland Kylix as remote client consumers of the Web service.

Changing three lines of code in the Web.Config could sabotage communication between our client and server applications. It is important to know who your clients are and how they are communicating with your Web service.

Obviously, had authorization been enabled in the Web.Config section of the Hutchings Photography Web service from the beginning, .aspx pages would have been created to allow consistent communication with that service. This way we would know what application our clients would be using—our application.

To enable the Visual Basic .NET application, go into the Web.Config section of the Web service and change the security setting we put in place earlier in this chapter to allow anonymous users, using the following code. Try running the application once again (see Figure 11.22):

```
<authorization>
   <allow users="*" /> <!-- Allow all users -->
   <!-- <allow users="[comma separated list of users]"
      roles="[comma separated list of roles]"/>
      <deny users="[comma separated list of users]"
      roles="[comma separated list of roles]"/>
   -->
</authorization>
```

Figure 11.22 Visual Basic .NET allowing all users.

Allowing and Denying Users and Groups

You now know the authentication limitations between Visual Basic.NET and its ASP.NET counterpart. Let's look at how to allow and deny members based on their Group affiliation.

Using Administrative Tools, Computer Management, add two new members, Josephine and Mary Lou. Add them to the Users Group. Then, edit the Web.Config file to allow the Group Hiawatha to access the Web service.

```
<authorization>
    <!--<allow users="?" /> Allow all users -->
    <allow users="JosephineM"/>
    <!-- <allow roles=""/>-->
    <deny users="?"/>
    <!-- roles="Users"/> -->
</authorization>
```

Try this out by running the application and logging in as this new member. Also try changing the role to either allow or deny the Users Group.

Summary

There are many different types of authentication available to use with .NET and IIS. IIS offers authentication methods such as Basic and Digest. SSL can be incorporated with these types of authentication to make them more secure.

In addition, the .NET Framework includes other ways to authenticate and authorize an individual that can increase the security of a Web page or Web service. The available methods of authentication using the .NET Web.Config file are Windows, Forms, and Passport.

Basic Windows Authentication is the most widely used form of authentication. It is less secure than other forms of authentication, but not every Web service or Web site requires the highest level of security.

The IIS Internet Services Manager is one way that you can set permissions for authentication and authorization. The other way is through manipulating the Web.Config file. This increases mobility because the Web.Config file is in XML and can be modified on the fly without compromising the stability of your Web service.

It is fairly easy to build your own Web service to support a wide array of different users. Web services support various HTTP communication types, such as SOAP, GET, and PUT, making it more malleable for developers on other platforms and for software development tools to access .NET Web services.

In addition to authentication and authorization, the Web.Config file hosts many different ways to add life to your Web site, including the ability to direct session state, statistical analysis of your Web service or Web site, data connectivity option, cookieless sessions, and more.

Testing the Web Service/
Performance Optimizations

So, you got your Web service running, it returns the right data, you registered it at www.xmethods.com, and you even have it on a production server. There is nothing else for you to do, right?

Because you made it this far, we're going to assume that you understand the need for testing or at least want to know more about what can be done. We hate to throw out a cliché, but spending the time now will save you time later. There's always a project or sales manager pushing for a product to get out the door. Then it is released too early, and there are several issues with the product that could have been resolved earlier. Sure, the product works great in-house with 5 to 10 users, but what happens when the product is used by hundreds, if not thousands, of clients? Performance testing is an important part of the development cycle.

Performance

There are several issues to take into consideration when optimizing performance. A Web service should be thought of as just another Web application.

Things that you would do to optimize a Web application and a Web service are much the same. We'll go into some detail of what those things are.

Web Service Clients

Web services do nothing without some form of a client. This can be an end-user application, Web browser, or another, consuming Web service. Because Web service clients are what the end user will interact with, performance is important. Users want information, and they want it now. But how can this be done?

Asynchronous Service Calls

The easiest way to consume Web services is by using synchronous calls; that is, your application waits for one call to come back before working on the next one. For some applications this is sufficient and maybe even preferable. Anything traveling over the Web is, almost by definition, slow—at least from the perspective of the CPU. If you happen to be making a large number of calls to any number of Web services you should use asynchronous service calls. Asynchronous service calls invoke a Web service, then move on, performing some form of work or invoking another Web service method. With asynchronous calling, the main or invoking process may not be able to guarantee when the remote operation is complete. This generally results in an increase in code complexity, but your application can become far more efficient.

There are several good times to use asynchronous method calls. Consider the following:

The main process of the application is controlling a user interface. If your application is using synchronous calling, the user interface will seem to freeze until the calling process returns.

The calling method takes a large amount of time.   Calling it asynchronously will let your application move on to other nonessential processing.

The client application needs to make one or more calls to remote services.   Calling several services at once will take less time.

This may sound like something that every client application should implement, but not all applications will benefit from asynchronous method calls. A Web service that returns a user identification number, then requires that identification number for all other subsequent method calls wouldn't work. You do not know what the identification number is, so you cannot make the next call.

In the old Windows way of programming, creating multithreaded applications could become a daunting task; but thanks to some new objects in .NET, this has been simplified. To make an asynchronous call, .NET provides a new object type called IAsyncResult that handles much of the complexity for us. Declaring a variable of type IAsyncResult is an object that polls for completion and is used to return the results of a method call. The code used to consume one of the Hutchings Photography Web services is shown here:

```
IAsyncResult Async;
com.hutchingsphotography.webservice.HutchingsPhotographyWebService serv
= new com.hutchingsphotography.webservice.HutchingsPhotographyWebService();
lblStat.Text = "Processing";
Async = serv.BeginReturnThumbs(textCat.Text, textSub.Text,
textLice.Text, textKey.Text, "", "", null, null);
while (Async.IsCompleted == false)
{
// We can go and do something else here
lblStat.Text = lblStat.Text + ".";
}
lblStat.Text = "Finished";
DS = serv.EndReturnThumbs(Async);
```

This code is similar to the synchronous calling method, but instead of calling and waiting for the service to return, the IAsyncResult object returns from the call immediately. The IsCompleted property returns True when the asynchronous operation has completed.

Callbacks

Another way to use asynchronous calling in your client applications is to use callbacks. Notice that two additional parameters were passed into the ReturnThumbs method; both of them were set to null. The first parameter is actually a reference to a callback function, and the second is used to pass information about the asynchronous state. To create and use a callback is relatively simple, especially if you've used Win32 API callbacks before.

First, you need to create a callback function. Pay special attention to the signature of the callback function. Note that it returns a void and takes a System.IAsyncResult as a parameter.

```
private void MyCallBack(System.IAsyncResult Result)
{
DS = serv.EndReturnThumbs(Result);
}
```

To call it, we just change the way we call BeginReturnThumbs to add the new parameter, this callback function:

```
AsyncCallback Mine = new AsyncCallback(MyCallBack);
Async = serv.BeginReturnThumbs(textCat.Text, "", "", "", "",
"", Mine, null);
```

When the method is complete at the server, MyCallBack will be called. It won't be this easy if you're not using .NET. The .NET Framework does quite a bit under the covers to make this work.

Web Service Servers

There are literally thousands of things to optimize to make sure that your Web service is running optimally. We can't mention all the ways in this book, but we will mention several that will put you on the right path.

Error Handling

Errors occur in software programs. Error-free code is extremely rare—there are so many elements that it becomes impossible to track down all of them. What matters is what happens after an error occurs. Does our Web service take it in stride, or does the error shut down the service?

One of the basic elements in handling errors is checking values. If you create a Web method and it asks for an integer between 1 and 100, you will likely get numbers outside that range. What happens when you do not get an entire SOAP packet? Network errors happen, and we shouldn't assume anything. If we don't get what we need, by all means ask for the information again. Bounds testing and error checking are especially important.

Because writing code to check for every possible situation isn't possible, one thing that we have in our tool box is the Try-Catch-Finally statement. Because Exceptions are Thrown, we want to Try a piece of code, Catch the errors, and Finally do things that need to be done whether or not we received an error. The Try-Catch statement looks like this:

```
try
{
// "TRY" to run some code here
//   This is where an exception could be raised.
}
// Any number of Catch blocks can go here for specific errors
catch (Exception e)
{
// All exceptions descend from Exception -- catches any exception
```

```
// You can actually catch many different types of exceptions
// here simply by using multiple Catch statements.
}
finally
{
// Clean up after ourselves
// This executes regardless of whether we had an exception
}
```

If there is any error thrown in the Try block, the system searches for the associated Catch block in the order that they appear in application code until it locates a Catch block that handles the exception. A Catch block handles the exception if the type is the same or derives from the exception thrown. If there is no Catch block, the exception is then passed up the call stack. If the exception gets to the top of the call stack and there is no matching catch that handles the exception, the default exception handler handles it and the application terminates. This is not what we want our Web service to do! We want to catch the exception somewhere in our Web service code and return information back to the client, not crash our Web service completely.

The Exception object has several useful members to help us determine what caused the error:

Message.   This is the error message that explains the reason for the exception.

Source.   This is the name of the application or object that caused the error.

StackTrace.   This describes the content of the call stack, with the most recent method call appearing first. The stack trace is captured immediately *before* an exception is thrown.

ToString.   This is the most user-friendly version of the error message.

The Try-Catch-Finally statement is structured exception handling, meaning you can have one or more associated handlers specifying the type of exception to handle. This is different from previous, pre-.NET versions of Visual Basic, which used the unstructured On Error statement.

One feature of the Try-Catch-Finally statement is that you can choose to consciously throw another exception from within the Catch block. It will then move up the stack until some other Catch block can handle it.

NOTE Do not initialize variables inside a Try block because the Try block is not guaranteed to be completely executed. An exception can occur before the block is completed. The result is a compiler error.

Scoping the Results

Scoping the results deals with making sure the data that you are sending your clients is data they need. That last statement may sound obvious, but there are a couple of items worth noting. Let's take into consideration the overused travel agency scenario.

You've provided a Web service that lets users authenticate who they are and book a trip (providing airfare, car rental, and lodging). What happens when you get a user that just wants to rent a car or just book a flight? You don't want to have your Web service returning additional information that the user doesn't need. This forces the server to do extra work—time that could be put to use on another process.

Instead of providing one Web method that returns flight, car, and hotel information, you can create three additional ones. These additional methods return only the flight, car, or the hotel information. Internally these Web methods can be calling the same functions, but the additional method limits the return to what is needed by the client. This prevents unnecessary processing on the server and reduces the number of data packets traversing your network.

If you choose to create additional Web methods that limit the scope of a response, it can still be a good idea to include a monolithic one as well. You don't want to create a Web service that requires the same information (user authentication, for instance) to be passed again and again for a common Web service method call. Having a broad number of Web services, including ones that conglomerate the most-often-used methods, limits repeated trips to the server.

Remote Dependencies

If at all possible, try to limit the number of remote dependencies of other Web services when designing and implementing your Web service. Clients can access those remote Web services just as easily as you can. Because they can use asynchronous callbacks, it would end up being more beneficial for them because they wouldn't be waiting for you and because it removes the extra overhead from your Web service. The clients will also be able to make the calls they need and not the ones that you think they want.

If at all possible, host every Web service that is necessary for your Web service to run on the same server because network connections can be plagued with trouble at any given moment. If your Web service has to make several trips to other servers, your performance will degrade exponentially as traffic increases. At a minimum, make sure that the Web services are on the same domain or are near each other in the same physical location. At last resort, if you must call a Web service hosted by another firm somewhere on the Internet, be sure you have good error handling.

IIS Server Configuration

There are a number of things to take into consideration when configuring your Web server for improved performance. Following are some observations on what you may be experiencing and on things to think about when implementing your Web service.

Logging

By default, IIS keeps a log of all the visits or requests to your server. This can help your system administrator track practically everything. While this can be a good thing, file I/O processes consume a large number of CPU processes. If you choose to keep a log file, make sure you're capturing only the information you need. IIS 5.1 gives you plenty of logging options that can bring your Web server to its knees. One option in particular that you should watch out for is on the option to log the host Extended Logging Properties. This performs a reverse DNS lookup for every machine that connects to your Web service. While this can be useful for tracking mischievous users of your Web service, this takes time and precious CPU cycles. (See Figure 12.1.)

Keep-Alive

Keep-alive is an HTTP specification that allows for greatly enhanced server performance. By default, an HTTP client connects to a server and makes its request; then the connection is closed. If the client has to make several

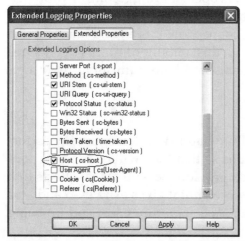

Figure 12.1   Extended Logging Properties with HOST option checked.

Figure 12.2   HTTP keep-alives enabled and set to a 900-second timeout.

requests to a server to get what it needs, the client has to make several connections. This takes time on the server as well as the client because several
separate connections may need to be made for each element. These additional requests and connections require more server activity and resources,
decreasing server efficiency. (See Figure 12.2.)

Because keep-alive is enabled by default, you may want to check on the
amount of time that the connection stays open. During testing of your Web
service, check the amount of time it takes for your Web service to respond
across a high-latency (slow) network connection. It is a good idea to make
sure that the timeout is at least equal to this amount of time. This ensures
that the client's connection is not terminated before finishing the use of
your Web service.

Performance Options

IIS runs as a service on Windows. By default, Windows gives a performance boost to foreground applications so that they will be more respon-
sive to the end user. Windows XP also provides several visual effects that
will degrade performance on a Web server, but it gives extra eye candy for
the user of the machine. Because your Web server may just end up being

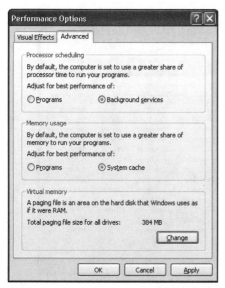

Figure 12.3   Advanced performance options.

locked in a server room, this is unnecessary and can be turned off. IIS performance can be improved by disabling these extras. To get the Performance Options on Windows XP, right-click My Computer and select Properties. Select the Advanced tab, then click the settings button under the Performance section. On the Visual Effects tab, make sure the option Adjust for Best Performance is selected. If you select the Advanced tab, you should then see a dialog box like the one in Figure 12.3.

Under the processor scheduling section, make sure the Adjust for best performance of option is set to Background services. You may also want to consider setting the Memory usage to System cache rather than to Programs. If your machine is set up to be a server, setting the memory usage to System cache will improve IIS. Setting it to Programs will allow your applications to run faster; but because IIS is a server and not an application, this will not benefit your Web service.

Unnecessary Applications and Services

Running other processor-intensive applications on the same machine that is running IIS will also degrade system performance. Applications like Exchange and File and Print Services should be placed on a separate server so that IIS has full control of your server's resources.

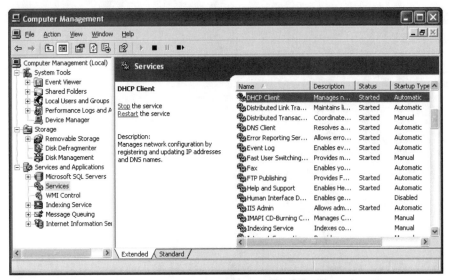

Figure 12.4 The Services snap-in in Computer Management.

By default, Windows installs several services that are not necessary for the performance and use of your Web service, or more specifically IIS. (See Figure 12.4.) These services should be stopped and set to start manually or disabled entirely. This does not mean that you need to go through the list of services and stop everything. You should be fully aware of the service dependencies *before* you begin to disable any services. A good practice is to disable one service, then monitor the effect it has on your system.

You can open up the Service Properties and select the Dependencies tab (see Figure 12.5). This will show you any other services that depend on the service you have selected as well as any other services on which the selected service depends.

The following services are not required on a dedicated IIS server. You may have other unnecessary services running that were installed along with other products. Finding those services that are unnecessary for you and your particular installation is a matter of trial and error.

Alerter.   Notifies selected users of administrative alerts.

ClipBook.   Enables ClipBook to store information with remote computers.

DHCP Client.   Manages network configuration by registering and updating IP addresses and DNS names.

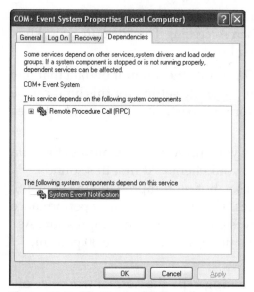

Figure 12.5   The Dependencies tab.

Human Interface Devices Access.   Enables hot buttons on multimedia devices.

Messenger.   Transmits Net Send and Alerter services messages between clients and servers.

Net Logon.   Supports pass-through authentication of account logon events for computers in a domain.

Network DDE.   Provides network transport and security for DDE.

Network DDE DSDM.   Manages DDE network shares.

Print Spooler.   Loads files to memory for laser printing.

TCP/IP NetBIOS Helper.   Enables support for NetBIOS over TCP/IP.

Workstation.   Creates and maintains client network connections to remote servers.

Additional Optimizations

There are other areas to consider when improving the performance of your IIS server, including the following:

SSL or Secure Socket Layer slows the performance of IIS significantly.   SSL should be used only with those Web services where needed. To make sure SSL is removed for a particular virtual directory, uncheck the Require Secure Channel When Accessing This Resource checkbox on the Secure Connections dialog box.

Enable bandwidth throttling.   This limits the amount of data that the Web service can dish out. The appropriate setting for this limit can be found only after trial and error for your particular server and Internet connection speed.

HTTP Compression.   This allows your IIS server to compress the data to reduce the download time for your clients. At first this sounds great and may be an option you set, but by compressing the data, IIS will take additional CPU resources. This in itself can affect performance and eliminate any benefit that was gained from the compression. As a general rule, if your CPU utilization is already above 80 percent, compression should not be used.

Allow connection and resource pooling.   By the normal workings of TCP/IP, a server will open up a connection when a client requests one. What you can do with IIS is create a pool of connections, so when a client requests a connection it is immediately given one from the pool. This also makes DLLs from Web services easier to reference and speeds connections to databases.

Use the cache whenever possible.   Caching pages on the server can keep the server from having to process repeat requests. For instance, in the Hutchings Photography Web service, we can have the server cache the ReturnReferenceTables response because that will more than likely not change between client requests. This will prevent the server from having to perform the database lookups for each individual client.

Component Services

Component Services or COM+ is a developer tool for building three-tiered transactional Web applications. Using Component Services you can integrate and manage clients, servers, and database connections. For example, you can use component services to manage ODBC connections to provide high-performance database access as well as share these data sources among users.

The core of component services is the Microsoft Distributed Transaction Coordinator, which manages transactions. Transactions are groups of business processes that must succeed or fail together. Think of transactions when you go to the ATM banking machine. You enter your ATM card and your PIN, then withdraw or deposit money. If the ATM machine subtracts the amount of money from your account but then is unable to disburse the money to you, the transaction has to be cancelled. That is, the amount you desired to withdraw is then added back into your account. If any portion to the transaction fails, the whole transaction must fail, and any completed portions must be rolled back.

Web services are managed by COM+. You can use this fact to your advantage. Your Web service can be run with three different levels of protection. (See Figure 12.6.) Select the level of application protection by selecting your Web service in IIS administration, then going into the properties for it. Here are the three levels:

Low (IIS Process).   This means that your Web service is running in the same process space as IIS; if your Web service crashes, IIS goes down with it. Basically, this means that there is no protection for an out-of-control Web service.

Medium (Pooled).   This allows your Web service to be pooled with other applications, but separate from IIS.

High (Isolated).   This option sets your Web service as an isolated process in it own address space, managed by Component Services.

Having your Web service under the control of COM+ allows COM+ to restart your Web service if it fails. As mentioned, if your Web service goes out of control, it is possible to stop it and still keep your Web server (IIS) running.

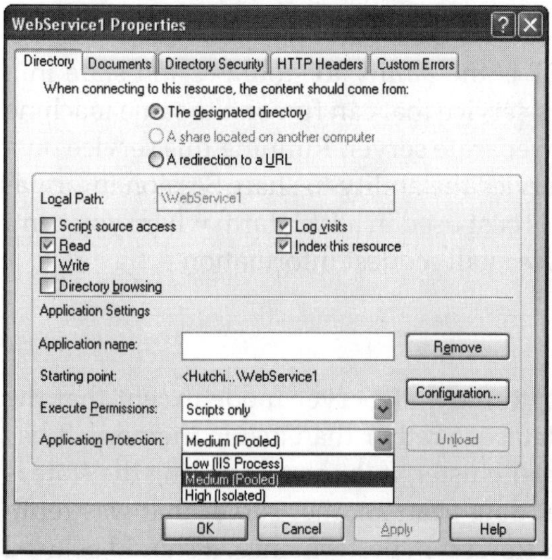

Figure 12.6   Component Services options for your Web service.

Session Management

Session management in Web services is a performance implication that you should consider carefully. With .NET, session management is easier, but that doesn't mean you should use it indiscriminately. The .NET runtime treats Web services as a type of ASP.NET Web application, so your Web services have access to the same state management functionalities as other ASP.NET applications. In many cases you won't need to manage Session state in your Web service; Session management is disabled by default. Because Session state management can have a serious impact on system performance, access to the Session object is enabled only at the method level. You should disable access to Web service methods that do not require access to the Session object to improve performance.

If for some reason you have to keep Session state in your Web service, you need to figure out how you will store that Session state. There are three general options to storing session state: in-process, StateServer, and the SQL Server method. Each of these options is discussed in a separate section next.

In-Process Mode

With in-process Session state, state is managed in process and, if the process is restarted, then the state is lost. This is the fastest way to store session information, but it should be used only in those situations when the user is guaranteed to hit a single server or will always be redirected to the same server (as in a Web farm), or when session data is not critical.

StateServer Mode

One of the new features in .NET is the ability to store Session state in a StateServer mode. StateServer is a service that can run on the same machine as the Web server or on a totally separate server. Running this service on a separate machine gives a Web service the ability to share Session information in a Web farm. This method is best used in a Web farm where you can't guarantee from which server a user will request information.

SQL Server Mode

The SQL Server mode is similar to the StateServer mode except that the state is stored in a SQL Server database rather than just in memory. It has the benefit of being in a SQL Server cluster; if the server storing the state is unavailable, it could request that data from another server that was replicating the data. This option is the slowest in performance. It should be used when the reliability of the data is pertinent to the Web service.

Session state can easily be handled in .NET, but it is often best to design your Web service using a stateless model. You will notice better performance and will not have to worry if your Web service needs to scale out to a Web farm.

Performance Tools and Monitoring

There are several things you can do to optimize, but how do you determine what needs to be optimized? Luckily for you, both Windows and .NET provide tools that can make it easy to view what is going on in your system. Let's explore these tools in the following sections.

Event Viewer

At first glance the Event Viewer may not seem to be all that useful for monitoring system performance. The Event Viewer (see Figure 12.7) displays information about hardware, software, and system problems as well as security events. The Application log contains events logged by application or services. The Security log records events such as valid and invalid logon attempts. The System log contains events logged by Windows system components, such as a failed driver during system startup. Using the Event Viewer, you can check for error messages regarding applications that are not responding. It can also show reasons for poor system performance.

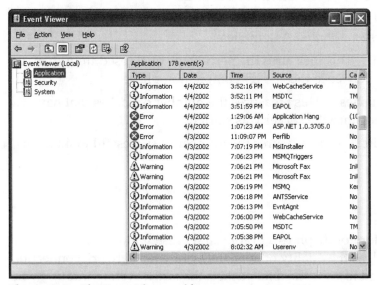

Figure 12.7 The Event Viewer with some error messages.

System Monitor

The System Monitor (see Figure 12.8) can take snapshots of your systems performance at selected intervals. The System Monitor uses counters to track the usage of system resources. You'll find that more than 85 .NET-specific object monitors have been added to your system after the .NET Framework is installed. Some of the counters you may be interested in are these:

Memory Pages/Sec.   This measures the rate at which pages are read from or written to disk to resolve hard page faults. If your system is accessing the disk for information, access will be much slower. You should want this to be less than 15 pages per second.

Memory Available Bytes.   This measures the amount of physical memory, in bytes, available to processes running on the computer. This value should never go below 8 MB.

Memory Committed Bytes.   This measures the amount of committed virtual memory, in bytes. This value should never go above 75 percent.

% Processor Time.   This is the percentage of elapsed time that the processor spends to execute a non-Idle thread. This value should be below 75 percent.

System Processor Queue Length.   This is the number of threads in the processor queue. This shows ready threads only, not threads that are running. The value should not be above 2.

CLR Rate of Classes Loaded.   This measures the number of classes loaded per second in all Assemblies.

% Time in JIT.   This measures the percentage of elapsed time spent in JIT compilation since the last JIT compilation phase.

File Cache Flushes.   This measures the number of caches that have been flushed since the server was started.

File Cache Hits.   This measures the number of successful lookups in the cache.

Network Monitor

The Network Monitor displays a graphical representation of network performance as well as the quality of availability of your network connection. It can also be used to view the data packets that are traveling through your network.

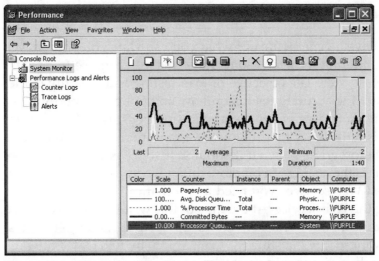

Figure 12.8   The System Monitor tracking pertinent system resources.

Task Manager

The Task Manager (Figure 12.9) can track the running processes on your system. You can also use it to view the resources that the processes are using. Unlike the System Monitor, which shows snapshots of your data, the Task Manager shows an immediate overview of system activity and performance as well as statistics about memory and processor performance. Task Manager can also be used to stop running processes, change the base priority of a process (give your Web server a boost here), or set the process to run on a particular processor (if your system has more than one).

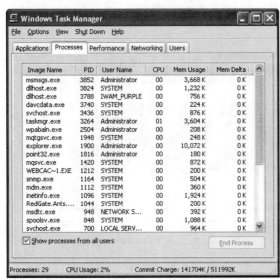

Figure 12.9   The Windows Task Manager displaying system information.

Web Service Stress Testing

Now that you have a general idea of what you can watch on your server, you may be wondering if there is something that you can use to test and check your Web service. The objective of load testing is to identify bottlenecks and to provide accurate results on how an application performs so that there are no surprises when the application goes live. With regular applications it is rather easy to test how the application works. You click a button. Does the program do what it should? If so, click the next button. With Web services the testing is a bit more difficult because there is no user interface. To test Web services you need a tool that can simulate multiple users accessing the Web service. At the time of this writing, there were two primary tools to test your Web service: Microsoft Application Center Test (ACT) and Advanced .NET Testing System (ANTS) by Red Gate Software. Each of these tools is discussed separately in a following section.

ACT

ACT comes with .NET Enterprise Architect Edition. It provides a simple interface for testing your Web service. (See Figure 12.10.) Some knowledge of VBScript or JScript can be useful, but it is not required. With ACT you can see how your Web server reacts when several hundred simultaneous users access your application at peak times. You can also use ACT to test the server-side components for performance, locks, and other scalability issues.

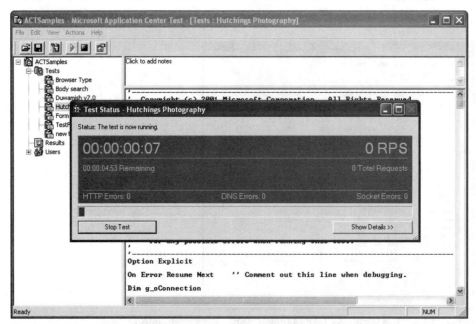

Figure 12.10 ACT performing testing on the Hutchings Web service.

After you load up ACT you can create a new test by selecting Actions, New Test. If you know what you are doing or just want to hack at it yourself, you can choose Create and Empty Test. If you want ACT to create the testbed code for you, select Record a New Test. You then select the language (it defaults to VBScript).

The next screen gives you the option to Start Recording to your Web service and invoke the methods that you would like to test. When you are finished, you click the Stop Recording button. ACT will then create a test script for you in the language that you selected. The test of the Return-Thumbs() method looks like this:

```
Sub SendRequest3()
Dim oConnection, oRequest, oResponse, oHeaders, strStatusCode
If fEnableDelays = True then Test.Sleep (10074)
Set oConnection = Test.CreateConnection(
"webservice.hutchingsphotography.com", 80, false)
If (oConnection is Nothing) Then
Test.Trace "Error: Unable to create connection to " & _
 "webservice.hutchingsphotography.com"
Else
Set oRequest = Test.CreateRequest
oRequest.Path = _
"/HutchingsImage.asmx/ReturnThumbs" + _
"?Category=People&SubCategory=&" + _
"LicenseCode=Flat&Keywords=&ThumbHeight=&ThumbWidth="
oRequest.Verb = "GET"
oRequest.HTTPVersion = "HTTP/1.0"
set oHeaders = oRequest.Headers
oHeaders.RemoveAll
oHeaders.Add "Accept", "*/*"
oHeaders.Add "Referer", _ http://webservice.hutchingsphotography.com/ + _
"HutchingsImage.asmx?op=ReturnThumbs"
oHeaders.Add "Accept-Language", "en-us"
oHeaders.Add "User-Agent", "Mozilla/4.0 (compatible; " + _
"MSIE 6.0; Windows NT 5.1; .NET CLR 1.0.3705)"
'oHeaders.Add "Host", "webservice.hutchingsphotography.com"
oHeaders.Add "Host", "(automatic)"
oHeaders.Add "Cookie", "(automatic)"
Set oResponse = oConnection.Send(oRequest)
If (oResponse is Nothing) Then
Test.Trace "Error: Failed to receive response for " + _
URL to " + "/HutchingsImage.asmx/ReturnThumbs"
Else
strStatusCode = oResponse.ResultCode
End If
oConnection.Close
End If
End Sub
```

Now, click the Start Test button and see how well our Web service holds up!

If you go to the Properties of your test, you can select the number of users you would like to simulate (up to 2,000), the duration of the test (up to 50 days), and the number of times you would like it to run.

One thing that ACT does is not useful for testing Web services, which is that it uses only HTTP GET. Because most Web services will be written to use the SOAP protocol, they may not even keep the HTTP GET.

ANTS

ANTS is a Web service load-testing tool that uses SOAP as well as the HTTP POST and HTTP GET protocols for its testing purposes. Instead of VBScript or JScript, ANTS provides Visual Basic .NET by integrating Visual Studio for Applications. This provides access to the .NET objects that you have been using to create your Web service. ANTS also allows you to create multiple scripts for the same test. This gives you the ability to make your tests a bit more real because not all your users will be invoking the same methods of your Web service.

ANTS can use state information so that you can set up any number of parameters for your script. In a live environment, your server will more than likely not be accessed by several thousand users all the time, so ANTS lets you perform spiked tests. The spiked tests simulate a surge in the number of requests it received, triggered by an unexpected increase in demand. ANTS can be run on several computers, with one acting as the controller. This allows ANTS to increase the numbers of simulated users exponentially.

After you load up ANTS you are presented with the New Project wizard, which has a few options that can help. The first option you are presented asks you if you want to test a Web service or a Web site. When you select the Test a Web Service option you are given the option to add a Web Reference. Enter the URL for the Web service; behind the scenes the tool runs the wsdl.exe to generate the necessary reference file. You are then asked for what computer you want to examine the performance counters.

You can then do two things: write the test script yourself or have ANTS create a test script for you. Here's a simple script you can use:

```
'create an instance of the Web service
Dim employeesService As New localhost.Employees()
'this will contain the ID of the employee we want to return
'information about
Dim employeeID As Integer
```

```
'Create a random number generator
Dim rnd As New Random()
'we're not interested in examing the data returned, so
'we won't bother using the DataSet returned by this call
'get a list of employees
employeesService.GetEmployees()
```

When the test runs you will see a screen similar to the Performance Monitor that comes with Windows. (See Figure 12.11.) This graphs the resource information of your server while testing the Web service.

You can add and remove any number of performance objects that you would like to track while the Web service is being tested. This gives you a better view of what your server is doing, and it may show limitations of the machine or Web service. When the testing finishes, you will see something similar to Figure 12.12.

ANTS slices and dices the data results for you in easy-to-read graphs. These results are stored as XML documents, so you can easily view and compare data from previous tests.

Whether you use a built-in tool like Microsoft Application Center or Advanced .NET Testing System by Red Gate Software (www.red-gate. com), load testing your Web service before it goes live is a good idea.

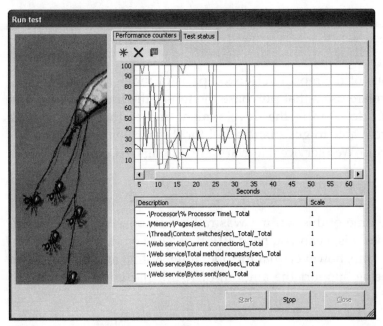

Figure 12.11   ANTS running a test.

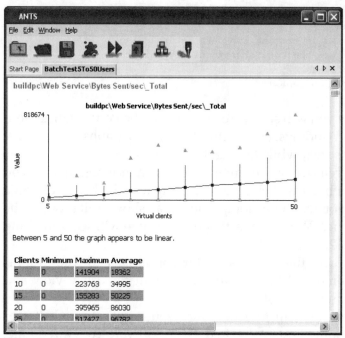

Figure 12.12   Viewing ANTS testing results.

Hardware

Hardware is one of the most overlooked parts of the performance equation. Sure, there are users that purchase the top-of-the-line hardware, but not all of them do. During the development and testing of your Web service, you were able to get a better feel for the hardware requirements necessary for your Web service. Here are a few things to consider.

Memory

Memory at the time of this writing was rather inexpensive, if not downright cheap. Does this mean you need 10 GB of RAM on that server? Probably not. Make sure, however, that the operating system and motherboard that you are using support the amount of RAM that you would like to install.

Hard Drive

A hard drive must deal with latency, which is the time it takes for the drive to locate the data that is requested. The first thing that is often overlooked is the speed (RPM) of the disk. Most of the budget drives out there are 5400 RPMs. This is fine for a file server or something else that does not need to access data quickly. For better performance, you need 7200 RPMs for IDE type drives. Also look at the buffer size; usually the more memory, the better the performance. If you can afford it, we recommend looking into SCSI disks and a RAID controller for your server. RAID can dramatically increase performance. Windows has built-in support for RAID 5, but this is a software RAID that gives the brunt of the work to your CPU, which is likely something that you want to avoid.

Central Processing Unit (CPU)

Because the CPU is the main brain of your server, it is important that you get one that can handle its workload. A CPU that is a few steps (100 MHz) slower that top of the line is usually a few hundred dollars less. Two slower processors can usually out-perform one faster one. Because CPUs can perform only one instruction at a time, having two processors to share the work can be a performance increase as long as your software can handle multiple processors.

One other thing to remember is that your software will eventually outgrow its hardware. But before you toss that old server into the garbage, consider clustering. With Microsoft Application Center 2000, clustering can be obtained on standard off-the-shelf servers. Once the servers are in a cluster they act as one machine, making it easy to administer and develop software for, because you don't need changes to your applications.

Database Optimization

It wouldn't be a complete chapter on performance and optimizations without mentioning database optimizations. Many Web sites, books, and other types of technical documentation discuss this subject. We want to draw your attention to one specific issue before closing this chapter: SQL Server's SQLXML classes. SQLXML allows you to write .NET code that takes advantage of the XML features in SQL Server 2000, namely the new keywords FOR XML AUTO, FOR XML RAW, and FOR XML NESTED. Returning XML from your database server can move the performance hit it takes on your Web server to create datasets, thus freeing some resources on the Web server.

Summary

Overall, performance is a big issue, and there are tons of things to consider. We've just barely touched on a few of them. Take time to explore further. You'll get more bang for your software and hardware buck!

Index